A Pride of Prejudices

Vermont Royster

A PRIDE
OF
PREJUDICES

ALGONQUIN BOOKS OF CHAPEL HILL
Chapel Hill, North Carolina
1984

ALGONQUIN BOOKS OF CHAPEL HILL
Post Office Box 2225
Chapel Hill, North Carolina, 27515-2225

Originally published by Alfred A. Knopf, Inc., 1967.

ISBN 0–912697–14–8

Algonquin Books is also the publisher of *My Own, My
Country's Time: A Journalist's Journey,* by Vermont
Royster.

FOR FRANCES

PREFACE TO A NEW EDITION

NOTHING seems deader than yesterday's newspaper. A newspaper story on the Super Bowl or a journalist's observations on some current controversy is dated and forgotten within a week, sometimes the next day. They are like jottings in a diary or a letter from a friend or kinsman about how things go in some distant place. Interesting at the time, but time has moved on swiftly, leaving these things the ephemera of a yesterday past.

Yet let a decade pass, or certainly a generation, and that old newspaper clipping, that faded letter, those diary notes, all these things can take on a new life. Our interest in them, and perhaps even their value, increases with the years, just as that old Tiffany lamp fell into scornful disfavor with the change of fashion only to find itself in time sought out to decorate the newest of homes.

There is a simple explanation for this journalistic phenomenon. As we live our daily lives we know how it is—in fact we are inundated with the news of events, and of opinions on it, to the point of boredom. But years later we can enjoy looking back to recall how the events were first recorded and viewed. Those too young to remember can find it interesting to learn how it was "in the olden days." Things written long ago can thus acquire a new freshness.

This phenomenon struck me anew looking again at the essays in this book, first published in 1968. The earliest of them were written in 1949, twenty years before they were gathered together. Nonetheless, there were readers who found it interesting in 1968 to share my observations and thoughts about wars or elections past set down as they were first written. That first edition went into three printings; and was widely and favorably reviewed.

Several years ago it went out of print, and since then I have been getting numerous requests for copies, but have had none to provide.

Now, some sixteen years later, comes this new edition by Algonquin Books. I confess that reading over these little essays I had the temptation, here and there, to rephrase a passage hoping to improve it, or to modify an opinion from later thought. I have resisted all these temptations. Every essay appears here exactly as originally set down, without benefit of hindsight.

Whether time and nostalgia give a new freshness to my account of Lyndon Johnson preaching a sermon or to my comments on the political game as played in a bygone time, I must leave to the reader. So too with my digressions on such topics as the male mystique or on sex and our robed judges. As I forewarned the reader of that first edition, I have never thought it necessary to be always serious about serious subjects, and I have always yielded readily to the meandering thought. I sometimes begin here, wander over there and end up in a place as much a surprise to me as to the reader. What surprises me most on rereading these pieces of long ago is how little things change. With the alteration of a name here and a date there almost any one of them would be timely in tomorrow's paper.

What has changed is *The Wall Street Journal* in which these pieces first appeared. In 1968 it was printed each night in eight printing plants across the country and its circulation was about a million. Today there are seventeen printing places in this country and it is also printed in Asia and Europe. Its circulation is in excess of two million, making it the largest circulation American newspaper. Though I am no longer its editor I continue to carry on conversations with its readers as a regular contributor.

So I invite you to share in these past conversations, here republished. As always, I welcome your company.

Chapel Hill, North Carolina　　　VERMONT ROYSTER
Spring 1984

FOREWARNING

THE earliest English periodicals to be spun from Gutenberg's galaxy spared little space for news of the "publick occurrences" but much to the prejudice of editors. The list of those ancient worthies includes such names as Marchmont Nedham, whose skill in invective has rarely been surpassed; John Milton, later to have some success as a poet; and Daniel Defoe, whose fiction was rich in verisimilitude while his accounts of events were rich in imagination.

Their prejudices were not confined to the policies of politicians. Under such titles as *The Spectator* and *The Rambler*, Joseph Addison and Samuel Johnson used the points of their pens to prick at the pretenses and pomposities of their age wherever found, the one with urbane humor and the other with more solemn preachments. They shaped the journalistic style of an era.

All these gentlemen shared the conceit that ideas were interesting and that in expressing theirs they were speaking to an audience both literate and interested. This journalistic habit, if not always the same felicity of expression, carried over into the press of the emerging American colonies.

In our early newspapers "news" was also sparse, and what there was was freely entangled with the editor's comments thereon. The other columns of these early journals were given over to poetry, sketches, and to essays, serious and satirical, on whatever subject struck the writer's fancy. The tone of many of these may be inferred from one regular series entitled "The Busy-Body Papers," written by a Benjamin Franklin, our first ambassador to France.

These American busybodies also conceived, at least well into

ix

the nineteenth century, that they too were addressing themselves to an audience interested in thinking about things. In the days before universal education the audience may have been narrower than that of today's huge circulation journals, but the writer shared with his readers a common literary and intellectual heritage which gave an especial cast to the dialogue.

This common heritage included, of course, the Bible and Shakespeare, two books that might be found in any covered wagon. Thanks to such standard textbooks as the ubiquitous McGuffey's Readers, the heritage also included at least a smattering of Roman history and dollops of Milton, Chaucer, Macaulay, Ruskin, Longfellow, Bacon, and their literary confreres. For all his faults, McGuffey treated children as unshaped but intelligent human beings. There was no truck with a "simplified vocabulary." Through McGuffey the children of a one-room Illinois school got their Samuel Johnson pure. They also at least brushed against the ideas of Edmund Burke, Blackstone, or Thomas Jefferson, as well as such older philosophers as Aristotle and Plato.

One consequence of this was that the journalist and his reader, even when they were both shy of formal higher education, had a common plane of reference. The journalistic essays of that day may have been sometimes as mediocre as many editorials of today, but they were of a different kind. The writer was not afraid that a literary allusion would go astray, or that his readers would depart if he took a day off from politics to discuss his personal philosophy of man, God, or society. The practice of "writing down" to the audience had not yet taken hold.

By the beginning of this century a number of things had happened to change the complexion of daily journalism. Among these were the Morse telegraph, the typesetting machine, and the rotary press, as well as the sociological changes wrought by universal elementary education. In combination they enlarged the newspaper's audience and—at least in editors' eyes—diminished the quality of the audience. The habit grew of accentuating happenings, preferably sensational ones, at the expense of reflection.

There were many gains from the change in newspapers; few people are as well informed about what goes on in the world as today's American newspaper readers. But the change did tend to displace the informal essayist, the man who simply wrote as a good conversationalist might talk on whatever topic came to mind.

Editors didn't drop the habit of venting their prejudices. The temptation, however, was to fire off conclusions as broadsides, the object being to keep everything short and simple. Even the more intellectual minded of the regular writers tended to restrict themselves to some special field—literature, the arts, or public affairs—out of the belief that the readers had compartmentalized interests. Sports belonged on the sports page, economics on the business page, and let each writer stick to his last. The trend is emphasized by the attention lavished on the few exceptions.

So perhaps the first forewarning for readers of this little volume of essays is that they are a throwback to a former time.

These essays are certainly journalistic; that is, they spring from the circumstances of the day. Many are in a familiar mold, passing comments on passing events and personalities. Some are reportage. They are nonetheless somewhat anachronistic in that the passing circumstance is merely a springboard for inviting the reader to let his mind wander, often rather far afield.

They also reflect the anachronistic conceit that the reader's interest is as varied as my own and that he is both intelligent and literate. There is likewise an assumption, as in conversation among friends, that not every thought need be earthshaking. A small observation can be interesting without being the final answer to anything. It is not even necesssary to be always serious about serious matters, and if it's a personal experience rather than a world event that spurs a reflection, is that too not grist for a conversation? It happens to everybody all the time.

Finally, these essays are old-fashioned in that I yield readily to the meandering thought. Some of them begin here, wander over there, and wind up at a place that sometimes surprises me as well as the reader. The journalistic tradition that a writer should get to the point quickly, avoiding nuances and digressions, is more breached than honored.

Perhaps it is also an anachronism that they should have originally appeared in a newspaper at all, especially one of mass circulation. That happenstance is due to the special qualities of *The Wall Street Journal* and the peculiarities of my own upbringing.

In 1936, when I first joined *The Wall Street Journal*, the paper's circulation was a bare 35,000 and it was just beginning to change from a specialized financial paper. Yet even then it had a trenchant editorial page and it kept a quiet corner where such men as Thomas F. Woodlock and later Willam H. Grimes could write about whatever came to mind. Today, with its million circulation and eight printing plants scattered about the country, the *Journal* deals in wider subject matter for a wider audience. But in writing about politics, economics, world affairs, and the social changes of the country it has kept its habit of aiming at an adult audience. It has also kept a space for comments on literature, art, theater, religion, or anything else of interest to intelligent men. And it has left a corner for essays such as these, fitting no journalistic pattern in shape or subject.

I arrived in that corner by a circuitous route. When I was born my father was a teacher of Latin and Greek at the University of North Carolina, Chapel Hill. Subsequently he took up law and in his autumn years was back at the university teaching law. But he never lost his first love, and he taught me the principal parts of Latin verbs before I could read or knew what they meant. A six-year-old can delight in chanting *tango, tangere, tetigi, tactus.* He started me on formal study of Latin at the age of eight.

Greek waited until my teens when I was shipped off to the Webb School in Tennessee, an old-fashioned place that still required four years of Latin and two of Greek before Will Webb would say you were ready for college. When in due course I arrived at Chapel Hill, I took Latin and Greek as "snap" courses to help hold up my grade level, crowding the rest of the curriculum with history and English literature. Spare time was used for the student newspaper and the literary magazine and for radical political activism that tried the patience of Dr. Frank Graham, then the president.

In the depression years of the mid-1930's this educational background was itself a bit out of date. A nodding acquaintance with Euripides proved not a very marketable commodity. For a young man so inadequately prepared for life there was no recourse but journalism.

New York's major newspapers, which I importuned after some apprentice labors in North Carolina, showed an acute disinterest in my services. So there followed a temporary job with the City News Bureau, covering night court and police precincts, which lasted several months. Then a temporary job with *The Wall Street Journal,* which hasn't yet been terminated.

The rest was serendipity. The *Journal*'s staff was then small, and within a few months I was in Washington covering, seriatim, the Agriculture Department, Congress, the White House, the Treasury, and the burgeoning new regulatory agencies. Later, after time out for some unpleasantness with Germany and Japan, I became the *Journal*'s chief Washington correspondent, but inevitably drifted toward the editorial page out of a natural frustration at recording events with no license to express my opinions about them. Since being granted one I have never treated it as a limited license. Nor, happily, has the management of my newspaper; the proprietors have put up with my prejudices while by no means always sharing them.

By this time it may be superfluous to warn that the opinions expressed in these little essays are not necessarily the ones most frequently encountered elsewhere.

I have been called both a "conservative" and something referred to as a "nineteenth-century liberal." Both labels are, I think, inaccurate. Anyway, if conservative means, as it often seems to nowadays, an opposition to change for opposition's sake or a disposition to return the country to some imagined halcyon past, I beg to be excused. This is more an awareness that the past is as romanticized in history as youth is in memory than any want of awareness about the imbecilities of the present. My prejudice is that we might often better things by changing them.

There is much to be said for the nineteenth century, but who, really, would want to take the world back to it? Besides, the latter part of it marked a reversion among the intellectuals to the medieval philosophy of the all-wise king and his ministers who should manage all the people's affairs in proper fashion. That century's seminal thinkers, let us not forget, included the Fabian socialists and Karl Marx, all of whom were self-styled liberals.

Yet it is perfectly true that among my prejudices is a belief that our heritage from the past contains many values worth conserving in the twentieth century. I sympathize with the newest lament of the new liberals that the institutions of society, from huge universities to huge government, threaten the individual spirit; I only marvel at the lateness of their concern. That same past, I suggest now and then, offers us many practical lessons about the organization of society which we ignore only at a peril.

But if these modern busybody papers are in form a throwback to an earlier journalistic day, part of the anachronism is that of making passing observations without too much worry whether they fit into a political pattern, or even a consistent philosophical one. Absurdity is no respecter of political philosophies or the centuries of man. So most of all I hope the reader will find labels irrelevant.

Anyway, he is forewarned not to expect from these prejudices any denunciation of our century and all its works, nor an invitation to revel in those prophecies of doom so popular these days. I am often pessimistic about the immediate future, waxing indignant sometimes when our long heritage is abused or past lessons ignored. Who can avoid pessimism, looking at the state of the world and the behavior of the people in it? About the long future, however, I am stubbornly optimistic. Although mankind does forget old lessons to its pain, just as young people do those of their fathers, it always relearns them. It's comforting to remember that the Dark Ages only lasted five hundred years.

If after all this you still want to read what follows in this volume, I welcome your company.

V.R.

Contents

xvii

CONTENTS

CONTENTS

I

A DASH OF IRE

THE USES OF GRUMBLERS

O F all the statements that came to hand as the shiny New Year replaced a worn-out 1964 the most provocative one was from that gadfly of the Negro Muslims, Malcolm X. Asked what he planned to do by way of celebrating as midnight brought in the calends of January, he remarked, "I shall stay home contemplating some of the disasters ahead."

Whether this marks him as verily a Daniel come to judgment is something, as the saying goes, that remains to be seen; prophecy is not an especially dependable commodity. But it certainly shows him an un-American breaker of icons, a flouter of tradition, and not at all the sort of fellow who would be a welcome addition to the celebration.

For it is a well-established tradition, doubtless reaching back to the dawn of the English common law, that all New Year's statements must be cheerful, looking not only upon the bright side of the present but forward with optimism and confidence to all the bounties yet to come. To do otherwise, in ancient days, was to disturb the King's peace. To do so now would disturb everybody's peace of mind.

Thus the Secretary of Commerce, if he would honor the tradition, must always foresee a bustling year in trade. The Secretary of the Treasury must assure us that the dollar is sound as a nut. The Council of Economic Advisers must find patterns of new growth in their charts. The Secretary of Defense must see peace for our time. And the President, as provider of all things for all

3

people, must combine prophecies of both peace and prosperity. Those prominent in private life must do as well. Labor leaders, pausing between strikes, must promise their followers that next year's contract will be better than the last one. Civil rights leaders, having for twelve months denounced the snail's pace of progress, must see in the new year the rewards of patience. In every brokerage house the sluggish market must be hailed as consolidating a firm base for an early penetration of the all-time highs. And it would be pure treason for any corporation president to tell the stockholders, flat-out, that he foresaw a lousy year.

All this, to be sure, requires some nimble rhetoric, but the trick is lots of "althoughs" and "howevers." Thus: "Although the situation is far from stable in Saigon, recent developments give hope . . ." Or: "The deadlock in the United Nations will require much patience; however, the new attitude of the Soviet Union suggests . . ." "Although there are some economic indices that bear careful watching, a continued care to avoid budgetary surpluses promises . . ."

Of course it's questionable whether most of the people speaking these sentiments—and they are exact quotations from official statements—believe a word of them, except perhaps in that brief moment of self-hypnosis every man falls into when he has just uttered something he imagines people will listen to.

At any rate, it's hard to imagine a man of such perception as Adlai Stevenson being anything but depressed by what's going on around him in that steel and glass mausoleum on the East River; or Secretary McNamara, having spent a hard day over the cables from Saigon, being as indomitably cheerful supping with his wife as duty demands that he be in public.

It's even hard to imagine most of the public being taken in by these pleasant deceits. The holiday recess at the UN won't keep the Congo out of the newspapers for long. A successful skirmish in Vietnam, happily coinciding with the season of hope,

4

won't bring complete forgetfulness of that tragic business, especially in those homes where the telegrams arrive expressing the Secretary of the Army's deepest sympathy.

Yet the tradition persists because the notion persists that those who speak cheerfully, like Pollyanna, are the only bearers of good cheer. Hardly anyone perceives the virtues of grumbling. This is strange because, as Joseph Wood Krutch has observed, the ability to worry is the most praiseworthy of human accomplishments, praiseworthy because it is essentially an optimistic occupation. To be sure, there is also a good bit of fraud in the grumbler. To some extent Malcolm X is putting on an act. So too, though, are the less flamboyant grumblers, like editorial writers or politicians out of office. They aren't really confident of all the disasters they may see ahead, and few of them would wager hard money on the arrival of their worries.

Still, this doesn't obviate their social usefulness nor diminish their contribution to the public happiness. The man who goes off to a dinner party in the confident expectation of a delightful time risks a real crusher to his spirits. Dragged reluctantly by his wife, he has at least a fair chance of a pleasant surprise and—should that happen—of joy unknown by those Pollyannas. Of course if the ill wind does blow, he isn't crushed; it's no more than he expected.

There's another thing. What American society would there be, great or small, if men hadn't grumbled about governments of old and a little tax on tea? Who but the grumblers fled West to people the Pedernales and the prairie? And why would Lyndon Johnson spend an hour growling about the state of the Union except for knowing that it is not bright talk but dark mutterings that move men to action against the wind?

So here's a small word for a little happy grumbling about the British pound, the situation in the Congo, the mess in Vietnam, the prevalence of taxes, the permanence of inflation, corruption in

5

Washington, crime in the home-town streets, and all the other little things we carry forward unchanged from 1964 to 1965. Most of them will not eventuate in the contemplated disasters, especially if they are contemplated with the proper merry melancholy.

Such anyway were the cheerful sentiments with which I had planned to toast the New Year until the lady of the house, as she dragged me off to the midnight revels, grumbled that honesty just spoils everybody's fun.

January 6, 1965

WHAT INDIGNATION?

I T'S been a couple of hundred years since the English went to war because they were scandalized, and half a century since a French government quaked over a little matter of lying and forgery in high places.

Since the Dreyfus affair and the War of Jenkin's Ear there's been no dearth of scandals, some of which have made loud uproars and consumed reams of newsprint, but it's a rare thing nowadays when they have any more political consequences than the titillation of the public. The French have had Cabinet officers chasing nymphets, the British have had Foreign Office officials chasing not only Communists but each other, and of course there was the delightful Profumo affair which the staid English seem to have accepted with relief because it at least involved opposite sexes.

Meanwhile we've had our own passing scandals. Nothing lately has quite touched Teapot Dome, in which some wheeler-dealing Cabinet officers tried to steal the country blind, or the juicy morsels provided by the extramarital activity of Warren Harding. Both of these things contributed to history's low opinion of Mr. Harding, and a couple of jail sentences did come out of the Teapot tempest. But for all the national attention to these scandals, there's no evidence that very many people were scandalized enough to rebuke anybody via the ballot box.

So it's been ever since. At the time there was much outcry over the blatant immorality of Harry Hopkins's political doctrine

7

of "spend and spend, tax and tax, elect and elect." It never hurt Mr. Hopkins, who continued as the gray eminence at the White House, played a major role in the wartime deals with the Russians which afterwards gave so much trouble, and was the posthumous subject of an adoring biography that won a Pulitzer prize.

To be sure, other public servants, including gray eminences, haven't been quite so lucky. A crony of President Truman's went to jail for a felony and a close adviser of President Eisenhower lost his job for slipping on a rug. Again, however, there's no evidence that any of these scandals, for all that they had their noisy day, had any appreciable effect on the political fortunes of the political leaders upon whom the scandals breathed.

Herewith, then, a minority report. The substance of it is a suspicion that a recent Washington scandal, involving the nocturnal peccadilloes of President Johnson's close friend and confidant, won't have much of any political effect. It's a nasty business, all right, and because it involves sexual mores it will probably raise more noise than Billie Sol Estes and Bobby Baker combined. Any way you look at it the halo on Lyndon Johnson's head as the great moral crusader against the wickedness of Barry Goldwater will doubtless be tarnished. But the question is whether the American people will get indignant about the right thing, which is not what happened one night at a YMCA but an attitude toward moral standards in public life of which this case is but one hapless example. The question, indeed, is whether the American people any longer have the capacity to get really indignant about anything.

Whatever you may think about a man's sexual habits, there are other immoralities more worthy of public censure. Yet only a few years ago a man high in the councils of state was convicted of perjury in a treason case and the widespread reaction, especially among those who lay claim to intellectual leadership, was that even if he was guilty the act ought not to be too terribly condemned because, after all, that was a time when "everybody" was being kind to Communists. In rather wide circles there was less indignation over the thought of a man's betraying his country than over his betraying his wife.

And where, really, was the public indignation over Billie Sol or Lyndon's Bobby Baker? Billie himself got convicted of various misdemeanors, but there was no great demand for a thorough airing of the circumstances that made those misdemeanors possible. As for Bobby Baker, only a few Republican Congressmen seemed interested in finding out what happened. At any rate, the Democrats tried quietly to quash the matter and if that caused any outrage among the electorate it certainly wasn't an uproar.

Even over the highest offices people are pretty tolerant, and you don't have to go back to Warren Harding. A man who spent all his life on the public payroll can end up several times a millionaire and the fairly common reaction is that that just shows how smart he is.

More subtle moral questions make no dent at all. People go to the polls and vote for a man for Senator for no other discernible reason than that he's the brother of, or was once a secretary to, a national hero. A governor of a state can be under indictment for using his party power to defraud the public; the prosecutor may put the ex-governor in jail but the public asks no accounting from the man's political party.

This phenomenon, if that's the word for it, is one that can't all be blamed on Lyndon Johnson. Senator Goldwater can fulminate about the moral and ethical climate of Washington, and be right, but it's doubtful if it will get him very far in the present climate of the country. Why blame it all on politicians when the president of a huge national union can milk the treasury, stand convicted in two courts, and arouse no indignation among the majority of the union's members? The prevailing view of the members seems to be they'd have done the same thing if they'd had

9

the chance, and anyway didn't Jimmy do a lot of good things for his followers?

A lonesome judge can get indignant about whiskey-drinking parties for teenagers, preliminary to manslaughter, but not the suburban parents. Mobs—without regard for race or creed—can disturb the public order, smash shop windows, and bash heads, and respectable people will lament police brutality because the mobs acted in a good cause. And among most of those we trust to teach our young, "Puritan ethics" are as laughably outmoded as McGuffey's Readers.

So we wonder if this latest bit of scandal will prove of such great political moment. No doubt the poor fellow is going to be giggled at, even pilloried, for his human failing. This want of charity will miss the point, which is not whether men sometimes succumb to weaknesses of spirit or flesh—there but for some kind of grace perhaps go we all—but what it means to government and society when immorality of all kinds is shrugged off as accepted behavior among those we thrust to honor and trust.

Personally, I'd like to think that morality and ethics in governnment officials could still be a telling issue in any campaign. But neither the record nor the times give much hope that it will be.

October 16, 1964

A MONSTROUS THOUGHT

You can hardly pick up a newspaper or magazine these days without reading about the uprootedness—sometimes it's called the alienation—of the younger generation from the society of their elders.

The new generation, so runs the diagnosis, have nothing to cling to except their own alienated selves. God is dead. The family is in decline. Their country is no longer an inspiration. The moral code appears a pointless hypocrisy. The ancient virtues of thrift, duty, work, obligation invoke no response. And so on through the catalogue.

This mood, if that's the word for it, is blamed for just about everything: long-haired boys, pantalooned girls, revolts on the campus, LSD, teenage vandalism, sexual license, cornflakes art, draft-dodging, and what-have-you. Nor, so you read, is this an isolated American phenomenon. *Time* magazine in a recent issue reported that London too is "switched on . . . everything uninhibited and kinky is blooming at the top." And this moved Henry Fairlie of the British *Spectator* to write, in a *New York Times* article, that it was all too true, and very, very sad. Mr. Fairlie laid the blame in the same places: young people in Britain, he said, "do not understand the point to which their long history has brought them and . . . do not know where they are going."

It would be a bold man, looking around him, who would deny all this. Doubtless the symptoms are exaggerated because the alienated hipsters are noisier; good behavior, like good news, attracts less attention than the bad. All the same, thēre's enough in the diagnosis to give pause. But the worst part of it is that once you pause, your thoughts are apt to run further than just the new generation. You may think about your own.

If God is dead, He was buried not by the young but by the old. The decline of religion is no new phenomenon. What is new is that the theologians themselves now assault it in the very places where, presumably, the love of God is to be taught. Even frocked bishops question Him in the pulpit, while neither they nor their congregations apparently see anything odd in this juxtaposition. If young people, looking about with their first adult eyes, think the family declining, or take the preached moral code for hypocrisy, where save among their elders would they see the examples to deny the precepts?

Once upon a time the old were not only honored but cared for by their own. In how many households today do grandparents dwell? When young people see their parents eager to have their parents "not be a burden," or at most a burden to be borne by all out of the public treasury, pray why should that inspire them to a closer sense of family?

Or take the matter of sexual mores. For years the "double standard" has been under assault, and not without logic. But all the articles about it in all the popular magazines would equalize it not by raising the one but by lowering the other. What we have taught is not equality in virtue but in license. And the lesson has been explicitly preached not merely by scribblers in magazines but by many presidents and teachers of the very schools to which we send the young to learn a manner of living.

Perhaps this new manner of living is an advance in civilization, although many of us have some gnawing doubts. The certain point, however, is that the effect is not without its cause. This is true also in the other ways in which the new generation is shown the society in which they have been reared. If you had to take your view of America from your daily diet of reading or watching the TV screen you might well conclude yourself that it is a pretty dreadful place. To hear it told, we fight in a distant place only out of arrogance, or to make rich the munitions makers. The auto companies recklessly endanger our lives out of greed. The drug companies hoodwink us all, and the doctors gouge the poor. The newspapers, in their eagerness to sell copies, deny us the right to a fair trial when we stand accused.

We have, so it has been dinned into us, laid waste the beauty of the countryside, polluted the air and the waters. Our land is a land of poverty and racial oppression. Our economic system, controlled by prices and motivated by profit, is dubious in morality and makeshift in operation. Our politics is corrupt and our politicians venal.

These views of our country are not the uninspired imaginings of the young. Each line above was limed, in article or speech, within the past fortnight by some elder who has claim to the public attention. In fairness it should be said that those who speak thus probably do not intend so black a picture, wanting only less poverty, more beauty, yet safer cars, or better medical care. Rarely, however, are they content to say so; they suppose that to ask improvement they must denigrate the whole. The effect is profound on impressionable minds. Its depth is measured in a haunting phrase of Max Lerner's, a perceptive journalist of liberal mind. Asking what it is young Americans can feel deeply about, he was moved to write: "Not America itself, nor its history, since patriotism of such depth would be a monstrous thought."

Why? Why would no English poet speak today of his other Eden, demi-paradise, where a happy breed of men dwell on a precious stone set in a silver sea? Nor an American one cry Hail, Columbia, happy land, where humanity with all its fears hangs breathless on its fate? Somehow we have contrived—we of the older generation—to paint our self-portrait not warts and all but

13

warts alone. To take the mythology out of religion, we have killed not only God but the spirit of man as something more than a beast to feed and procreate. To take the jingoism out of patriotism, we have not only destroyed the icon of manifest destiny but gratitude for the land that has blest us and pride that its people made it bright beyond compare.

Perhaps we older ones can strike the balance, knowing that if there be blotches, yet in no land are men less oppressed or richer in what others dream of, and so be unashamed to love our country; the truly monstrous thought is that with pen and voice we have made the young think that to do so is monstrous.

June 20, 1966

BILLIE SOL AND THE SUGAR

THE late W. C. Fields, that astute student of the larcenous heart, discovered that you can't cheat an honest man. So don't give all the credit to Billie Sol Estes. To be sure, he lifted the old shell game of the Texas county fairs—now you see it, now you don't—to magnificent heights. A man who can play sleight-of-hand with huge liquid fertilizer tanks by the simple device of switching serial numbers faster than the eye can see, well, he deserves a place alongside such super performers as the great Ponzi or Ivar Kreuger, the European master whose matches burned the most sophisticated fingers of Wall Street.

But Billie Sol had a lot working for him. For one thing, none of it could have happened if the quick buck hadn't exercised a certain charm for a number of earnest farmers, hard-headed moneylenders, and devoted public servants on the government payroll. Possibly none of them intended anything really dishonest (who would sell his soul for a suit from Neiman-Marcus?) and it isn't yet proved that anybody did anything illegal. It's merely that sleight-of-hand requires the sucker to look the other way, and what will divert the gaze quicker than the promise of an "easy thing"? Another part of the Fields theory is that where the sugar is there will the flies gather. So there is the rather elementary fact that the Agriculture Department takes billions of dollars every year from all the people and pays it out to some of the people. The Department also disposes of other things of large monetary value, such as crop allotment, from one man to another, and you have done someone a real favor.

15

In fact, there was quite a bit of scandal some years back over the grain storage program. Billie Sol just showed more imagination in putting two and two together, the attraction of sweets scattered about and the little touch of larceny that always lurks in the mortal heart. The combination is a sure-fire mixture for scandal, and though at the moment it centers on the Agriculture Department you can find the mixture almost anywhere in the federal government today. The government not only handles more than $100 billion every year; it has all manner of other goodies to give away. Profitable television licenses. Urban renewal programs. Copper stockpiling contracts. Favorable income tax rulings. There is today hardly any area of the national life, or any part of the economy, where the decisions of public officials— and sometimes the actions of government clerks—do not mean money in the pocket for somebody.

In the days of Teapot Dome a scandal in the federal government could stun the nation precisely because it was rare. And it was rare because the opportunities for anything more than a little fudging on a channel-dredging contract were rare. Today government scandals roll around with the inevitability of the equinoxes. And while they create some excitement, you can hardly say the populace is outraged.

And for me that's the saddest part of the whole affair. I agree with President Kennedy that some people will always succumb to the temptation for a little bit of larceny. What's sad is that Washington's reaction was more embarrassment than shame, the country's response more a chuckle than a roar. What's saddest is that everybody is so interested in the government's sugar that hardly anybody minds the flies.

For to be fair about it all, in a day when workers get paid for not working and farmers for not farming, it almost seems natural to get paid for a fertilizer tank that isn't there.

May 24, 1962

POVERTY BOOM

IT's truly astounding how much poverty has boomed in this country since the accession of President Johnson. Of course poverty has never been a stranger to us. Even the most affluent society has its dispossessed, those who for one reason or another find themselves apart from the general prosperity. Some by their own doing. Some by inadequacies of mind or spirit beyond their power to rectify. Some by misfortune which they neither caused nor can correct. All of them, even the slothful, are worthy of compassion and have a call on the help of good men. In this country the response to that call has always been phenomenal, not only for our own unfortunates but for those in faraway places.

But for all that, the poor have never been so much with us, or at least so much in the mouths of politicians. You can hardly pick up a newspaper or tune in the TV set without hearing about this blight of poverty, usually presented as some enormous new discovery made betwixt last November and last night.

So that proverbial man from Mars, or even a worldly reader in Paris or Moscow, might well conclude that poverty is seeping like a plague through this rich, capitalist country. You can well imagine what pleasant reading it must be for those whose job it is to tell bleak masses elsewhere how terrible life is in the United States.

Almost everybody knows this is a distorted image but hardly anybody dares say so for fear of being damned as a heartless wretch. This is what makes the poverty boom such a marvelous political ploy. But it doesn't make it any more honest. For the implication in all this political propaganda is not simply that there are those poor amid plenty, which is true, or that there are those who for whatever reasons are without much hope of improving their lot, which is also true. The implication is, first of all, that misery embraces a fifth or more of the whole population and that the word "poverty" here used describes the same condition as poverty in Asia, Africa, or even parts of Latin America. The second implication is that in all the years of this country, until this Congressional session, nobody has done anything about it.

If you want to see how dishonest this is, spend a few days in one of the slums in New York, or any other of our great cities. There, believe me, you will find poverty by the standards of the greater part of the nation. But there also, believe me, you will find the tempest-tossed from other lands to whom this "poverty" is something they fled to from something far worse. If you don't believe that, go from the Latin slums of New York to the slums of Latin America.

Or take a tour through the poorest section of the barren Appalachian hills. If you have compassion, this will nurture it. But match this with a visit to the poor of almost any of the lands where our Peace Corps is now working; better yet, match it if you can with a journey through the byways of the Iron Curtain countries. There you will see misery of a wholly different order.

And while you are thus journeying, try one across your own country. Not one of these airplane trips that whisks you across a continent in a few hours but a slow journey by car or bus. Then ask yourself if a fifth of the nation is, really, ground down in the hopeless circle of poverty. These same journeys will also give you a better idea of what America has done to war on, if indeed not yet to conquer, the affliction of the dispossessed. The welfare payments in a New York slum give yet a standard of living that millions in the world would envy. Moreover, for years now Americans have taxed themselves to rebuild cities, sometimes even whole countrysides, as in the Tennessee Valley. Look, as you journey, at the houses, hospitals, schools, colleges, and camps sprouting like mushrooms over the landscape. Look, most of all, at what the American economic system, with all its creaks and groans, has done to make our definition of what is poor a marvel to the world. In no other place does the laborer in the factory, the clerk in the counting house, the waitress in the coffee house, the drayman on the road, or the longshoreman on his pier—all those who before and elsewhere have been numbered among the poor—enjoy so much as the reward of his labor.

We have our poor, indeed we do, and no good man would halt our efforts to make them fewer. Yet what is this new poverty program, hatched by the Administration in a hundred days amid the distractions of Vietnam and Panama? Search as you will you will find nothing new in it, save for the creation of a new commissar of poverty. Whatever the arguments about outdoor camps for boys, urban renewal, labor retraining programs, federal aid to education, area redevelopment, work relief, loans to farm families and all the rest, the program does not "chart a new course." This is what is claimed for it by President Johnson, while others assure us it is the first salvo in an all-out attack that is going to obliterate poverty forever. Anyone who questions the honesty of the advertising is as bereft of political friends as lonesome George.

What the same government is doing to worsen the lot of the poor will hardly be mentioned at all. Only old fogies today are concerned by continuous billion-dollar deficits and the steady erosion of the dollar to pay for them. A little inflation, so we're told, is just a price we have to pay for prosperity.

Yet if, as Walter Heller says, all those with income less than $3,000 are poor by American standards, what will sooner make poorer those handicapped in life than a still further cheapening of those dollars? What more cruel to those who must live on social security, a pension, an insurance policy, or a lifetime's savings?

Still, we find this poverty program utterly fascinating. First time we ever heard of a party running for re-election by running down what it's done for the country and telling the folk they never had it so bad.

March 24, 1964

A BLOW FOR LIBERTY

JOHN Garner of Texas, who rose to fame as Speaker of the House and sank into obscurity as Vice President, has always liked to strike a blow for liberty.

In his Capitol days the instrument for such symbolic gestures was a bottle of corn-squeezings, which he would set upon his desk whenever he had like-minded guests, were they Democrats, Republicans, or indigent journalists. It was a fitting way, I always thought, to toast the common man in his fight against oppression by the high and the mighty. At the time I encountered Mr. Garner the country had just escaped from the dark age of prohibition, with which the self-righteous had oppressed the people. But his instinct must have told him that repeal would not end the matter, an insight which ought to earn him a small niche in any Hall of Fame for philosophers.

For even today you can take almost any current issue—ranging from taxation to diplomatic relations to antitrust policy—and sooner or later you will find that it's got entangled somehow with the spirits of grape and grain. And the victims nearly always turn out to be those who would raise a toast to liberty.

The matter of taxation need not be labored. Any time a governor, President, or Congressman wants to extract a few pennies more from the working man's budget he hikes the tax on these beverages. Without these levies a good bottle of Scotch or Bourbon would cost you in the neighborhood of a dollar, even at the dollar's depreciated value. The difference between that and what you actually paid last Saturday is tribute levied on the simple pleasures of the poor.

But take also diplomacy. Among Secretary of State Rusk's headaches two big ones are General de Gaulle and the Common Market. De Gaulle is being ornery all over and the Common Market has just hiked its tariffs on U.S. farm products. So what do we do to retaliate against the Netherlands, Belgium, Luxembourg, etc. for their bad treatment of our chickens and such? We hike our tariffs on French wines and cognac. This is known in diplomacy as a double coup; it's supposed to punish the Common Market countries in general and France in particular. But of course the only victim is the American who likes brandy with his coffee. The only person whose heart is gladdened is the grape grower of New York and California.

And you must not suppose that the commercial entrepreneur is any less reluctant to oppress the drinking classes than misty-eyed reformers or hard-bitten politicians. Indeed, if you want to see monopoly at work—and the ill-workings of our supposed antimonopoly public policy—you can hardly do better than study the retail liquor business.

In the popular mythology the root of monopoly is confined to Big Business. No doubt it would be rooted there if it could be, for you can set it down as axiomatic that any group of men in any line of endeavor will, if they can, try to fix their returns and keep out all newcomers who might lower them. But today Big Business is scared witless by the Justice Department. Today it's the little fellow with the wit to carve out nice little monopolies.

Naturally this isn't confined to the liquor business. Many craft unions have tight monopolies, unmoved by the fact that there are jobless men eager to work at the trade. In many cities, as in New York, the taxicab business is a closed corporation; you can only hack by paying several thousand dollars to buy a medallion from one of the privileged who already has a license.

And all the Fair Trade laws, in whatever guise they come,

are simply endeavors to enforce a fixed-price structure on the customer who comes in the door. It's just that it works better in the liquor business. In a number of states this business is in fact a monopoly of the state. In others the private entrepreneurs have gained laws which either limit the number of retail stores or fix the selling prices, or both. The result, as you might suppose, is that the prices to the working man in these places are several notches higher than in free-trade places. One of these latter, incidentally, is the District of Columbia, where the nation's politicians buy their own liquor cheap.

How far the high and the mighty will go if given a chance was illustrated recently in New York State. Uncle Sam, as any tourist knows, is benevolent enough to let you bring in a pittance of foreign spirits duty free. It's not a huge amount, and judging by the statistics the tourist imports didn't put much of a dent in New York liquor sales. It was the principle of the thing, I guess.

Anyway the dealers sneaked through a law prohibiting local residents using the mail for this nefarious traffic. They sold it to the legislators with the same argument used to keep up retail prices and to limit the number of stores—namely, that thus they served as the guardians of the public sobriety. This is simply a particularly effective variant of the generalized argument of all these little monopoly groups, from the cab drivers to the Fair Traders, that by jacking up prices or controlling the market the controllers are protecting the public from all sorts of terrible things that would happen if the public had a free choice of prices and market places.

Is there a public outcry about any of this? Do you read diatribes against these little monopolies from those politicians fulminating against the wicked monopolies of Big Business? Not so you notice. All that saved New Yorkers from this latest monopoly effort was a court decision which said that the state couldn't interfere with foreign commerce.

Still, the customer can give thanks for that, although it's an irony that in a country where every politician professes a desire to protect the consumer we have to turn to the courts for succor. We owe our rescue from Fair Trade, you'll recall, more to judges than to legislators.

Perhaps Mr. Garner was unnecessarily flamboyant. But his gesture to the common man was fitting. Amid the great affairs of state it would be nice if some other politicians would take time, now and then, to strike a real blow for liberty.

March 4, 1964

24

THE THEOLOGY OF CHANGE

NOBODY—well, hardly anybody—reads St. Thomas Aquinas any more. Mostly he wrote about man's relationship to God, a subject lately fallen into disfavor if indeed it's not unconstitutional. Moreover he liked to look at the long-range effects of the moment's pragmatic decisions, which is not only unfashionable but· today considered downright tiresome. Yet the young nephew of Frederick Barbarossa was no recluse from worldly affairs. Tucked away in his great *Summa Theologica* are many shrewd thoughts about such secular matters as man's relationship to man and such practical problems as the mundane laws of the state. In fact, in different times the good St. Thomas would have made an excellent lawyer, or even an editorial writer.

He liked to range from one subject to another, searching always for the heart of the matter and then compressing his thought into short compass, thus offering something for both the reflective and the hurried reader. That's still an art more widely honored than practiced. It was in one of these paragraphic asides that he grappled with the ageless question of how immutable should be the civil laws men make for themselves. Certainly it is a question that troubles many people today, a time when many of our laws are undergoing great and frequent changes at the hands both of the lawgivers and the law's judges.

"Nothing," said St. Thomas, "can be absolutely unchangeable in things that are subject to change, and therefore human law cannot be altogether unchangeable." He was, then, no man

25

to have truck with the argument that just because something was decreed by some Founding Fathers it must remain henceforward immutable. Here is one antique philosopher who might be quoted by the most liberal advocate of change to cope with "modern" problems.

"In speculative sciences," he observed, "we see that the teaching of the early philosophers was imperfect, and that it was afterwards perfected by those who succeeded them. So also in practical matters.

"For those who first endeavored to discover something useful for the human community, not being able by themselves to take everything into consideration, set up certain institutions which were deficient in many ways; and these were changed by subsequent lawgivers who made institutions that might prove less frequently deficient in respect of the common weal."

But the good Saint, unlike some other good men, was not bemused by the thought that laws were the answer to every ill or the straight road to the good society. Since human law is framed for human beings, "the majority of whom are not perfect in virtue," he thought it futile "to forbid all vices from which the virtuous abstain." And that man of long ago was perceptive enough to notice that in the very changes of the law, even when "something better occurs" to the lawmakers, there are sometimes, as with good medicines, unwanted side effects.

"The mere change of law is of itself prejudicial to the common good," he observed, "because custom avails much for the observance of laws. . . . Consequently, when a law is changed, the binding power of [all] law is diminished, in so far as custom is abolished." Consequently, the laws men adopt "should be as enduring as possible."

Here, then, are ancient observations whose truth we learn anew. For it is now being observed by many men that we are in times when respect for the binding power of the law is, if not yet demolished, at least eroded. The evidence of it is found not merely in the violence of the street, though that be growing, but in the lost respect for both law and custom among the young and the resignation with which their elders accept scandal even in high places.

The most dramatic instances of great change in our laws are, of course, those being wrought both by judges and lawgivers in the relationship between white and Negro. Here, surely, are changes long overdue in customs and institutions which, to borrow St. Thomas' phrase, have been "deficient in respect of the common weal."

Yet we are finding, just the same, that law alone is powerless to end those vices of prejudice from which the virtuous abstain. The law can make a hamburger available to all comers. It cannot make all men accept all other men as brothers. So it is that sometimes there is a bitter taste in the law's victories.

Moreover, the very manner and swiftness of the change has brought its unwanted effects. If one law and one custom can be overturned overnight by one set of judges, how persuasive can one be in urging the binding power of other laws and customs? For the habit of swift change takes its hold upon the judges and lawgivers not only in great things but in small. Public disorder, which it was once the duty of both law and custom to suppress, becomes acceptable if it is done in good cause, or at least retribution for it is to be abated.

And in even less weighty things. One year the tax laws prohibit thus-and-so; the next it is allowed; and perhaps—who knows?—the year after it will again be proscribed. Judicial rules on questions much more prosaic than great constitutional issues are themselves hardly less mutable; a widespread complaint of lawyers today is that they do not know from one court session to the next what the law is.

From this comes that modern dilemma of how to balance

change and stability, no easier struck now than in the days of St. Thomas. The civil law, like human custom, cannot be altogether unchangeable; both must yield at times to the "changed condition of men." Yet when the faith in change becomes an idolatry of those who make both laws and customs, who need be surprised if it infects those who are asked to obey them? How, in the simplest case, do you restrain teenagers from exuberant disorder when they see that elsewhere disorder is inveighed against neither by law nor custom?

Frankly, I don't know where the answer lies. But it is rather ironic—is it not?—that this great modern dilemma, now being discovered in surprise by practical men, should have been re-marked upon long ago by a man in an ancient monastery.

December 22, 1964

OF MEN AND ANGELS

THE late Thomas F. Woodlock, whose thoughts on things were a feature of *The Wall Street Journal* many years ago, was wont to return often to a search which was once thought worthy of the perplexity of philosophers. The search was to answer the simple question: What is Man?

The question was implicit whenever he wrote, as he did voluminously, on very practical matters that seemed remote from metaphysics—on monetary policy, for example, or speculation in the stock market, or on foreign policy problems of war and peace. "We chatter fatuously of dictators and democracies," he remarked on the eve of World War II, "as if it were merely a matter of governmental forms or, even, economic theories that is in question. It is not rival forms but rival substances that face each other— the most fundamental of all ideas, man's idea of his own nature, man's concept of himself and his destiny."

So he urged his readers to see the brewing war as a conflict over the nature of man. And so he saw many political issues, as a reflection of the conflict over whether the state should be the master or the servant of men.

Sometimes at Christmastide he would state the question explicitly: Man is either nothing more than a collection of atoms shaped in the form of an animal, or he is the Man of the Psalmist, "a little lower than the angels . . . crowned with glory and honor."

Today the very form of the question would strike most people as quaint. To our generation angels are no more prevalent than witches. As for its substance, enlightened intellect is supposed to have settled that. In the graphic words of a scientist eminent in Woodlock's day, the anthropologist S. J. Holmes: "All natural traits and impulses of human beings must therefore be fundamentally good . . . Cruelty, selfishness, lust; cowardice and deceit are normal ingredients of human nature . . . Intrinsically they are all virtues."

This is no mere recognition of the natural frailties of men. In that "scientific" view of Man, cruelty and deceit are not treated as imperfections which we may all be brought to simply because we are not gods; the plea is not even that these are failings to be understood and forgiven. What is claimed in this view is that sadism and dishonesty are virtues to be acquired as they are useful. For animals—is it not so?—love and lust are one, and being one are indistinguishable.

Such, strangely, is the modern view preached under the aegis both of scientists renowned for their knowledge and philosophers reputed for their wisdom. It is not only a rejection of angels to aspire to; discarded also along with Man's divinity is the conception of Man's uniqueness or that his destiny is any greater than that of beasts.

Thus Socrates, the rationalist, is thought as outmoded as St. Paul, the mystic. Spinoza, to whom man's special status was the human mind, is as out of the common course today as Buddha, who saw in Man a special spirit. The concept of Sin, which for Thomas Aquinas was the fruit of Man's first disobedience, is as insubstantial as the Superego, which to Freud was the inner measure by which Man tells good from evil action and which, in lieu of God, punishes the way of the transgressor.

If this were a correct view of Man, then why indeed should anyone lament the animal behavior of men? Yet lamentations are being heard in the land, and the sound of them come from strange places. Clerics who debate whether God is dead give sermons decrying the mores of their flocks. It is no longer unusual to find articles in the intellectual magazines, both popular and esoteric, bemoaning the alienation of man from society and the crumbling of society's ethics. A recent issue of *The American Scholar*, one of the more reflective quarterlies, is mirror to such reflections. In a single issue here is Joseph Wood Krutch sadly puzzling over the modern cult of the Marquis de Sade. Storm Jameson, in a little essay on the writer in contemporary society, confessing that the attack on conventions "which can be gay and salutary" begins to shock "when it becomes an attack on self-respect and decent self-love." John Morris expressing pleasant surprise at a writer who can use words like "gentlemen" and "honorable" without "somewhere a trace of irony."

Finally, there is Hiram Haydn offering a jeremiad against our society, "in which violence and cruelty and vindictiveness flare openly every day" and where sexual exhibitionism concentrates on "sadism and fifty-seven kinds of perversion."

Mind you, these are not the voices of the bourgeoisie. All these writers have impeccable credentials as intellectuals—rational, progressive, and nonmystic. The heralds of the Enlightenment have joined the Puritans at the wailing wall.

While that in itself is interesting, the strange thing about it is that these new criers of "O Tempora, O Mores" seem to see no connection between the ideas about Man and the behavior of men.

Yet if Man, in the words of the anthropologist, is no more than "a predator whose natural instinct is to kill with a weapon," can we logically decry the instinct which, being natural, is thereby virtuous? We may fear the predator for ourselves, as the lamb does the lion, but if it be true that Man is nothing but another animal, as modern philosophers assert, then what moral reason can there be for condemnation?

An old man is sliced up on a park bench by a pack in human

form for the joy of seeing him bleed, and we are begged by public leaders to have sympathy not for the dead but for the unfortunate young with nothing else to occupy their time. A tortured woman stands on a windowsill and the gathering crowd yells "jump" for a lunch-hour thrill. Why not? Lust, cruelty, selfishness are indeed instincts we share with the beasts. But if this be all, as the new philosophy dreams, then what point is there in kindness, courtesy, charity, chastity, respect, or honor?

Still, if wise men today lament the consequences they may one day look to the causes. And if they do not recover the vision of the Apostles, they may at least share with an ancient pagan the view that "humanity is poised midway between the gods and beasts." That, after all, is not too far from where once the angels dwelled.

December 23, 1965

II

POLITICAL GAMES

THE PERILS OF POLITICS

You can set it down as a firm principle that nothing more disturbs the even tenor of political life than the perils of a re-election campaign. The nearest thing to it is the frustration of being a governor asked to govern amid a large and loud opposition among the governed.

"A most wretched custom," old Cicero remarked long ago, "is our electioneering and scrambling for office"—a sentiment shared, albeit for somewhat different reasons, by every man who holds an office anywhere.

Consider, for example, what a disruption it is to General de Gaulle to have to turn aside from his work of reshaping France, the Common Market, and the Western Alliance in order to scramble for votes against provincial politicians hardly anyone ever heard of before. Or what a frustration to Harold Wilson to have every plan for the whole of Britain hang upon the health of a single member of an almost equally divided Parliament. How much better affairs could be managed with a solid majority and a sure space of time before again that dreadful business on the hustings.

So you can set it down as a firm rule that every man in office is in favor of longer terms in office. And that those whose office is to direct the affairs of a village or a nation will look longingly at an arrangement less conducive to opposed councils and better designed to give them authority commensurate with their conceived responsibilities.

35

In short, from their own points of view President Johnson is logical in proposing that terms in the House of Representatives be made coincident with the terms of the Presidency, and the Congressmen are equally so in welcoming the extension of their terms from two to four years.

As a matter of fact, there are some undeniable merits in the idea. Election campaigns are as much a disruption to the country as to those seeking re-election. Not only the partisans of the candidates but the people who must decide have their attention diverted from their normal affairs. The division of the country is acerbated. And it is an expensive business for taxpayers.

In this country with its fixed dates for elections they sometimes come inopportunely. In two of our major wars we have paused in mid-battle for Presidential campaigns, and though in neither case did the people abruptly change leadership it could have happened and there are many who think it unwise to risk such a political upheaval in time of war. To some thoughtful people, too, the frequency of elections for our House of Representatives forms a particularly troublesome case. The question caused a good deal of debate among those drafting the Constitution, and Mr. Johnson is not the first one since then to suggest changing the arrangement.

One argument for changing it is the contention, not easily gainsaid, that some Congressmen are reduced to half-time legislators. That is, they must devote a good part of their second year to persuading people to re-elect them, a disproportionate diversion compared with four-year Presidents and six-year Senators.

It is also perfectly true, as President Johnson said, that it takes time "to master the technical tasks of legislating," time wasted for a Congressman elected one year and tossed out two years later, although by this argument all incumbents ought always to be re-elected.

Finally, it's true that biennial elections can handicap a President in what he wants to do. Several times in recent history a President of one party has had to face a House with a majority from the other party.

Thus run the arguments. But they also run squarely into the fact that what is complained of is not the result of thoughtless happenstance but thoughtful design. Unlike parliamentary-type democracies we have fixed terms of office precisely because there is wisdom in making the governors return to the people whether it suits their convenience or not. And we use different terms for different parts of the government with the wise intent of minimizing the risk from unchecked majorities, especially ones based on fleeting political passions.

The Senate never changes altogether at one election no matter how momentarily popular the President who is chosen. We may someday end up with a one-party government, but it cannot come to us overnight in a moment of excitement. The conscious design in having interim elections to the House is to guard against the possibility that a President, once elected, should "have his head" for four full years with no chance for the people to express their judgment on his policies or actions. In these days, when wars and other great events can come so swiftly, four years can be a very long time.

The arrangement, adopted only after prolonged consideration of alternatives, knowingly accepts the troubles of frequent electioneering for Congressmen and the possible frustrations of Presidents from seeing the House captured by another party. Perhaps it is curious, but it is nonetheless true, that this arrangement has served the country well for more than a century and a half. Biennial electioneering has really caused no great difficulty, even in wartime. It hasn't deterred able men from serving—or kept them from being rechosen over and over again; two members of the present House have served longer than the most senior Senator.

What the President proposes is to abandon, not merely to

37

modify, this tested system. The idea isn't to extend House terms on a staggered system, as in the Senate. He wants the term of every House member to be concurrent with those of the President. This would almost surely mean that every winning President would win the House also and be assured control of it for his full term. Without doubt that would make every President's political task easier and every Congressman's life less perilous.

What it leaves in doubt is whether the people will be better governed by reducing their opportunities for voting in order to reduce the perils of politicians.

January 20, 1966

SERMON ON THE HILL

Tom Sawyer's Uncle Silas, if Huck Finn has it right, could preach the dad-blamedest sermons you ever heard. Within the family and among the neighbors he was just plain folks and about the humblest man you ever met. Aunt Sally used to boss him around right awful. But the minute he got up in the pulpit something different came over him. He'd get a-holt of the text and really lay into the congregation on how they ought to behave. For the first ten minutes or so he'd have them riveted because he usually had a point. But it was mighty hard for Uncle Silas to know when to stop. Just when the people thought he'd wound it up and it was time to sing the hymn, Uncle Silas would recall something he'd forgot to say, or maybe just think of a new way to say what he'd already said, and before you'd know it he'd be meandering all over the state of Arkansaw. By the time he got through, the way Huck put it, half the congregation would be nodding, the other half would be fidgeting, and all of them would be so tangled up they couldn't find their way home in daylight.

Sometimes, it seems, it's that way when Lyndon gets a-holt of a real good text.

There's hardly an editor in the country who can disremember the President's talk last spring in the rose garden at the White House. Mr. Johnson was only going to say a few words of welcome to the American Society of Newspaper Editors. Before it was over the visitors had heard a half-hour sermon on civil rights, poverty, education, and the Bible.

Millions of folks got a sample of the President's technique on their TV screens when Mr. Johnson went up to talk to Congress about civil rights and such things. This time the President had sure enough got a-holt of a real good text—next to the Bible there ain't nothing holier than the Constitution—and you sure have to admit that his point about civil rights was superpluperfect. He had both law and morality on his side, and there warn't a decent member of the congregation didn't know he was dead right.

In fact, it didn't take him more than about fifteen minutes to convince them. In that first quarter hour he was sharp, concise, forceful, and moving in words well chosen by somebody who knew how to put them down on paper. If he'd a-quit then he'd have had himself another Gettysburg address, and the Congress would have risen up and enacted the morning paper into law, just like they once did for Franklin Roosevelt.

But just about the time the applause was deafening and everybody was ready to stand up, that far-away look came over his eyes and he lifted his head up from the text. Pleased as Punch with the reception he was getting, he wanted to get in a few more licks.

Anyway, he said it all over again. He reminded us twice that it was a hundred years since Abraham Lincoln, and twice pointed out that a hundred years make a century. At least three times he told us that the right to vote was fundamental to democracy and that men ought not to be bigoted, just in case the point escaped us the first time around.

Then having disposed of bigotry, he took off on poverty and disease. Neither one of these would be banished by the law he was proposing, possibly not by any law the Congress could pass, but you can hardly deny that they're fit subjects for any sermon.

Next he went back to Cotulla, Texas, to show us how it is to walk with the poor. In 1928, of course, he never dreamed that he'd be rich and President of the United States. But America is a place where a young fellow can exceed even his most fondest dreams, whether he starts from Cotulla or Abilene, Kansas, or Independence, Missouri. The important thing is for Presidents to use their chance to help people. And he let us in on a "secret," as if he feared nobody had suspected it. "I plan to use it."

From Texas he moved on to Buffalo, Birmingham, Cincinnati, and Philadelphia to remind us that this is one nation and we ought to all put our shoulders to the wheel, open the city of hope to all people, and work together to heal the wounds.

Judging by the applause, although by now it was somewhat wearier than before, hardly anybody took exception to this, Republicans or Democrats. The only thing you could notice, scanning the floor of the House, was that the Democrats in full view up front seemed a bit more alert than those half-hidden in the rear.

Certainly nobody in that peaceful, historic chamber could take exception when he recalled that men from the South were at Iwo Jima and men from the North have carried Old Glory to the far corners of the world and brought it back without a stain on it. Or that in Vietnam today men drafted from the East and from the West are all fighting together without regard to religion or color or region of the Great Republic.

In fact, he couldn't be faulted for leaving anything out. He approved of demonstrations to provoke change and stir reform but advised us to turn away from violence and respect law and order. He said we should preserve the right of free assembly but shouldn't holler fire in a crowded theater. On the way he took a couple of swipes at President Roosevelt and President Truman, one of whom came to Congress to veto a veterans bill and the other to draft railroad workers into the Army. Not to criticize but to emphasize that his own appearance in the great chamber was to serve the people out yonder in the fifty states.

"I want to be the President who helped feed the hungry," he

II · POLITICAL GAMES

said. "I want to be the President who helped the poor. . . . I want to be the President who helped to end hatred among his fellow men and who promoted love. . . . I want to be the President who helped end war among the brothers of the earth. . . . I want. . . ."

It made you feel kind of sad to see the Congressmen and the gallery getting a bit glassy-eyed, and to read in the *New York Times* that one third of the TV audience tuned him out that last half-hour. It was surely one of the elegantest sermons that ever was.

But maybe it will be like with Uncle Silas. The folks would sometimes get the jimjams and the fantods, but they got the message and nobody could be gratefuler or lovinger. They knowed all the time his heart was in the right place.

March 19, 1965

OLE CASE AND THE GOP

Some of them big fellows," ole Case was saying, "just want to stand up there and knock the cover off of the ball or stand on the mound and see how hard they can throw it."

No doubt about it; managing the Mets would make a philosopher out of anybody, and Casey Stengel was scattering his words of wisdom like confetti, while the sportswriters scrambled to sift the pearls out of the syntax.

"They don't wanna learn," said the perfesser, explaining why his side mostly got clobbered. "They don't wanna learn to watch the infield and outfield so they can run smart if they get on base. They don't wanna learn how to ketch a man off base and pick him off."

He brooded for a moment, or so it says here in the dispatch from St. Petersburg. "We have young men on this ball club who have been highly educated at the best universities and can memorize every batter in the league, but what good's it do when they can't get the ball over the plate?"

It was, take it all in all, a real meaty press conference, especially when you compare it to some of those that take place in Washington. And it struck me that a lot of people in the political leagues could learn something from ole Case. Much of what he said about the Mets would fit the Republicans and explain why, more years than not, they get nosed out for the pennant.

In any business the pros will most likely take the amateurs and, it's like Casey says, you don't get to be a real pro just by getting all dressed up and swinging hard. "Our uniforms was big league, they cost as much as anybody else's, but the fellows in them was just make work."

Yet the Republicans, take it over the years, have always had a predilection for amateurs in the political game, however good they may have been at other things. President Hoover probably understood the problems facing the country as well as any man of his time and he was a far better President than anybody gave him credit for. But certainly one of his handicaps was that he was a latecomer to politics, the Presidency being the first elective office he ever held.

Alf Landon had somewhat better political credentials since he had been elected governor of Kansas, but this experience had come late in life and in 1936 he was up against the greatest political pro of the century. F.D.R., lest anyone forget, had been in politics since he was a young man, in Washington, in the Albany legislature, as a Vice Presidential candidate, and as governor, all before he got elected President.

The Republicans next turned to Wendell Willkie. Mr. Willkie was one of the most charming men you ever met; he had a flashing mind, striking personality, and an impressive grasp of the issues considered in the abstract. But in politics he was the veriest sort of amateur, and the Republican front office surrounded him with the most motley collection of amateurs imaginable. He swung for the bleachers every time but never came close to hitting the ball.

Tom Dewey you'd have to set down as a pro, like Richard Nixon after him. And as you may have noticed, each of them missed only by a hairsbreadth and in each case it took a real pro team to topple them. Both Truman and Kennedy, the winners, knew how to ketch a man off base and pick him off.

Eisenhower, of course, was the exception to test the rule, winning with natural talent and flair. But it often seemed he didn't

44

know the political infield from the outfield, and his amateur's attitude toward politics proved costly to the Republicans; they failed to use his eight years on base to build up a good running team.

So here the Republicans are now, with spring training already started, and every reporter covering the game puts the odds against them. Ambassador Lodge, who has shown well in the exhibition games, is viewed in the locker room as a nine-to-five player lacking the Durocher spirit. Senator Goldwater works at it but seems to lack the knack. Governor Rockefeller shows his lack of seasoning in the minor leagues; he throws hard but doesn't always get it over the plate.

Governor Scranton has certainly had varied experience and his batting average is very good. The question here is whether he has his heart in the game, or is sort of a "gentleman bowler" who doesn't want to play if he thinks the team's chances aren't good. That leaves Mr. Nixon as almost the only full-fledged pro in the starting line-up, and he's been in a slump.

Arrayed against them is a team led by a Texas leaguer who started politicking practically in his cradle; Lyndon Johnson's years in politics about equal all the Republicans' combined. To follow him in the batting order he can turn to people like Senator Humphrey, thoroughly experienced both in Congress and on the hustings, or Attorney General Kennedy, young, but a hard driver and a tough campaigner. And the Democratic ranks are full of men to whom politics is a lifework, a full-time profession.

Maybe that's the secret. Too many Republican leaders act as if politics were a thing they got into out of a sense of civic duty, or from late-blooming ambition. Too often Republican politics is a sometimes affair all down the line; quadrennially they whip up the team spirit but between times they are busy with other business.

To many Democrats politics is their livelihood; Lyndon John-

45

son hasn't been off the public payroll since 1932. They work at it, fair weather and foul, and take the trouble to learn the intricacies of the steal, the double play, the bunt, and the sacrifice. They take the long view; even while losing one game they're plotting how to win the next. Most of all, they play together even if they don't happen to like the manager of the moment.

The one view is the amateur's, the other the pro's. And it's like ole Case says, If you gonna win in the big leagues, you gotta learn the trade. Otherwise you just stay in the cellar.

April 14, 1964

LANDSLIDES

O N the day after election—it fell on November 6 in that halcyon year of 1928—the political wreckage of the Democratic Party was strewn far and wide.

Poor Al Smith had managed to lose all but two states in the East, the entire West and Border states, and even five of the traditional Dixie strongholds. No wonder that in the aftermath of the landslide a great national magazine carried a famous article echoing the gloom of the newspaper pundits. The Democrats were dead.

They had been slain, or so it seemed, by a concatenation of circumstances. First of all, there was the matter of prosperity. Smith tried to suggest that not all was well, as indeed it wasn't, but the idea was hard to sell to people who had fat pay envelopes and saw easy money almost everywhere. Especially so since the Republicans in the popular mind had the image of the Grand Old Party of the workingman, the farmers, the Negroes, with a consistent record not only of prosperity but of peace. Since 1860 only two Democrats had ever been elected President; the last one was Woodrow Wilson, who got in by political accident and then got the country into a war.

Then there was the business about prohibition. The platforms of both parties endorsed this experiment, noble in purpose, and pledged full enforcement. But Governor Smith was a blunt, outspoken man, and the Democratic resolutions committee had hardly finished its work before the governor pulled that plank right

47

out from under the convention with a statement implying that the noble purpose wasn't very practical.

In their hearts most people knew he was right. But when Mr. Smith talked about "fundamental changes" it made him sound like a radical tinkerer with the Constitution, and in that happy time nobody was in the mood for extremists. As Will Rogers aptly put it, folks were willing to stagger to the polls and vote dry. They also seemed to be in a mood to decry low-level politics while lapping up smears. It was one of the dirtiest campaigns to date. Hoover was more dirtied four years later but even in '28 there were efforts to tar him with the Teapot Dome scandal because he had been guilty of association with the guilty. Smith was smeared with everything handy.

One story of the day, for example, was that the Happy Warrior was often high on bootleg booze and that sometimes it took two men to prop him up on a platform to make a speech. "Do you want a drunk in the White House?" And there was that picture of the governor standing at the entrance to the Holland Tunnel with the astounding explanation that this was going to be the basement to the Vatican when President Smith brought the Pope to America. This was typical of the bigotry, both social and religious, that backlashed both ways. It was said Hoover couldn't have a strong foreign policy because he was a Quaker, and that Smith's foreign policy would be run by the cardinals. Priests passed the word to vote for Smith because he was Catholic and Protestant ministers preached against him for the same reason.

Finally, as a factor in that Democratic debacle, there was the personality of Al Smith himself, surely one of the most colorful politicians of the century. Born in the shadow of Brooklyn Bridge, Smith left school before he was thirteen and turned to Tammany politics as one of the few careers then open to an uneducated man. Working his way up through the machine ranks, he first got himself elected governor of New York in 1918, lost in 1920, and returned to office in 1922. In 1924 he was a leading candidate for the Presidential nomination, for which he was proposed by a young New York aristocrat, Franklin Roosevelt.

During this pilgrim's progress he grew in stature but he could never quite outgrow some of the deficiencies in his education or the mannerisms of his origins. He never quite understood the virtues of the carefully worked out, formal speech and he rarely used it in the '28 campaign. He preferred the off-the-cuff speech in which he flayed away at whatever came to mind.

This proved effective with the listeners in his personal presence and gained him followers far more enthusiastic than those of Mr. Hoover, who was somewhat colorless but encouraged a sense of confidence. But Smith's speeches too often read poorly when set down in newsprint. And on that new-fangled contraption, the "raddio," he sounded perfectly dreadful. So he struck a good many people as a dreadful prospect for the White House, with his derby hat, his cigar, his accent, his unintellectual way of discussing public issues. As with prohibition, he spoke a lot of common sense about a lot of things but all too often it came out seeming oversimplified.

Recollection, that sometimes frail reed, suggests that people rather liked Al Smith (later he was certainly immensely popular), but that for one reason or another they just couldn't see him as President. Probably any Democrat would have lost in 1928, there being a tide in such affairs, but Al Smith was the wrong candidate running on the wrong issues at the wrong time. And that turned defeat into debacle.

Ah, well. The magazine that tolled its obituary over the Democratic Party is now extinct while the Democratic Party, as you can see this morning, is still quite alive.

Moreover, that noble experiment which upon one November morning seemed untouchable to every politician in the land is now long gone and happily forgotten. A bare four years later both political parties were embracing the "fundamental changes" which had seemed so extremist when first mentioned out loud by a man willing to speak his mind, good politics or not.

One moral of this tale, if you must have one, might be that there is a substitute for victory. Al Smith never got to be President, yet he ended a popular delusion, changed a major policy of both political parties, and led the way to an amendment in the Constitution. Few Presidents, come to think of it, can claim as much.

As for the Democrats, maybe they were lucky, since 1928 was followed relentlessly by 1929. Anyway it's a reminder to the Republicans of 1964 that in politics landslides aren't always fatal.

November 5, 1964

POLITICAL FANTASY

Y ou can set it down as a general rule that when American voters choose a political leader they expect him to solve their problems. Not just ease them; end them. Else, what's a politician for? And he'd better solve them—or else.

Do we think our district isn't getting enough urban renewal money out of Washington? Get a new Congressman. Is the city traffic in a hopeless snarl? Get a new mayor. Is the state's farm-land suffering a drought? Get a new governor. Are we frustrated by foreign policy or is the domestic economy faltering? Get a new President.

There is more to this than a feeling, often quite reasonable, that altering men may alter policies and that one policy may make a better contribution to the public weal than another. We ask the new man to solve the problem altogether, and if he falls short of that we are quite apt to toss him out at the next election.

The politicans, of course, abet this idea themselves. The man out of office always has to hold out a solution to the problem that the incumbent has manifestly failed at, even at the risk of booby-trapping himself after he's elected and can't find the remedy either.

All this can be pretty amusing, and jokes about it are a part of our folklore. But it has its sad side too. For imbedded in this attitude, shared by people and politicians alike, is a firm convic-tion that for every problem there exists a solution. More, that for nearly every problem there exists a political solution. All that is seemingly required, therefore, is that we find the politician who has found the solution. Then our troubles will be over. The rub is that the premise is wrong. There are some problems for which there is no solution. There are others for which, if there are solutions, they lie in the slow application of time-consuming remedies. And yet others for which the apparent cures are breeders of new ills.

The treachery that lies in supposing otherwise is not merely that we are betrayed into disillusionment, heartbreaking though that can be. The disillusionment, once it comes, can paralyze those actions which, while far from solving a problem, can contribute much to its amelioration. And it can also (indeed it has in other times and places) leave people an easy prey for charlatans.

The war in Vietnam may serve as an example. You can argue, according to your lights, that the better course is to withdraw, to blow up a bigger war to get it over with, or simply to continue our present course with bulldog tenacity. The illusion lies in supposing that any of these courses will "solve" the problem that Vietnam represents, which in reality is the problem of Asia.

The point is not that one of these courses may not be better than the others but rather that none of them would write *finis* to the problem. Yet in something that touches all of us so closely as a war this is not a conclusion any of us readily accepts. That is why so many people turn longingly to anybody—some to the hawks and some to the doves—who professes to have the simple, quick answer.

This propensity for the simple solution has also betrayed us, to choose another example, in the race problem. That much has been done in the past decade to ameliorate the situation of the Negro in a white society is surely plain. That much more can and will be done over the next decades is equally certain. But it ought to be clear also to anyone who gives that problem a moment's real thought that there is no political leader anywhere, white or Negro, who has a cure for it that he can pluck out of his bag, plump into law, and so write *finis* to that problem.

The false hopes have already proven costly. Many Negro people, disillusioned, are turning away from their thoughtful leaders to charlatans. Many white people are likewise turning to politicians who seem to promise that the problem will go away if it is just ignored. Either way, the disaffected are reflecting a belief that political measures can resolve a problem which, if not ultimately insoluble, cannot in fact be solved by political remedies. And the tragic part of it is that meanwhile the wise course of slow, steady progress toward a better—if not a perfect—situation is being impeded.

The examples could be readily multiplied. In the economic field disillusionment has set in with "perpetual inflation" as the nostrum for perpetual prosperity. But the idea persists that our political leaders could, if they were just clever enough, take all the pains out of economic life and spare us all toil and trouble.

President Johnson, so report the political dispatches, is in political trouble because he hasn't solved Vietnam, the race problem, or our economic woes, all of which is incontrovertible fact. Perhaps you need not waste sympathy on him, since he asked for the judgment by posing as the master politician who would solve all those problems. But you might spare a moment of pity for the next Republican candidate, whoever he may be. For he has got to promise the electorate that he has, somewhere in his pocket, just the right medicine for each and every one of these ailments.

This fantasy that for every problem there exists a political solution is largely responsible for the drift toward paternalistic (or socialistic, if you prefer) government. In its extreme form it helps account for that phenomenon of the twentieth century, the totalitarian government. Hitler came to power because he persuaded Germans that all German problems had political solutions and that he knew what they were. A similar fantasy nurtured Lenin,

Mussolini, and Castro.

But maybe one fancy deserves another. And one pleasant dream is of a major party candidate for President of the United States who would confess that he wasn't sure what to do about Vietnam, that he had no magic formula for racial problems, that he had small hopes of abolishing poverty overnight, and that regrettably he wasn't omniscient enough to abolish every economic woe—that he could, and would, only pledge himself to do the very best he could to meet each problem and try to make it a little less woeful.

Fantasy, of course, is the only word for such an idle dream. Such a candidate would be honest, novel, and wonderfully refreshing. And he would almost surely get clobbered.

October 7, 1966

SULLY WITH THE FRINGE ON TOP

E VER since Xenophon took leave from the Socratic school and got mixed up in the Persian wars, men whose talents or luck put them at the center of public affairs have unlimbered their pens to serve up their version of history hot off the griddle. Sometimes the history has been written by the men who made it. Caesar did it for the Gallic wars, and undoubtedly would have added his version of the founding of Imperial Rome if something hadn't happened to him on the way to the forum. In our own time Winston Churchill often gave the impression he ran World War II just so he could write books about it. Presidents Hoover, Truman, and Eisenhower—not to mention half the generals of recent wars—have told us how it looked to the men who had to make the decisions.

Secondary characters, those whose only claim to fame is their nearness to the great, have also capitalized on their luck by turning chroniclers. Who would remember Madame de Pompadour but for her proximity to Louis XV? Or William Herndon, except that he was Lincoln's law partner? And the practice has its virtues. Of course you need to remember that President Grant's history of his own Administration may have a certain bias, and that Hopkins's diaries aren't unprejudiced when they mention Morgenthau, Wallace, Ickes, or other contemporaries of the Roosevelt era. Yet trivia, even gossip, can be as much the stuff of history as a state document once you have the means of giving it perspective.

Just because it does need some perspective, however, there's virtue too in the reticence which has often prompted thoughtful men to wait a while before they put to print every keyhole revelation. A decent interval lets tempers cool and avoids the danger of idle gossip's injury. That's why once the fashion was for public men to bequeath their private papers to a musty library to lie unopened until long after the great events in which they participated.

Once; no more. Nowadays a man appointed aide to a commanding general or assistant to a President sharpens his pencils, and probably buys a tape recorder, before even reporting for duty. The idea is to get there fustest with the mostest memoirs.

The memorialists of the inside-the-Kennedy Administration are off to a good start. Two of these, Ted Sorensen and Arthur Schlesinger, Jr., have already gotten fanfares of publicity, and the odds are strong that others are quietly scribbling away on their own versions of who said what to whom. This is a tribute to President Kennedy, who while he paused briefly on the scene left nonetheless an indelible mark. It's not so clear what else these hot-off-the-griddle books are tribute to.

Perhaps for future historians they'll prove a real contribution to history. The difficulty is that all most people are noticing now are the juicier morsels. We are told, for example, that the man who is presently President of the United States got the opportunity to be President only by the grossest sort of maneuvering. Lyndon Johnson, you gather from the gossip of Mr. Schlesinger, was viewed by Mr. Kennedy as about on a par with a "riverboat gambler." He supposedly offered Mr. Johnson the Vice Presidency as a gimmick to get party unity, expecting he would decline.

No one can know whether this gossip is true. But true or not, it sullies the memory of President Kennedy, which was doubtless unintended by the gossipers, and casts a slur on the present President, which doubtless was intended.

Then again we're told that President Kennedy wanted to get

rid of the man who is still Secretary of State on the grounds that he was incompetent. The concrete evidence cited for this by historian Schlesinger is that Mr. Kennedy exploded to his wife, "Jacqueline, damn it, Bundy and I get more done in one day at the White House than they do in six months at the State Department." After this bit of husband and wife conversation comes a lengthy analysis of the shortcomings of Secretary Rusk. Here Mr. Kennedy is not quoted; the words are Mr. Schlesinger's. All the same, since Mr. Schlesinger purports to be writing history, the inference most people draw is that when he speaks of Mr. Rusk's "blandness" or his lack of "command" the judgments are not just Mr. Schlesinger's but also those of President Kennedy.

In history this gossip may not matter. For the present, the Secretary of State is left under the stigma that his President had lost confidence in him. What results, then, in both cases, is character assassination by gossip. Neither Mr. Johnson nor Mr. Rusk can answer, and President Kennedy can no longer explain. And it's all so cruelly pointless.

There's something more troublesome, too, about all this than possible wounded feelings. A man in public life has to expect a certain amount of gossip, and it's always true that our versions of history are colored by who's the most articulate protagonist. But imagine, if you will, the effect on the public councils if every man asked for a private opinion must look around the table and wonder which of his colleagues is the eager diarist biding his chance to rush and tell all. Who then would be frank, toss out a tentative idea, play the devil's advocate among the courtiers?

It is hard to imagine anything more destructive, not merely of men's reputation but of the public weal, especially when what is reported for the delectation of the multitude is sometimes nothing more than what one man says another man said a President said about somebody else.

The raw material of history lies in the recollections of men who were there about what happened within their purview; history is served too when men set down afterwards the reasons why they did what they did. It can even be served when those who were there set down their personal opinions, on their own responsibility, of others who played their role in the event. Out of such raw material one day, hopefully, comes the truth.

Quite apart from the question of good manners, though, it's a little hard to see what is served by sullying men with gossip dressed up in the tassels of history.

August 8, 1965

SHOW BIZ ON THE HUSTINGS

IN all this political confusion we're almost persuaded to plump for Fredric March as President of the United States.

If you'll drop by the neighborhood movie house where they're playing *Seven Days in May* you'll see what we mean. The show is pretty melodramatic, all right, but so is the political scene these days, and take it all in all we think President March handled all those awesome responsibilities as well as anybody.

First off, he looks like a President, which is important in the television era. He has the deep-lined face of Lyndon Johnson, the strong jaw of Franklin Roosevelt, the expressive eyes of John Kennedy, and the finest political profile since Warren Harding.

Moreover, President March is obviously a man of character, driving himself mercilessly in spite of the doctor's warnings, never losing his grip on his principles even while showing the utmost skill in the rough-and-tumble of political infighting. Finally, he is an extremely articulate President and his skillful handling of a crucial TV press conference beats all the other hopefuls hollow.

If anybody wants to object that this is just show business, we'll remind him that acting has always been an important part of leadership. Julius Caesar rallied his troops with histrionics and so did Winston Churchill a beleaguered nation. Modern technology is just making thespianism more important.

Whatever President Hoover's other virtues or failings, he wasn't photogenic and he didn't have F.D.R.'s resonant radio voice or commanding presence. Just about everybody is agreed that the turning point in 1960 was when Kennedy outpointed Nixon in their joint TV appearances.

As for the objection that Mr. March's articulate lines were written by others—including Fletcher Knebel, a journalist with a longer Washington experience than any of the current Presidential aspirants—we'd answer that Thomas Jefferson, no mean hand with words, scripted for President Washington. In more recent times the White House has been haunted with ghost writers; Sherwood for Roosevelt, Sorensen for Kennedy.

As for the objection that President March's movie performance was improved by the fact that the final version was but a fraction of what was photographed, with scenes rearranged in the viewing room and any flubs left on the cutting room floor—well, we give you President Johnson's recent TV performance, that Sunday night conversation with three professional journalists.

It was a very fine performance, as we remarked at the time. Mr. Johnson was the very picture of a President, grave, thoughtful, informed, and albeit showing just the right touch of human frailty. One of the most effective parts of the performance, as a good many of the critics noted, was the little soliloquy on freedom in America with which the show ended. It was sentimental but not too much so, and it was placed perfectly for the final fade-out.

Still, Mr. Johnson had no less the benefit of rearrangement that Sunday evening than did Mr. March. The professional producers of President Johnson's TV show shot a good third more of film than the audience ever saw. Then from the eighty minutes of raw material they cut it down to sixty minutes of running time.

Naturally we don't know what was left out, but judging by what was left in we doubt if it was anything Mr. Johnson said of great significance. Since TV is a form of show business, we suppose the cutting decisions were made just to improve the tempo, give a little better display to the better scenes, and perhaps sharpen the dramatic effect of the more moving ones.

This certainly was the reason behind the rearrangement of scenes. The question you heard about the Bobby Baker case, so our TV friends tell us, originally came near the end of the show. But this put it out of sequence with some other questions about a President's political troubles and furthermore made it a little anticlimactic after such subjects as poverty and Vietnam. So it was moved up in the cutting room.

Another shift made an even more profound difference in the drama of the performance. In the original run-through the soliloquy on freedom was in the middle. Afterwards it was obvious that in terms of dramatic structure and impact on the audience this scene would make a fine ending. Which is where it ended up.

As an old play-goer I wouldn't fault any of these decisions. If you are going to put on a show, especially one an hour long, there's no reason why you shouldn't make it as interesting as possible. The presence of artistry doesn't necessarily mean that the finished version gives any less of a true picture of the man in the White House, because whenever he's on public view, no matter who he is, he is playing a role just as we all are when we don our best suits and go a-calling.

Moreover, selection and rearrangement is a proper function of journalism. A reporter writing about a President's press conference doesn't recount the questions and answers seriatim; he may omit some entirely. It's not at all unusual for a TV news show to show snippets of speeches or interviews. What's a bit disturbing is the fact that the vast majority of the viewers of this conversation with the President didn't know the manner of its staging. It's one thing for a newspaper to print excerpts from a President's press conference, to choose a comparable example, when they are so labeled. It would be something else to announce "the text of the press conference" if in fact it was cut; worse if the questions were rearranged to suit an editor's literary fancy.

The label "prerecorded" seems hardly enough to avoid misleading viewers, nor is it enough to rely on the possibility that every watcher keeps up with the TV gossip columns where the show-business aspects of the White House might be mentioned.

Nobody can separate the Presidency from the performing arts; nor should they, for the men as well as the ideas that move us are reflected in images. All the same, if the Presidency is going to be turned into just an adjunct to show business, don't be surprised if some people someday decide to choose the pro over the amateur. If manner is to become all that counts, might as well plump for President March. Best performance you ever saw.

March 24, 1964

"GOOD" POLITICS

D IP into either political party, Democratic or Republican, and you can find almost any political philosophy you wish—men who preach economy or spending, managed currency or sound money, the planned economy or free enterprise, a return to local government or a bigger federal government, the welfare state or rugged individualism.

This cross fertilization of politics perturbs many people because it is irrational and because it seems to mark a degeneration from the good old days when the parties stood on principles. Yet to Herbert Agar, who in his book *The Price of Freedom* has done a comprehensive study of party politics, the picture of the parties all fouled up is simply normal. Furthermore, Mr. Agar finds this good. In his view politics and principles don't mix.

As to the normalcy of this tossing of the political salad—so that both parties seem to offer the same menu with a slightly different sauce—the evidence is fairly convincing. Rare have been the times when the two major parties in American politics have demanded that the voters make a decided choice on a matter of deep principle. As to the rightness of this habit—that is a matter still open to debate.

Mr. Agar argues that compromise is the only safe road for a democracy. Therefore the aim of each party should be to avoid setting group against group—which means offering a little something to everybody—and the "great" leaders have been those who understood this and acted upon it. This is an interesting view, if not a novel one. But it leads to strange places.

Theodore Roosevelt was the last of the Republican Presidents to be a master of "group diplomacy," the method by which a President builds and maintains an inharmonious party. The last master of group diplomacy was another Roosevelt, but this time in the Democratic Party. The argument is that the Republicans can never return to power until fate gives them another such master—a Lincoln, a McKinley, or a Roosevelt.

The technique of group diplomacy is familiar. It means that the politician promises something to varied groups of voters, the farmers, labor, small businessmen, racial groups, veterans, and so on. The offering to each must be delicately balanced so as not to offend another group, and also in a way that does not alienate the larger, amorphous strata known as the middle class—i.e., all interests must be "compromised."

It follows then that such a leader cannot indulge in the luxury of standing on principle. For example, he cannot oppose subsidies to farmers because he would alienate the farm vote, yet he must keep the brakes on these subsidies lest he lose the workingman's vote. He must, for another example, be strong for "civil rights" but not so forcibly strong as to split off sectional groups. At all costs he must avoid irreconcilable issues.

The obvious lesson in failure is our Civil War and its aftermath. Lincoln, the compromiser, came too late to avoid the clash, and possibly even he could not have avoided it because the party of Calhoun would not compromise. And Lincoln died too soon to bring compromise to the problems of the reconstruction.

So much for the record. There remains the question whether compromise has ever settled anything or merely postponed the issue. There is—perhaps more important—the question of where this "group diplomacy" leads us in the end. The destination is certainly amoral, and it might even be immoral. If Mr. Agar is right that the only successful party is the one that promises a little something to everybody, we move to a point where both parties must promise everybody. And with both parties promising everybody, then the more successful party will be the one who promises most. The results are not pleasant to think about.

Those who believe in this pragmatist view of politics take their comfort from the fact that it means both parties in this group diplomacy are giving the people democracy. This may be true, but if so it is the ultimate in cynicism, for it means that the people will not accept any issue except who-gives-most.

The Civil War could have been avoided by a compromise which retained slavery in half this country (this is what Lincoln favored) and the upheavals of the late nineteenth century over free silver could have been prevented by a compromise with the inflation. A clash on principle brewed one revolt and almost a second one. But would we have been a better, greater nation for such compromises? And is it true the people refused to face an issue of principle when it was set before them?

Perhaps politics and principles don't mix. But the men who believe so don't seem to have much faith in the democracy they are busily defending.

March 17, 1950

III

POLITICAL PEOPLE

THAT COMFORTABLE MAN:
L.B.J.

THE neighbors' TV had just been flipped off and the menfolk were discussing what President Johnson had just said about Southeast Asia and General de Gaulle when the lady of the house came bustling in to empty the overflowing ashtrays. "Maybe he doesn't know what to do about Vietnam," she remarked, "but he's such a comfortable man." It drew a laugh, but the more I think about it the less sure I am what anybody was laughing at.

The unrehearsed script for the Sunday night conversation with the President might well have been written by the same writer who does Dr. Kildare. The topics all dealt with ailments—poverty in America, communism abroad, death and taxes—and all the symptoms were discussed with proper clinical gravity by young men seeking answers.

If there were any answers, they escaped us. But just like Dr. Gillespie, the man in the black rocking chair listened gravely, nodded an occasional agreement or now and then pointed out a consideration overlooked by the questioner. He never showed impatience, but always gave the feeling that he had thought about the matter beforehand and was patiently awaiting a few more X rays or the pathologist's report from Saigon before making any momentous decisions.

And just like Dr. Gillespie, he showed a few flashes of human frailty beneath the stolid exterior. Asked about his smoking, the President said that he had given it up as a health measure but confessed that he still missed it every day.

69

All in all it was nothing like President Kennedy. None of the young doctor's flashes of wit; rarely a smile, and even then a rather sad one. None of the feeling that the older man was right up to date on the latest cure for Castroism.

So it was such a performance as could be easily faulted, or even ridiculed, by those who think that Presidents, like doctors, should know all the answers for what ails us. Still, the more I reflect upon it the more I suspect it's one of those performances that will please the audience if not the critics, and that it may well settle down for a long run.

That's because I've always had a suspicion that the appeal of youth and vigorous action lacked staying power in politics. In fact, I always thought it was only a small part of the appeal of President Kennedy, albeit the one that attracted the most attention. Thus he was least successful in his first days in office when he seemed to be attacking every problem at once with undiscriminating vigor, but appeared to grow in stature later as he grew quieter and, paradoxically, less sure of the answers.

One difficulty with youth in politics is that it is not a very durable quality, and is therefore good for only about one election. But the greater difficulty is that none of us—even young people themselves—really put as much stock in it as we all pretend to. We are all excited by youth and vigor, the young because they share it and the rest of us because we remember it. We all like to talk about the young men taking over, but it's more than a joke when the young doctor is advised to grow a mustache or wear glasses. When we must put the great affairs of life in another man's hands, we almost always turn to the mature—even the fatherly—image.

Of course, maturity is not wholly a matter of age. President Kennedy after the Bay of Pigs was only a few days older but he was never again so youthful. President Johnson is not really so much older than Mr. Kennedy was. And yet that Sunday afternoon he appeared to be, and what is more he was willing to appear to be.

Moreover, he appeared quite willing to let Senator Goldwater or Governor Rockefeller be the ones with the quick, sure answers to the problems that beset the Presidency. If he was imitating anybody it was not so much President Roosevelt, his idol of long ago, as President Eisenhower, whom he now much admires. And if there was one secret to President Eisenhower's political success —it certainly was a secret from most of the political writers—it was the fact that the country just felt comfortable with him.

President Johnson, let's face it, is not the most dashing man we ever had in the White House and perhaps not one very greatly to enthuse the populace. It would be hard at the moment for anybody to decide whether they approve or disapprove of his political philosophy because hardly anybody right now can be sure what it is.

But if Mr. Johnson succeeds in making the people feel comfortable with him in the White House, that will be a very uncomfortable development for the Messrs. Goldwater, Rockefeller, Nixon, Romney, or whoever else tries to take him on.

March 17, 1964

MAN OR MYTH?
GEORGE ROMNEY

LANSING, MICH.

I F you go about Michigan asking political questions you'll come upon an intriguing one yourself. In boardrooms and union halls the conversation usually comes back to this poser: Is George Romney real?

Naturally the question has nothing to do with his flesh-and-blood existence. Thousands of Michigan schoolchildren, trooping in daily lots through the hideous state Capitol, have shaken the governor's hand. On a weekly schedule he holds open house for all and sundry to pay him a visit; now and then—enough times to make legends—he has actually been able to put a happy ending on some woeful tale.

He's been highly visible too throughout the state, a sort of Haroun Al Raschid on an internal combustion carpet. And of course the state legislators here, whom he's constantly bedeviling with proposals to remake Michigan, haven't been able to ignore him, though they try hard. Neither have the Democrats. The latest polls put the Republican governor well ahead of any and all of the Democrats willing to joust with him.

For all that, however, Governor Romney remains something of an enigma to his supporters, his opponents, wandering journalists, and assorted members of the Republican National Committee, all of whom from time to time have mentioned him as a possible Republican Presidential nominee.

The puzzle doesn't lie in the fact that the governor mixes strong, and highly critical, opinions of the direction of his party and the nation with repeated assurances that he's only interested in continuing as governor of Michigan. This balancing act is par for the course among politicians.

What puzzles friend and foe is that the governor mixes his disclaimer of national ambitions with actions which make it seem he might really mean it. This makes him appear a very unreal politician indeed. Furthermore, he not only utters little sermons about the call of civic duty to do what he can to untangle the mess in Michigan but his political actions are aimed almost solely at that task. Even when he makes an outside speech, as he recently did to the nation's editors in Washington, he talks about Michigan, not the national sins of the Democrats.

There are other things that give Mr. Romney an air of unreality as a political animal. In a world where work is done over tinkling glasses in smoke-filled rooms, he neither drinks nor smokes. His Mormon sense of clean living also gets him early to bed and up at daybreak. This isn't from practical considerations of health, which even a politician might understand, but from religious views of personal conduct.

There are, it's true, practical advantages in his habits. Mr. Romney, clear-eyed in the dawn, is often several steps ahead of those who sluggishly roll to work in mid-morning. The disadvantage, which lies in the human suspicion of the sanctimonious, he avoids by not preaching his practice on others, a forbearance even more remarkable than asceticism.

This combination of tolerance and personal Puritan ethics carries over into his politics. He can talk about Michigan's fiscal affairs in practical terms and demonstrate the practical advantages of solvency, but he rarely leaves it at that. He also sells solvency as a moral virtue, like clean living, and he sells it with as much fervor as he once sold Ramblers.

Preachments about moral virtues, spiced with little religious touches, are of course not unknown in political speeches. Lyndon Johnson uses them too. But when they come out of Mr. Romney they sound peculiarly sincere; the audience is more apt to marvel than to choke. This kind of politics, with its overtones of McGuffey's Readers, frequently draws scornful sniffs as either naïve or phony. Yet the scoffers have to admit that the governor has won most of his fights, given Michigan a new constitution, a new fiscal program that has lifted it out of bankruptcy, and imbued the countryside with a new sense of confidence. In his struggles with the legislature, which is hardly a model one, he's always on the brink but never quite falls.

All this bewilders the hard-bitten. In Detroit's cocktail lounges the politicians will treat you to long discussions about the Romney "angle." About how he shrewdly waited to run for governor until things in Michigan got so bad they couldn't get worse. About how he's waiting out '64 to wait for '68. Or, paradoxically, how he's angling for the Vice Presidential nomination now to get him out of Lansing while he's still ahead.

This is perfectly plausible talk, if you are talking ordinary politics. Mr. Romney certainly has enough troubles left to want out of here. There are reasonable odds that 1964 isn't a Republican year nationally, and a Vice Presidential candidate isn't tagged as a loser like the head of the ticket. Witness Mr. Lodge.

You can make an equally good case that it would be smart to stay here and build for four years hence. And you can have fun arguing which course would be smarter. The trouble with such speculations is that Mr. Romney may not fit the ordinary political mold. Perhaps—just perhaps—he isn't engaged in a devious game of political maneuvering for his own ambitions but might—just might—be what he pretends to be, a man who actually believes

74

the Mormon teaching of his childhood and is engaged in politics from a sense of civic duty.

Even if that's true, it's still uncertain how he would fare in the national glare. His views on the specifics of many issues are as enigmatic as his image, and his talents haven't been equal to pulling order out of Michigan's tattered Republican ranks. Still, two shaky institutions—American Motors and the state of Michigan— have prospered better while he was around, which is something.

So there is a George Romney. And if people here are still debating whether this image is real or a phantom, a visitor from the outer political world finds it refreshing that such a debate should be.

May 18, 1964

75

SELF-PORTRAIT OF A
PRESIDENT: HARRY TRUMAN

O N April 12, 1945, Harry Truman became President of the United States by circumstance. On November 2, 1948, he became President by right of election. In the contrast between these two events there lies the key to the strange, and, certainly fascinating, story of the two men who were President Truman.

Thinking back to that first April, if you can close the mind to what happened afterwards, there is no reason to doubt that a humble man came to the White House. Not only does the adjective and the attitude dominate the first volume of his memoirs written long afterwards; it shows in the correspondence of the time, including the famed letters to Mama and Mary, and in the recorded actions. This was a man to seek advice, to listen to it, to struggle with decision. He was a man who felt overwhelmed by destiny but wanted to meet it as best he could.

In 1948 it was the country that was overwhelmed, with all its prophets confounded. The man who proved all the wise men wrong and himself right was Harry Truman. And although the country did not then know it, it was therefore a different man of the same name who went back to the White House.

For that reason, though Mr. Truman himself may not know it, his second volume of memoirs is a wholly different book from the first volume, which described his early Presidency. It has a different leading character, a new assortment of villains, and an altered spirit. Here is no view of the world seen through humble spectacles.

76

The second Harry Truman did not, of course, burst full bloom upon election night. Indeed, one of the things that makes this volume so interesting is that the watchful reader can observe the first Truman being gradually submerged by the man who was extremely confident, and always supremely right. There is only one place in all this book where Mr. Truman entertains the faintest notion that he might have been wrong, and that was about something that happened in 1939, long before he dreamed of the Presidency.

Open the book at random and on one set of facing pages you will find phrase after phrase: "I gave positive direction . . ." "I therefore insisted . . ." "I compelled . . ." "I had to stop . . ." "I ordered . . ." "I had to watch them all the time . . ." The monotony of the rhythm is such that in the single span of forty-two lines there is the beat of seventeen first person pronouns.

Against the background of this beat there begins to emerge the motif of the developing Truman. At least two years before the 1948 election he already saw himself being assailed by such an assorted cast as Bernard Baruch, the American Medical Association, General Wedemeyer, the Democratic Congress, Chiang Kai-shek, the British, General Hurley, the meat packing lobby, and Henry Wallace. By the time the Republican Congress came in and was abetted by the Southern Democrats, Harry Truman saw himself as left alone to withstand the onslaughts against the Presidency and to save the Republic. On his own reckoning he vetoed more pieces of major legislation in three years than his predecessor did in three terms.

This growing sense of his own role prepared the stage for 1948. It does not take a psychologist to recognize the effect of that year's event on the personality of Mr. Truman. For here he was, presumably disgraced and beaten, abandoned by two segments of his own party, setting out against odds which even his best and closest friends told him were hopeless. Yet set out he did, with pluck and vigor and an inner confidence built on the

77

ability to submerge all doubts about his own essential rightness.

The effect of that victory on Harry Truman was electrifying. Whereas before he had doubts to submerge, afterwards he felt himself justified beyond question. From that moment the memoirs take on a new tone because Harry Truman was a different man. From that moment Mr. Truman began to lose all patience with anyone, from a music critic to a General of the Army, who would differ with the man who had been right when everyone else was wrong.

What is fascinating about all this is the ingenuous way in which Mr. Truman sketches in this self-portrait in his own story. He admits that MacArthur did not understand war as well as he. The Supreme Court, in the steel seizure case, did not understand constitutional law as well as he. Adlai Stevenson did not understand politics as well as he. And if these people had just listened to the new Truman, all would have been saved.

What is curious about all this is the fact that Mr. Truman the author manages to reveal all in undisguised fashion and yet leave his central character, Mr. Truman, warm, understandable, and even appealing. It is the kind of artlessness that is the despair of Hemingway or Steinbeck. The secret, whatever it is, is the same one that confounded the pollsters and proved the despair of Mr. Dewey. Perhaps it lies in the candor with which Mr. Truman displays a direct egoism that other men may feel but are too inhibited to express.

Whatever it is, it makes the reading of his memoirs a memorable experience. Unlike most statesmen's memoirs, their value lies not so much in the dull study of history as in the narrative drama of stirring events and the fascinating character study of the extraordinary man at their center.

Indeed, the historians will have some trouble with these memoirs and the reader who comes to them ignorant of the times will get a strange picture of their history. This is so not only because some of Mr. Truman's asserted facts are disputed by a distinguished list of former friends and associates—including MacArthur, Baruch, Byrnes, Francis Biddle, Leo Crowley, Admiral Leahy, Generals Wedemeyer and Hurley, and Henry Wallace—although these disputes naturally put the truth in doubt.

The picture is also made strange by some startling omissions. For instance, Mr. Truman manages to tell the story of his Administration without discussing the greater controversies over the Hiss or the Harry Dexter White cases. Likewise with the mink coat and tax scandals. They are dismissed in a phrase ("flyspecks on the window") and the names of many of the major actors do not even appear in the index.

Similarly, he tells the events leading up to the Korean War with quotations from many documents but leaves out of the account the vital statement of Secretary of State Acheson just six months before that war which put Korea outside our claimed sphere of defense. The unwary student would never suspect that this had anything to do with the origin of the war. He thus seems to ignore the things he does not want to remember, as though he feels that if they can just be forgotten then they never happened.

All this, of course, is a pity, for it deprives the future of a fair and earnest statement of Mr. Truman's point of view and the reasons for his actions in many particulars. It actually creates a distortion which could be unfair to Mr. Truman himself. The earlier Mr. Truman, the man who tried to act honestly and conscientiously, cannot really have disappeared so completely as Mr. Truman's latest writings sometimes make it appear that he did.

Historians, as well as his contemporaries, will debate the wisdom of many of his actions. But Harry Truman was President of the United States at a great moment in its history and there can be no question that many of his actions had a profound importance to that history—the unleashing of the atom bomb, the reversal of the pro-Russian policy, the decision to fight in Korea, the creation of the North Atlantic Alliance, the Berlin airlift, the Marshall Plan, and the Truman doctrine.

Among these are some things for which posterity will give him great credit. Reading these memoirs one cannot help but wish at times that he had not been so preoccupied with the image in the mirror; posterity might have had then a better glimpse of things as they were. As it is, someone else will have to do the real job of recounting the accomplishments and failures of the Truman Administration. Mr. Truman cannot measure the one because he cannot see the other.

But for all that, Harry Truman has done one job that will help the historians and instruct his contemporaries. He has offered some candid clues to the two men who were President Truman.

March 6, 1956

STALIN: A SURMISE

JOSEPH Stalin of Russia has been looked at through many eyes. He has been examined, probed, dissected, and analyzed by friends and enemies, by statesmen and churchmen, by serious scholars and by ordinary men with a hope to understand. Yet the man remains an enigma. To some he is genial Uncle Joe of the Kremlin, or a paralyzed prisoner of the Politburo, or even a great leader cast in a heroic mold; to others he is the power-mad scourge of the East, a murderous and malevolent man without morality or a touch of redeeming grace. Yet he surely cannot be all of these, and he probably is none of them.

Still the search goes on, for men still hope that by solving the riddle of Stalin they will come to some understanding of that mysterious force in the East that has already enslaved half the world and threatens all else. It is a hazardous search. Whoever touches the man is destined to raise a storm; his latest biography has already been assailed as both a vindictive attack against and a subtle apology for him.

The reason is plain. We live with the legend that great men are good and villains bad. Our leaders, if they do good, must be all noble; if they do evil, they must be all villainous. Hence tyranny, murder, and oppression must be explained in terms of the tyrant, and to suggest that the tyrant is not unalloyed seems to apologize for the evil.

But—and here begins the enigma—one cannot look at this man closely without some admiration mingled with the hatred, fear, and condemnation. At least he seems to have courage, ability, tenacity, and even a touch of devotion to an idea if not to men. And since these are qualities we ordinarily respect, the result is perplexity and confusion. With Stalin, of course, all is surmise. One surmise is that the evil which is the man's work has little to do with the virtues or vices of his personal life. One may surmise that evil is a thing itself and can enslave even men with great visions.

There was a time when men saw evil so. Stalin would have been no enigma to men who could understand the figure of Satan that stalks across the pages of *Paradise Lost*. And one may surmise that the older times were nearer the truth. Milton's Satan, who stood "proudly eminent" while "care sat on his faded cheek but under brows of dauntless courage" would pass for the faithful's view of Stalin. Satan was a "great and noble Commander"; he was a man not only of passion but of deep compassion for those "condemned to have their lot in pain." Even angels deemed it "a proud honor to uprear his mighty standard."

But there was no confusion in Milton's picture. Satan was clearly seen a spirit of evil. This was not because he was devoid of great attributes. It was solely because of one fatal flaw. Satan thought to stand as one with God and share the making of the universe. From this ambition all that Satan did, whatever his wishes, must turn to evil.

That Stalin, too, stands proudly eminent, no one can deny. There are many who will testify to his courage and to the fact that he is a great commander. Nor, to prove him a man of evil, does anyone need deny that he may have been, once upon a time, a man of compassion for men.

The life of Stalin, up to a point, was like others of the little band who gathered around Lenin and seized a revolution. All had seen inhumanities, inequities, and injustices. We do not condemn revolutionists as such; other men—Cromwell, Robespierre,

Washington—have made revolutions and yet left a rich legacy to mankind out of the blood they shed. And it is not necessary to deny that these Communist revolutionists, too, were moved to their rebellion by the best of motives.

What then, of the evil they brewed? Where did the crusade go wrong? Was it perverted by this man Stalin, a bad man, and his malevolent crew? Some would have us believe so, thus persuading us that the evil is in the personality and all can be saved by raising up "good" men to replace the "bad." Others would deny the evil altogether by attributing majesty and a far-flung vision to the men—today's tyranny is a passion for tomorrow's paradise.

But to judge this thing by its personalities is to misjudge it tragically. And the men who once saw evil plain would have understood why. The little band of Communists led by Lenin came—as all revolutionists do—to slay inhumanities. But whereas others came to strike off chains and set men free, the Communists came to remake the world into a world as they would have it be.

That was fatal error. When men are snared by the vision to rebuild the world, nothing but evil can ensue. If they are righteous, then those they believe are unrighteous cannot be tolerated. Indeed, as the Communists saw long ago, there can be no other church—for how can such men tolerate obeisance to any other aspirations for the world and man different from their own?

Not only will such men do evil, but in time they come to justify evil to themselves. Compulsion, enslavement, and even murder become the stepping stones up the altar. The recalcitrants who do not see are sacrificed to the Greater Good, slaughtered in all compassion by the men of vision.

Stalin appears monstrous because he sees clearly what Lenin or any other of the great leaders must soon have seen, that what must be done must be done. Had he done it less ably, there would have been no enigma. But then the world, or his part of it, would not have been remade. Milton's Satan saw that had he been "an inferior angel," there would have been no fall and no evil. And what happened here must happen whenever good men dream that if only they had the power they could achieve the glory, too, and lift men up to paradise.

It is not that all men who play with power—call it Communism or Statism or what you will—have bad intentions. What ends in tyranny may have begun with a vision. Nothing is so corrupting to a man as to believe it his duty to save mankind from men. He comes to evil because he must first usurp the rights of man and finally the prerogatives of God.

So the evil that is Stalin is no enigma, whatever his personality be. One may even surmise that his disciples are correct when they attribute to him the seeds of greatness; certainly a dream of remodeling the earth is a majestic dream. The monstrous error which condemns all such men is the fruit of one forbidden tree. Satan was an archangel who dreamed, too, of playing God.

October 6, 1949

TWO INCREDIBLE MEN:
CHURCHILL AND MACARTHUR

THE year was 1935—it doesn't seem like thirty years ago—
and everybody thought that the soldier's course was run. In
Washington that autumn day they paraded a guard of honor for
him, and the hero who had commanded armies went off in re-
tirement as adviser to a provincial constabulary.

It was the same year, so a date on the book's flyleaf reminds
us, that we read the autobiography of another man who had also
completed a full life. In his time he too had been a soldier, and
also a journalist of renown, a historian, a novelist, twice minister
to a king, key figure in a great war, and a politician to be reck-
oned with. Now the old man, as old men will, was rounding it
off with the tale of how it all happened.

The first man, of course, was Douglas MacArthur, and the
second was Winston Churchill.

What they had done before taxes credulity. Only a hack
writer turning out boys' adventure yarns would spin such derring-
do of the handsome young man, first in his class at West Point,
mixing with guerrillas in the Philippines, slipping behind enemy
lines in Mexico, winning five Silver Stars and the two stars of a
general in the trenches of France, all within fifteen years of being
a schoolboy. Becoming a full general and U.S. Chief of Staff, as
MacArthur did in 1930, seemed dreadfully anticlimactic.

Not even a pulp writer would have dared put Winston

Churchill's story in a movie script for Errol Flynn. It would have to come out like a Henty series—"Fighting Afridis in Khyber Pass," "With Kitchener at Khartoum," and "The Escape From the Boers." But G. A. Henty wouldn't dream of casting the same character as First Lord of the Admiralty and—of all things—Chancellor of the Exchequer.

What happened to them afterwards was patently impossible. You dare recount it only because it happened. The retired general was twice recalled to life, at Bataan and Korea, and twice gained victories for his country; it was left to others to lose them. The discarded minister saved his country from ashes; it was left to others to let its glory fade.

Yet for all the astonishment at such adventures, the most incredible thing is that in the era of the common man such men could be. Each was the son of a father who was himself an uncommon man and in turn the son of an uncommon father. The first Arthur MacArthur was briefly governor of his state and for years a respected federal judge. The second one, colonel of a battle regiment as a boy of twenty, became a general whose name was as much a household word in his time as the son's in our own. Lord Randolph Churchill, the son of a Duke of Marlborough (name famed by the Battle of Blenheim), was himself a queen's minister and mover of a nation's affairs.

So both Churchill and MacArthur were born with a heritage, not the least of which came from remarkable mothers. Jennie Jerome Churchill and Mary Hardy MacArthur were proud of the men they married, and in a way less now in fashion bequeathed their sons pride in family and a desire to honor it. A part of their inheritance was an uncommon mind. Churchill won no scholastic prizes as a schoolboy, but to a delight in history he brought incessant curiosity for its meanings and he mastered, as few men do, the structure of the simple English sentence. MacArthur, as anyone can testify who ever heard him speak, also

86

had the gift to articulate an ordered mind. His rhetoric, as sometimes Churchill's, might be a little overblown but whatever the subject the words went to the heart of the matter and, listening, you knew their clarity came from unmuddied thought.

Not the least of their inheritance were the genes of longevity, without which the rest would have been impossible. Both in youth were vigorous in body; in age they kept vigor of mind.

As striking as any of it is that each of these men inherited a nineteenth-century view of man and his destiny and with such a view made themselves towering figures of the twentieth. For each of these men, plainly, was an aristocrat—in birth, breeding, mind, and manner. Toward their fellow man theirs was the attitude of *noblesse oblige;* believing themselves superior men, and never deigning to hide their belief, they took it their duty to lead, their destiny to play great roles.

As men conscious of the past as well as the future, they saw the world not as if it were born yesterday but against the sweep of history. Thus Winston Churchill, surrounded by disasters at home, could spend an hour thinking about the Balkans. Thus MacArthur, fleeing Corregidor, was already reflecting on the world after victory.

This way of looking far ahead because they could look far back was noticeably absent in the other leaders, good or bad. Hitler dreamed of a great Reich but had not seriously thought of what he would do with victory if he won it. And much of our present trouble is due to the fact that Roosevelt's postwar planning dealt too much with the immediate, too little with past or future.

For much the same reasons, both MacArthur and Churchill unashamedly used words that today make many people wince— patriotism, duty, honor, loyalty, sacrifice, courage, and self-respect. You're struck with this reading MacArthur's memoirs; the sentiments sound old-fashioned. Yet reading them you know why MacArthur would rather be dismissed than fail to urge what he thought Korea required. Churchill sacrificed his political career in the 1930's, or so he and everyone thought, because he believed honor and duty to country required him to speak his mind on Hitler, alone if need be.

Men so endowed are likely to have a touch of arrogance. MacArthur, for all his admirers, could probably not have been elected to anything; Churchill would never have been chosen Prime Minister in ordinary days. Yet in each man's case, and several times, when a nation at war had need of uncommon men it turned to them. And every time the people found themselves well served.

Now their story is in the past and other men can only marvel at it.

March 31, 1964

INTERLUDE:
ADLAI E. STEVENSON

HISTORY is rich with men of stature whose own hour and that of destiny did not run together; their lives and the times were out of joint. One such man was a Democrat from the state of Illinois, who ran for President of the United States. Stephen A. Douglas was a man of good character, of great ability, and one with as deep a belief in the nation and the need to preserve her as had his Republican opponent. But across the land there was a great ferment, and the people chose a man who advocated little that was different in specific programs but who knew that differences in attitude can be fundamental. Earlier or later the people might have chosen differently.

Adlai E. Stevenson did not, I think, lose this election for himself; he did not lose, as some say, because he did not fight hard enough or because he fought with the wrong weapons. He did not talk over the people; the people understood what he was saying. But the people were no longer attuned to what he was saying.

Adlai Stevenson was defeated because he was forced to go the wrong way on the tide. He was defeated by his own party, which though it once spoke for the people, and will do so again some day, did not do so for the time being. Mr. Stevenson's attitude and the attitude of his party was perforce one of approval of all that is and has been in the Democratic Administration, and in this attitude there was a fundamental difference with Mr. Eisenhower and, as it turned out, with the people.

The supporters of Stevenson have nothing to be ashamed of in him and much to be proud of. No man could have better stated the cause of his party; no man could have so well demonstrated that his is a party that can claim allegiance from men of stature. And not the least of the things Mr. Stevenson's supporters have to be proud of was what he said in his dark hour of a post-election morning. His words, of course, were molded to a long tradition which accepts political defeat graciously, but those words also told of him that he understood the wisdom of that tradition. That which unites us is greater than that which divides us.

With no sense of disparagement but with a deep pride in the quality of men that this country can uncover in its crucial days, I think that nothing better revealed in Mr. Stevenson a quality for leadership than the manner of his yielding it.

November 6, 1952

ILLINOIS FISH FRY:
EVERETT DIRKSEN

VIENNA, ILL.

U NDER the hot sun of a southern Illinois Indian summer the crowd was mostly in shirt sleeves and galluses. They had come from all over Johnson county to eat catfish, to talk, and to listen.

The men had come from the fields in the early afternoon, for many were not shaven and nearly all were in their working clothes. The women were aproned, for they had to fry the fish and set the long tables inside the big frame meeting hall, but beneath the aprons they wore bright printed dresses mindful of the festivities. The passel of children were in T-shirts or simple pinafores save for one youngster in a white shirt and his Sunday suit.

The evangelist came, appropriately, in a rush and a cloud of dust. Besides his own car, there were two carloads of followers and the inevitable pickup truck equipped to take his voice and spread it loud around the countryside. Spread it loud and spread it far was what he asked. Everett McKinley Dirksen had come to wrestle with a very live devil as he has done some 1,500 times traveling 200,000 miles along the Illinois roadways. And he wanted the countryside to pay attention.

The countryside has certainly paid attention. Whether Mr.

Dirksen can pin down his personal devils, who in this instance are the Democrats and especially U.S. Senator Scott Lucas up for re-election, is a dubious matter. But there is no doubt that here for once is a Republican who is putting on a fighting campaign of evangelical Republicanism. To one exhausted observer it appears that if Mr. Dirksen can't do it, nobody could have.

In the space of two days Mr. Dirksen tore through the southern counties of Illinois with the militant fervor of Gideon pursuing the Midianites. Pinckneyville, Murphysboro, Anna, West Frankfort, Benton, Marion, Cairo, Vienna—the roll call of the south. Then with a whisk he disappeared in the direction of Kankakee far to the north. And all this in only two days. The Dirksen crusade has been under way for nigh onto two years and in that time he has been many times to every county in the state, at least once to practically every hamlet and crossroads where he could find a handful of people. Three speeches a day has been his average since midsummer, with four or five not unusual.

Sometimes his audiences are friendly, sometimes hostile, for he shuns no Democratic castle. He exhorts the faithful, cajoles the dubious, and charms the "wicked." But everywhere he sounds the trumpet and smites his enemies as one man. He is no prophet of complacency, of me-tooism, of compromise.

Mr. Dirksen charges in where—at least of late—other angels have feared to tread. He defends the Eightieth Congress, Mr. Truman's "worst" Congress. He upholds the Taft-Hartley law. He attacks extravagance in civilian spending of the government right down to some Democrat-proposed projects for southern Illinois where he speaks. He lambasts the Democrats' foreign policy that made the Korean War necessary and builds a war camp for a bigger one. He withholds no fire from Democratic promises of bigger gifts to farmers and new gifts for the townsfolk.

Here in Vienna the afternoon took on all the aspects of a revivalist camp meeting. It began quietly enough with a few words by the local candidates, from the school superintendent to sheriff. Mr. Dirksen, dressed in a worn but presentable business suit, started with a soft voice, a voice either naturally husky or made so from so much talking. The people sat expectantly, the women particularly intent. From here on Mr. Dirksen was a study in technique—the technique of the crooner, the vaudevillian or even, if you will, of the arouser. Bing Crosby could not have been more suavely folksy, Raymond Hitchcock more skillful with the local references, Billy Sunday more astute at playing on emotions.

But on subject matter there was no talking down to the audience. Mr. Dirksen spread out a big map and with it took his country audience to old Vienna, to Czechoslovakia, to Poland, and the Far East. His argument was that Russia had not won but had been given; and he tried to make what had happened in the past to the Old World pertinent in the future to new Vienna, Jackson County, Illinois.

By and by the women's fans came out and Mr. Dirksen's coat came off. As the farmers began to see "where your boys are" there was a stirring along the benches. As the map became "a testimony, if I ever saw one, to disaster and failure," there was applause and one old woman moved up front the better to see. As the rhythmic voice slipped into sarcasm quoting Truman's "I like old Joe—he's a very decent fellow," the applause was mingled with laughter.

Smoothly the preacher swung from far-off places to the country grocery store, evoking memories of O.P.A. and shortages and rationing, the things that come with a war. In a few minutes the women were helping him out and he picked up the impromptu cues with ease. Soon he was ready to shout: "This great administration has got you right back where you were in 1943! They've turned the clocks back!" And by this time he did not shout alone.

While the hour wore on it grew clear that the spirit had come upon Gideon and his trumpet blew louder. The people saw—

even if they did not believe in—the devils with whom he wrestled, and they could see too that they were strong devils because his tie slipped away from his collar and his hair grew ruffled as he wrestled.

After it was all over and the fish fry proceeded, one could not be sure that he had licked his devils. Everywhere Mr. Dirksen goes he blows a lonesome trumpet; there is no chorus from the GOP soldiers who should be with him. Here, in Vienna as in Israel, the twenty and two thousand were busy elsewhere and the faithful were not more than three hundred.

But when sundown came on a weary day no one could say there had not been a battle. And if it should come to pass that on election day his enemies, surprised, should have to ask, Who hath done this thing?—the answer in the book of Judges will be that Gideon alone hath done this thing.

October 24, 1950

THE VANQUISHED:
BARRY GOLDWATER

WHATEVER a man says in public, there is always a hurt in his heart when he has offered his services to his countrymen and they have rejected him. For Barry Goldwater, on the morrow of his defeat, that pain must be especially acute. He lacks the comfort of Adlai Stevenson, who could at least tell himself that he lost to a great popular hero, or of Richard Nixon, who could console himself with the thought that very nearly half his fellows did want him to be President.

Mr. Goldwater must know in his heart that he personally contributed to making a defeat a debacle, and that in so doing he not only lost for himself but made a shambles of his party. Most of all, there must be an aching wonder about what injury he has done to the political fortunes of the political philosophy in which he so deeply believes.

For Barry Goldwater, being a forthright man, is not likely to blink the stark facts of the electoral returns. Aside from his own Arizona he carried only five states, and those the wrong ones for the wrong reason. It surely does his party no good, and brings no comfort to a man of such good will, to see victory grow only in those places where it is nurtured by racial emotion.

The facts are equally stark in the contests of his Republican colleagues. Simple arithmetic shows that it was Mr. Goldwater, not Mr. Keating, who lost the New York senatorial race; in the face of that avalanche not even a million and a half split votes were enough to save Senator Keating. Much the same was true in Illinois, where the defeated Charles Percy ran ahead of the national ticket. And so it went all across the land. Even in those places where Republicans did squeak through it was in spite of, not because of, the party standard bearer.

As for the causes for all this, there is little comfort here either for Barry. It's true enough that Mr. Goldwater began with much running against him, the prosperity of the country, the emotional spill-over from President Kennedy's assassination (which the Democrats used crudely and blatantly), the natural inclination of Americans to give Lyndon a chance, and their normal disinclination to turn out incumbent Presidents. All this might well have beaten him, or any Republican, anyway. Yet it's also true that Senator Goldwater made a mess of his own campaign because he misunderstood some simple, fundamental things about American politics and the American people.

Barry Goldwater's high point was at San Francisco, where he won the nomination because a great many people—more, surely, than finally voted for him—shared an uneasiness about some of the things happening to their country and a yearning for a change.

The first mistake was in the art of party leadership. The selection of Representative Miller as his running mate was a blunder because, rightly or wrongly, he did not inspire confidence in a people made acutely aware of the mortality of Presidents. It suggested either a poverty of leadership within the party or too casual an attitude toward the office of Vice President.

The acceptance speech was a mistake in the same vein. It seemed to say that the convention victory meant unconditional surrender for those in the party who differed, as many always will in any political party. It hinted at both a want of magnanimity to the vanquished and too little tolerance toward diversity.

But perhaps Mr. Goldwater's greatest error was in misunderstanding the nature of the uneasiness felt by many citizens. These people, of numbers yet unknown in spite of the arithmetic of the

1964 election, are made uneasy by a government ceaselessly growing bigger and more powerful, by doubts that relentless depreciation of money is the magic potion of prosperity, that the good society is built on dubious public morals, or that a nation's safety lies in eager wooing of its enemies. But this isn't the same thing as a desire to repeal everything, without qualification or distinction, that has been done this past quarter century. In leaving the impression that this was his aim—whether it was in fact or fancy—the Senator stirred a different uneasiness among the people.

Nonetheless, not all Barry Goldwater's efforts will pass without an imprint. One evidence of this effect is that Lyndon Johnson felt constrained to appear more "conservative" in many matters than has been the Democratic wont. Another can be found in one of the polls of public sentiment made before the election by Louis Harris, a favorite pulse-taker for the Democrats. That poll rightly predicted the Johnson landslide. But Mr. Harris also uncovered some revealing things about the public's attitude toward some of Mr. Goldwater's ideas. An overwhelming 88 per cent of the voters, the poll found, agreed with Mr. Goldwater's plea that prayers in the public school should be restored. An even bigger majority—94 per cent—concurred in the Senator's view that the government has been seriously lax in its security regulations over government employees.

Perhaps these are peripheral matters. But there's nothing insignificant in the finding that fully half of the electorate shared Mr. Goldwater's concern about morality and corruption in government and said that on this score they had more confidence in him than in Mr. Johnson. Or in the poll's finding that 60 per cent of the voters agreed about the demoralizing effect of some of the government's welfare and relief programs. Finally, there is a deep significance in the revealing statistic that six of every ten voters agreed with the central thesis of Mr. Goldwater's philosophy—

97

namely, that the power of the federal government should be trimmed.

Here, then, is a contribution from Barry Goldwater. The landslide vote, as Mr. Harris prophesied, reflected a fear that the Senator would be too reckless abroad, at home too much a bull in the china closet. But what the people heard an honest man say made an impression that could linger long after the man himself has been dismissed. There have been other times in politics when this proved portentous.

Small comfort now, perhaps, for a vanquished man. But however poorly fought the battle there can be honor in it for those who strive, and in the war of ideas oftentimes the substitute for victory comes hereafter.

November 6, 1964

REQUIESCAT IN PACE:
J.F.K.

NEW YORK'S staid Carlyle Hotel, that January morning in
1961, was pretty much bedlam. The doorman, reception
desk, and the two flustered ladies at the elevator were obviously
overwhelmed by the reporters, photographers, Secret Service
agents, and political hangers-on that filled the lobby. Upstairs,
confusion was compounded. In the suite of the President-elect two
meetings were going on in different rooms with much bustling
back and forth. No one seemed to know that the Senator had
made a journalistic luncheon date. In fact, no one had bothered
to order lunch at all, and the young lady in the parlor accepted
with relief the guest's suggestion for steak (medium rare) with
mushrooms.

That seemed to satisfy Senator Kennedy when at last the two
sat down to lunch, possibly because he was preoccupied with
other matters. He was irritated by a recent *Wall Street Journal*
article "about my brother," the Attorney General designate. He
complained of being "too busy to think." He professed puzzlement
at fears among some of the business community that he was, as
he put it, "fiscally irresponsible"—and perhaps the journalist
could help him alter that image?

He explained that the Eisenhower budget, due a few days
later, would be balanced but that it would be a "phony balance"
because it depended on a postal rate increase and a hike in the
gasoline tax. As President himself, he said, he would endorse the

Eisenhower revenue requests but Congress probably wouldn't grant them. "Then there'll be a deficit and it will look like my deficit." Eisenhower, indeed, seemed much on the President-elect's mind. In commenting on the Southeast Asian crisis (it was Laos that winter), for example, he said quite frankly he hoped it would come to a head before he took over. The decision might have to be unpleasant, he commented, and "I don't have the confidence of the people the way Eisenhower does."

So it went—on Cuba, on the farm problem, on domestic economics, on the foreign balance of payments. He appeared to be a young man suddenly appalled by the complexities of the job he had won, and yet so engaging in his uncertainties as to stir instinctive sympathy.

The meeting was an inconsequential one, hardly worth a foot-note in history. So too was another meeting, almost exactly a year later, when the confusion of the Carlyle had given way to the order of White House routine. By then the uneasy air was gone. He seemed exhilarated by the job, and quite confident of himself although admitting, somewhat wryly, that there were problems he still didn't have answers to. But of such trivia are memories made, and what lingers is the impression of a warm, friendly man in whom the necessary egotism of a political leader was softened by humor and a frank recognition that he was still learning and growing. Ghosts from the Bay of Pigs still lingered in the Oval Room.

This private image of President Kennedy is not much differ-ent from the public one that existed until an autumn Friday in Dallas. Until then no one would have claimed that he was a great President. It was uncertain even whether time would prove him a good President. There had been the Cuban affair, mismanaged from youth and inexperience. There was also the fact that of all the enterprises thrown at Congress, by the wholesale and with impetuous enthusiasm, hardly any had come to fruition. The record was more of daring than accomplishment.

Abroad, the young President had lost some stature after his abortive encounter with Khrushchev and his rather humiliating visit with de Gaulle. At home, though it's easy to forget now, he was in deep political trouble. Barry Goldwater was much more eager for a match with Jack Kennedy than he was later with Lyndon Johnson. And yet . . .

Yet in memory and in fact President Kennedy had that rarest of qualities, the panache—or flair—that creates an image somewhat larger than life. It is undefinable but instantly recognized whether on sporting fields or the fields of politics. It was the sort of quality that made a journalist jot down, in that January before anything had been tested, his impression of Senator Kennedy as "a very impressive man determined to make his mark though still uncertain how."

That he did in the thousand days alloted to him. Not by his accomplishment but by the image he left of what might have been, an image compounded of youthful enthusiasm, confidence that the world can be licked by those who dare, and a knack for the beau geste when the battle goes ill.

If that image is the stuff of legend, it is no less worthy for all of that. We have too little of it not to cherish it when it comes our way, the more so when death leaves it unsullied. What a sad thing it is, then, when afterwards the living tarnish it. That seems to be what we are witnessing. First, in the name of preserving his memory, there was the effort to glorify him as such a man as never was. Then the rush of books for the self-glory of those who had touched him somewhere in passing. And of course all those men who raised his political banner to herald their own political marches.

Others have combed over every minute of that day in Dallas,

scavenging for every salable crumb of sensation, be it in imaginary plot and counterplot or in the real agony of raw emotions.

And what is one to make of the Manchester-Kennedy-*Look* magazine squabble? Here are no enemies of the late President trying to cut up his image with political knives. Here are his friends and kinsmen snarling at each other over whether their own words once eagerly uttered should now, regretted, be left unsaid. The object of all is to reap a harvest from the grave; the bickering is only over whether some words put down in cold print may injure the living.

Perhaps they may, and the more so for the titillation of each reader's imagination of what was left out. But the real victim is Jack Kennedy. Where ghouls gather there is no honor to the dead. A legend, like any other flower, needs a quiet time to sink its roots. If they will not have a stop, soon it will be hard to remember the man he really was. And for those who never met him, as for those who did, that will be a pity.

January 6, 1967

IV

LETTERS FROM
AN EDITOR

BLESSED IGNORANCE

O NE among the pleasures of a vacation is the privilege of not reading the newspapers from first day's beginning to last day's end. From someone who's spent a lifetime putting things in newspapers this will perhaps sound like rank heresy. And when you add to not reading the newspapers a firmness in not listening to any news on the radio, the confession will certainly earn you black marks among those who think "keeping informed about world affairs" is somehow a moral obligation ranking slightly ahead of obeying the Ten Commandments. Nothing will earn you such looks of surprise from such people as being asked your opinion on the Los Angeles riots and answering them with the query, What riots? When it further develops that you are totally ignorant of what's been going on lately in Vietnam, of the situation in the Dominican Republic, of the moves to save the UN from its financial crisis or, worse, of the rationing of air conditioning in New York City, the surprise of those who formerly thought well of you turns to consternation.

It gets a bit embarrassing. You expect one of your literary-minded friends to remind you of Oliver Wendell Holmes's remark that a man avoids sharing the action and passion of his time at the peril of being judged not to have lived. You even feel awkward under the glances of kinder friends who seem to be excusing you for this retreat from life on the ground that, after all, you are getting along in years.

Of course the retreat was only temporary, and the lack of

interest in "news" somewhat deceptive. It's just hard to explain to friends that at times some news is more important than others, which means that sometimes some things are more important than the latest dispatch from Saigon.

Robert Manry, that fellow journalist who fled the sedentary copy desk where he read all the Saigon dispatches, can hardly be accused of escaping life's perils by sailing the Atlantic alone in what was little more than a pram. But for some two months' time what happened in Los Angeles was only of abstract interest compared to the happenings within the four-mile circle of his horizon aboard the *Tinkerbelle*. Within that circle his problems were tangible, ones that he could confront with his own efforts. What could he do about Los Angeles, or Saigon? What, in all truth, did he or the world suffer from his two months' ignorance of disasters at the antipodes?

So it often is with the rest of us, and more times than we are willing to admit. On a beach or a mountain top you will be vitally interested in the weather. If you time the radio to catch the weather report and cut out the breathless bulletins about what President Johnson said to Hanoi, you aren't fleeing life. You're gaining a sense of proportion. It's not too different, really, in the workaday lives of most of us. Mr. Manry will find when he returns to Cleveland that for all the burst of excitement over his adventures the world he left will be centered exactly where he left it. The concerns of that world will be the traffic on Euclid Avenue, the pollution of Lake Erie, or the P.T.A. at Shaker Heights. The dollar crisis and NATO will rank somewhat after.

The cliché is that this is all one world. In real life there are as many worlds as there are inhabitants of it, and each man's world is very small indeed. This is true even at the vortex; in Vietnam a Marine's world is bounded by the boondocks, and the Congo is as unreal as outer space. Outer space, in turn, is briefly two men's world, but who will listen to an astronaut more than a curious

106

hour amid the pressing problems of the household or the shop? Yet every housewife, so it says in the advertisement, must read the complete news report of the world's daily disasters. Tune in every hour on the hour, the announcer declaims, or you won't know about the latest riot. And if you don't, how can you be a good citizen? Maybe so. But fresh from a surcease from incessant news, you might begin to wonder.

A little trick in this business, returning from a vacation, is to read the accumulated papers backwards. Working from the present to past, many earlier stories can be skipped because events have outmoded them. This leads to the rueful corollary—rueful at least, for a news-gatherer—that many of the stories could have been skipped in the first place. The suspicion grows that "keeping informed" is not only frequently time-wasting but often futile. Knowing that Singapore has seceded from Malaysia, and agreeing that it's a sad business, what do you propose to do about it?

If all this sounds like praise for ignorance, it isn't—quite. Some people need all the news they can get about the balance of payments, the shortage of water, or the fighting in Vietnam. All of us need to know something about all of these things, not lest we be vegetables but because some or all of these things may impinge upon the little world that is our own. Bad news, if it gives timely warning for remedies, is good news. But it is also true that the world can be too much with us. The tragedies, the disasters, the horrors are real enough; perhaps the greatest horror is that they are, somewhere, daily occurrences. They always have been and there's no relief in sight.

It does not follow, though, that there is a virtue in pounding ourselves with each of them every minute of every day. Nor that it's a disgrace for a housewife wrestling with diapers not to read *The New York Times* from cover to cover. And there's certainly something to be said for a holiday not merely from the cares of the office but the woes of the world.

107

In this business you have to admire David Lawrence for his unflagging indignation at the way the world is governed, Walter Lippmann for his inexhaustible passions at how it ought to be governed, Joseph Alsop for his matter-of-fact gloom about future battlefields, and James Reston for his middle-aged energy in helicoptering over present ones. All the same, there's something to be said for that copy-desk editor from Cleveland who turned the Atlantic into Walden Pond and for two months let the world go by in blessed ignorance.

August 23, 1965

HIDING A RAILROAD WRECK

O NE of the first stories I covered as a budding reporter was
a railroad wreck. I had my troubles because the attitude
of the road officials was that the less said the better, and preferably the paper shouldn't carry a word about it. They lost.

So ordinarily I would laugh off the outraged cries of some
airline press agents at the "publicity" given the recent plane hi-
jackings. The happenings did indeed get some notice in every
paper I read, and the gist of the press agents' complaint is that
this undermined public confidence in one of our vital industries
and, moreover, encouraged others by example to try a bit of
plane-snatching. Also bad for business.

But unfortunately, nowadays, the press agent's protective instinct has also become a common reflex in Washington. Not so
long ago, President Kennedy himself was extolling the merits of
journalistic self-censorship and hinting that if we journalists didn't
do it ourselves the government might do it for us. And since then
Cabinet officers, agency heads, and other bright young men in the
official family have been giving newspapermen more pointed private warnings.

All this is usually couched in phrases about giving away secrets to the enemy, which is a thing nobody approves of. But
when pressed, nobody names a bill of particulars against the newspapers for this crime. The specific complaints always relate to
something else. There was, for example, the Cuban affair. The
"publicity" given to the abortive invasion of counterrevolution-

aries, so we are told, did great injury to the prestige and dignity of the United States in the eyes of the world. You might suppose, from the indictment, that some newspaper reporter caused that bit of wreckage or that if the American newspapers hadn't mentioned it the world would have remained in ignorance of Washington's fiasco.

But this is not the only example. Washington reporters have been verbally spanked for publicizing disagreements within the Administration. Editors have heard that they are being "irresponsible" for criticizing policies of other governments that the State Department wants to be nice to. Press and radio have been privately criticized for giving too much advance publicity to space shots—except when the event turned out well.

Now none of these complaints, I hasten to note, has turned into any kind of Administration policy. But when politicians begin to talk like press agents, and the praises of self-censorship begin to be sung, it's time to reflect on what is involved. It's easy to retort that a wreck, whether on a railroad or on the beaches of Cuba, is no reporter's fault. But that misses the issue. The central question is, first of all, whether the American people should or should not know about the wreck that occurred on the beaches of Cuba. And then the question: Who has the omniscience to decide what the people shall or shall not know?

I would hardly deny that the news of the Cuba fiasco was a bad blow to our prestige. But the injury was in the event, and it would no more be possible to smother the news of it than, years ago, to hide a train wreck in which thirty people were killed. And the very act of trying, whether by self-censorship or government censorship, would in fact increase the injury. Indeed, it would turn the injury inward; for then it would not be just to our prestige abroad but to the very fundamental basis of our society, which rests upon the right of the people to judge those who run our railroad or our government. And patently they cannot judge if they do not know what has happened and what is happening.

If the Secretary of Defense and the Chiefs of Staff have a disagreement it is not just a piece of gossip to titillate editors. It is an important thing for the American people to know; more important, they should know what the disagreement is about, and why. If there are critical things to be said of a foreign government, it is important that the people hear them, however annoying to the State Department. Even the trivial is not unimportant. Public servants have been rightfully turned out of office when "invasions of privacy" disclosed they had peculiar friends. Serious faults in public programs have very often been corrected precisely by news that did our prestige in the world no good.

True, I would hardly deny either that sometimes things written in the press strike me as irresponsible. But I have known things I thought important to strike others as irresponsible. It is on this that all censorship founders, whether by government or by some committee of editors. Among my journalistic colleagues there is not one who I think has that infinite wisdom to say: "This the people shall know. This they shall not know." And I may doubt if any of my colleagues would attribute to me such omniscience.

So I sympathize with those in Washington who do not like to see their mistakes, their arguments, their plans, or their foibles noised about in the public forum. So too with my friends in the airline public relations offices who shudder at every headline about a hijacking. But the news of that wreck I covered years ago forced a railroad to improve its safety devices. And ever since then I've never believed that the public was well served by hiding news because somebody thought it was bad.

August 15, 1962

111

WAR NEWS

A JOURNALIST owes nothing to those who govern his country. He owes everything to his country. This is as true, when you think about it, in war as it is in peace, and it applies as much to the frontline correspondent as to the editorial writer pondering the policy of nations in his littered sanctum. The difference is that in peacetime there is rarely any difficulty, either for the reporter who writes or for the reader who reads, in deciding when the interests of the authorities and the interests of the nation collide. Most of the time they are the same, but in peacetime the journalist need never hesitate to write something that may injure the one if it will serve the other.

In war it is not always so simple, as both editors and readers are rediscovering now that the nation is once more engaged in fighting on a distant battlefield and when—once more—the news sometimes deals with battlefield reverses, planning mistakes, and logistical snafus. All of these things, one way or another, have lately been in the news about Vietnam. A Marine detachment is cut off and cut up, and sometimes we at home read about it while it's happening. Supplies are short because of inadequate port facilities. Or there is a flap because the right components for the right bombs don't arrive in the right place at the right time.

Such news is never welcomed by those in authority; at the very least it means harsh handling of a Defense Secretary by Congressional inquisitors. It's not always welcomed either by those on the battlefield who see their problems thus exposed.

Such news isn't comforting either to those at home. An editor's daily mail brings letters asking why we should air our troubles for all to see, and the question inevitably troubles those who report and edit the news. It's unlikely that in the months ahead the questions will grow less insistent. The only answer is that there is no simple one. Sometimes publicizing the truth about the conduct of military and diplomatic affairs may injure the country. At other times it is essential, if the country is to be truly served, that the public know the unvarnished truth even at the cost of bringing statesmen and generals into disrepute. For an honest journalist and his readers the anguish is in deciding which time is which.

In ordinary times stories about mistakes or hanky-panky in high places indubitably injure those entrusted with government; at times they may injure the government itself by impairing public confidence. Yet the nation is best served by exposure, even though it reach to the highest offices. In most cases this is true even in wartime. The Truman Committee during World War II uncovered a lot of peculiar goings-on, happily most of it of a minor nature, but no one would argue today (though some did at the time) that its revelations hurt the country's war effort. The exposure served the nation well, and incidentally put Mr. Truman in the White House. All the same, there's no denying that at times the consequences could be different. Imagine a foul-up in the production of ammunition. The interests of the country require an urgent correction. But it is not inconceivable that exposure—informing the enemy—might do severe damage.

For the battlefield reporter the dilemma is even sharper. How much should he report, day by day, on how goes the struggle—when on the one hand the information may comfort the enemy and, on the other, perhaps help correct the situation by arousing an informed public? After the event, how much should he report on how the battle was bungled, if that be the case? If there are

113

any uncluttered answers to these questions, no man has found them. There are, however, some pragmatic guides that might be worth pondering by both those who report and those who read the news.

The public ought not to ask for juicy morsels served up just to shock or titillate, any more than a reporter ought to serve up gore and foul-ups just to catch headlines. Every man knows that battles are bloody, and most such stories are written to show that the reporter was there and to demonstrate his skill with rhetoric. They are mostly read to feed the same appetite as Technicolor blood in a James Bond shark pit.

As for foul-ups, they are endemic in the best-run armies. The sit-at-home's desire to read and go cluck-cluck ought not to over-weigh the thoughtful reporter's judgment whether there is any purpose in making a sensation out of war's inevitable confusion. Still, that's not the whole of the matter. It's no accident that the Pulitzer prizes for journalism, which have now passed their fiftieth anniversary, are heavy with awards for reporters and editors who disturbed authority by what they published. It has been so in war as in peace.

Recent awards have marked no exception. A newspaper was honored for exposing the record of a man the President would make a judge. An editor was chosen for his comments on U.S. foreign policy, which included some dissent from the prevailing view in the White House about the war in Vietnam. The war photography and the war reporting which won awards were hardly comforting to anybody in their vividness.

Every reader, if he will pause to reflect, will recognize that a newspaper serves illy when it keeps silence about the bunglings of generals or the ineptness of other officials, even if that may include the President. The reporter or editor who does so out of kindness to the individuals concerned, or out of some mistaken idea of "responsibility" to the government, is not merely being cruel to those risking the hazards of battle. He is really being irresponsible to his country's cause. The test is no more than this: Does this story you read merely serve to satisfy your appetite for sensation, or does it speak of things the public needs to know in order that men, knowing it, can put things right or guard against recurrence?

Doubtless the distinction will fret us till the end of time, and draw troubled letters to troubled editors. From that, among free men, there is no escape. But do not fear that the journalist will go far wrong who remembers that his duty is not to those who govern but to his country.

May 24, 1966

DISTURBERS OF OUR WAYS

RALEIGH, N.C.

HUNDREDTH birthdays, among institutions as among men, are things worth celebrating, and the accidents of history have made the past twelvemonth memorable for centennials among newspapers. The most notable of these for sheer longevity was the recent anniversary of the Hartford *Courant,* that New England institution which marked the passage of not one but two centuries. The *Courant* can lay claim to being the oldest newspaper of continuous publication in the country, having been born when Connecticut was still a colony of the English crown.

But in other ways the first centennial of the Raleigh *News and Observer,* celebrated here with due festivities, is just as remarkable. Born in 1865, in a devastated land among a defeated people, it had a less than auspicious beginning and suffered many tribulations merely to survive. Survival, of course, is cause for celebration, as it is on the birthdays of venerable men. It is also the occasion for asking what has been done with so long a life, and for a wondering why it is that while the years have taken so much toll of others, these still live.

Part of the answer is always simple good luck. Yet for a newspaper that alone hardly suffices, for it must draw its sustenance from the community in which it lives, and when that is withdrawn nothing will save it from the graveyard. So for a newspaperman at the festive board the celebration is touched with some unease. What is this thing which, in his own livelihood, separates the dead from the living? What is a newspaper for, anyway?

It's been aptly said that any successful institution is the lengthened shadow of one man. By the record, this is particularly true of a newspaper. Nobody ever heard of one that made its mark from the inspiration of a committee or a board of directors. Name them off, the great—or once great—newspapers of the country. Behind each one, giving it its vigor, its personality, its force for good or ill, has been a single man.

Joe Pulitzer of the old *New York World*. Adolph Ochs of *The Times*. Colonel McCormick of the *Chicago Tribune*. The right man can make a little newspaper in a little town be heard across the land. So did William Allen White of Emporia, Kansas, and Carl Magee of Albuquerque, New Mexico. It was Magee's tiny paper that brewed the tempest known as Teapot Dome.

This was certainly true with both the *Courant* and the *News and Observer*. You won't find Thomas Green in many history books, but he was the remarkable character who founded the *Courant,* which in turn helped make a revolution. Josephus Daniels didn't found the *News and Observer;* he bought it at a bankruptcy sale. All he did was match the man to the paper and put the paper on the map, journalistically and financially. Ever since young Josephus walked into the paper's print shop in 1894 people have constantly talked about the paper, occasionally praised it—and steadily cussed it. Locally, it's sometimes referred to as the *Nuisance-Disturber*. It's an apt name, whether used with affection or acerbity. Josephus earned it by being a disturber of the peace, successively, of Raleigh, Wake County, North Carolina, and eventually the whole South.

Personally he was a kindly man. Politically and professionally he was about as tame as a wildcat. In the fashion of an earlier

117

day he didn't try to be "reasonable" in an argument and he wrote with a slashing pen that sometimes wounded good men as well as bad ones. He could be stubborn, dogmatic, cantankerous—and to a good many of his readers from Raleigh eastward to the sea, just plain infuriating. No matter. He had the notion that a newspaper, especially one in a state capital, ought to print the news of what went on whether anybody liked it or not. This meant telling the readers who got engaged or married or who won the prize at the State Fair. It also meant, sometimes, the news of who got divorced or who got drunk and wound up in jail. And always it meant telling the people what the mayor was up to, and the legislators, and the governor. Not always politely, either.

The good that came out of this may have been a by-product, but it was inevitable. For one thing, it got people to reading the *Nuisance-Disturber* in preference to its blander competitors, a little thing of which newspaper business managers might take note. For another, it fostered the habit among those in high places of looking skittishly over their shoulders. That habit has played some part in the fact that North Carolina has never had one of those long and shameful scandals in its state government that have plagued so many of its neighbors.

Equally important, it stirred up the populace. Through the newspaper the people of New Bern or Kinston felt a community of interest with each other and with the people of Raleigh. They became aware that they had common problems, and were aroused to think about them even if only to disagree with Josephus on what to do about them.

Some ancient sage of the craft once remarked that the only purpose of a newspaper was to print the news and raise hell. Inside the flippancy is a kernel of truth. Curiously, it doesn't seem to matter much what an editor raises hell about. Of course it's better to be on the side of angels, if you know which side that is. But Colonel McCormick and Josephus Daniels each managed to make healthy and long-lived newspapers that served their community well, although each followed a different set of angels.

We live now in blander times, and Heaven only knows whether these newspapers will live to the next centennial. The *Courant* wouldn't dream of fomenting another revolution, and the *News and Observer*—though rarely— has been known to say a kind word about a Republican. Nowadays extremism in support of principles is thought a vice. Yet as the birthday candles are blown out, you wonder if the rules are really changed. If a newspaper is good for anything it's only to be a nuisance to our conscience and a disturber of our ways. And for those who fail in that, the graveyard still awaits.

May 17, 1965

RHETORICAL QUESTION

How can the widely respected editors of a paper like *The Wall Street Journal* be convinced that they are talking nonsense?"

The question, of course, is intentionally rhetorical. Its poser assumes that everybody will agree the talk is all nonsense, as everybody agrees on the postulates of Euclid. He also subsumes that nothing can really be done about it. Nobody expects to improve the reasoning processes of morons. Even the touch of flattery isn't much comfort. Where's the honor of being "widely respected" when the clear implication is that this merely reflects the prevalence of fools? In some circles, so we judge by Her Majesty's honors list, the Beatles are as widely respected as atomic physicists.

The question is also familiar to anyone who wanders from the quiet of this editorial sanctum into the wider world, particularly through the world of Washington or the haunts of liberals among the groves of Academe. Often it's couched in softer language, but our old friend Thurman Arnold—who in his book *Fair Fights and Foul* puts it in this blunt form—is no man to pull his punches. However phrased, it comes down to the same thing. The editors of this venerable journal, or at any rate some of them, aren't simply mistaken on some questions, as even so rational a man as Mr. Arnold might sometimes be. The charge is that they spout not merely error but pure nonsense.

That makes it an intriguing question to the victim. Few men, save perhaps the venerable Mr. Arnold or youthful penmen of political science, expect to be ever infallible. No man likes to think himself a jackass. So you start running down the long list of public questions on which, over the years, successive editors of this journal have expressed some views in hope of finding this nonsense so it can be cured.

You might begin, appropriately enough, with antitrust policy, since this was Mr. Arnold's own métier years ago when he was the Justice Department's famed trust-buster. Here you find the paper's comments almost boringly repetitive in their support of the antitrust laws and in their criticism of all monopolies, whether instituted by business, labor, or government.

It's true enough that the editors have begged leave to doubt that attacking mere bigness, as trust-busters have sometimes done, is always the same thing as busting up monopolies, and have out-Heroded Herod in thinking labor monopolies as bad as those of industry. But if doubting that present antitrust policy is perfect constitutes nonsense, it's hard to know what to think of Mr. Arnold's comments on it in his book. During the depression trust-busting was his talisman for setting all things right; now he is having some second thoughts.

Or take civil rights and civil liberties, a talisman not only of Mr. Arnold but, and rightly so, of all those proud to call themselves liberals. Does the nonsense lie in the fact that *The Wall Street Journal*'s pages instantly hailed the removal of the segregation barriers in the nation's schools or, despite misgivings about particular clauses, have favored federal legislation to make all citizens equal under law? Or perhaps the paper was being nonsensical, as well as quixotic, when it defended the right of Paul Robeson to a U.S. passport, Communist or no, simply because he was a citizen?

The question of which view is nonsense is devilishly hard to grapple with. In foreign policy the editorial columns did, to be sure, support the postwar British loan, aid to Greece and Turkey, and the Marshall Plan, all of which admittedly took a lot of the taxpayers' money. The paper also supported President Truman when he went into Korea and President Kennedy when he confronted Khrushchev over Cuba. Perhaps wrongly, but not without considerable agreement from outspoken liberals.

In delving back through the yellowed pages in the file you can find some criticism of such things as the later developments in the foreign aid program, some doubts expressed that the UN would prove a viable instrument for U.S. foreign policy. These views were, confessedly, not too popular at the time in certain circles. Now some of these same doubts are being expressed by liberals of impeccable credentials, which may suggest only that it's nonsensical to be premature.

So you come next to economic policy, which is probably what the darts are aimed at. For it is certainly true that as far back as any readers of this paper can remember it has argued for a government budget within the resources of the government. And it is certainly true that in some quarters this is thought plain silly. Yet even here the question gets slippery as an eel. If you review the reports of successive Councils of Economic Advisers or the budget messages of Presidents you find a curious refrain. While the immediate deficit (there seems to be always one) is defended, it's allegedly accepted only to get the country moving again so that we can get back to a balanced budget. There's usually also a warning of the inflationary dangers if the deficit policies advocated get out of hand.

Translated, this says that it's nonsensical to be for a balanced budget but also nonsensical not to be for one. Which makes it a little hard for anybody, including an editor, to find out where the sense lies. So you end up pretty frustrated. To get absolution from the indictment should you advocate that the government simply print all the money it wants to spend, abandon your devotion to the dignity of man and the rights of each one under law, stop talking about the need for freedom in the arts and excellence in education, desist from criticizing businessmen who are greedy or union leaders who are arrogant, cease speaking about the encroachments of tyranny on men's liberties?

Which of these is nonsense? Or are they all?

About the only thing for good-natured men to do is not to let the frustration take the fun out of the argument, fair fight or foul. And in the face of so all-encompassing an indictment enter a plea of *nolo contendere*. With some hopes of a Scotch verdict.

July 1, 1965

FREE BICYCLES

THE tangled affairs of the Curtis Publishing Co. inspired a delightfully nostalgic story in *The Wall Street Journal* which included a very distinguished list of former workers in the *Saturday Evening Post* vineyard.

Not counting Benjamin Franklin, who got his head start for the lead in a Broadway musical by peddling the weekly when it was called the *Pennsylvania Gazette,* the *Post* can lay claim to launching the careers of U.S. Senators, such as Robert Kennedy, and tycoon merchants like Stanley Marcus, who started out hawking it from door to door. But when this newspaper's reporter was burrowing through the archives for his story, nobody called his attention to one of those boyhood salesmen. Namely, me.

It was nice in later years to join the authors' circle and have something in common with James Fenimore Cooper, Joseph Conrad, and F. Scott Fitzgerald. But by that time, possibly, the *Post*'s standards weren't quite so high. In the halcyon years, circa 1925, the magazine dripped so much prestige that a boyish *Post* salesman could be, and was, invited to lecture on his experiences before the local Chamber of Commerce. As with most experiences, those proved to be more educational than anybody realized at the time. A look backward now over so long a span suggests some passing thoughts about the nature of the American economy, the ever-changing demands of society, and some special thoughts about one particular industry in that economy and society, the publishing industry.

The first lesson was about competition. When the first bundle of magazines arrived, a natural sales area seemed to be the state office buildings surrounding the capital square not too far away. The *Post* proved in high demand all right, but this also proved to be the territory of an older and bigger boy. A few sales were made by the appeal of youth and a ragamuffin appearance, not a solid base then or now for building a durable market. In the parlance of the trade, a good many copies had to be "eaten."

This was an introduction into the difference between gross and net, or the illusory aspect of the thing called profit, a distinction that still escapes some academic economists. This lesson was reinforced with the discovery that *Post* copies (they were fat in those days) were so heavy that you needed to ride the streetcar to and from the market place, which used up the "profit" of quite a few copies.

Then there was the business about the free bicycle. Memory fails as to how many copies at a nickel apiece were needed for that bonus from the circulation office, but there's nothing feeble about the recollection that it took so many weary months they seemed, in childhood's telescoping time, to be measured as years. The only solution, finally, was to get there fustest with the mostest, which wasn't too easy for a plump little boy with an affinity to laziness, and to have read the magazine so as to be ready with a fresh sales talk adjusted to the appetites of busy men or kindly old ladies. From a pre-teenager in knickers the summaries must have been pretty fascinating.

And of course none of this would have worked if the *Post* hadn't offered what the customers wanted. It had, for its time, a perfect product, and a mere description of it sounds like the formula for today's TV—a large dose of entertainment containing a mixture of soap-opera stories with an occasional first-rate one, a dash of sports and personality pieces, and a smidgin of articles on public questions, most of them probably not as profound as they seemed.

That, indeed, is the fashionable explanation for the decline of the *Post;* TV, it's said, is the villain. This may have a kernel of truth, but it begs the question. The publishing business, unlike the buggy industry, hasn't vanished from the scene. There are other magazines doing quite well. The explanation is much simpler, though it's not one readily welcomed by either businessmen or economic planners. Not only are the needs of people constantly changing, so also are the means of filling those needs. Sometimes a particular business declines because it does not meet the change. Sometimes it declines because, no matter what it does, something else can meet the need better. When that happens, you can have the sadness of nostalgia but there's no point in weeping.

Since publishing is our own business, all of us in it feel sad when the *Literary Digest,* the *American Magazine, Collier's* and the rest pass on, or when the *Saturday Evening Post* falls from its once high estate. It can be a little frightening too. There but for good fortune perhaps someday go *Time, Newsweek, Life, Look, The New York Times,* the *Chicago Tribune* or—heaven forbid—*The Wall Street Journal.*

Indeed, it sometimes seems that publishing is the most fragile of industries, possibly because it must make and sell a new product every day. What is nonsense is for politicians, and academic observers of the economy, to get all in a lather when a town becomes a "one newspaper town" or the nation has fewer "magazines of substance" than it had on some particular date years ago. The fallacy here is the same as when the economic planners note that some other segment of the economy—farming, say, or coal mining—is declining in importance and job opportunities and then rush forward with grandiose plans to save it. If there are fewer coal miners in a West Virginia town than there were a

126

quarter century ago, it's because there are better fuel resources and better jobs elsewhere. If there are fewer dirt farmers, there may be a loss in romance, although dirt farming is more romantic to those who write about it than do it. There's no loss to the nation's diet.

Still, there must be a lot of middle-aged men around silently sending good wishes to the *Saturday Evening Post* and hoping for a speedy recovery. And it's not all from romance, either. Some of them are indebted to it for an early lesson some people never learn. Ain't no such thing as a free bicycle.

November 18, 1964

THE FUNCTION OF
A NEWSPAPER

FOR some elections past the majority of the newspapers have in their editorial pages supported the Republican candidate. In most of these same elections the majority of the people have voted for the Democratic candidate. Wherever editors gather, these incontrovertible statistics—which might be verified again next election—are repeatedly brought forth and used as a springboard to some remarkable conclusions. Frequently our own colleagues use them for self-flagellation; should they not do so, some outside critic is sure to seize upon them as a whiplash for shortcomings. The latest to fret over the sad estate of the fourth estate is former Governor Stevenson.

The newness of what Mr. Stevenson says lies only in the urbanity of his wit. For the burden of it is again that newspapers have a duty to influence as well as to enlighten the people and that since the statistics show a failure to influence there is demonstrated thereby a failure to perform their duty. In Mr. Stevenson's bright phrase, we have not lived up to our invitation to greatness.

Of course one might comment that what Mr. Stevenson complains of is good fortune for Mr. Stevenson. If the statistical majority of newspapers were able to influence public opinion, which he says is their proper function, then his party would not now be in power and Mr. Stevenson's own political chances would be poor instead of good.

Or if one assumes—as Mr. Stevenson possibly does—that the majority of the people in this case are wise and the statistical majority of newspapers are foolish, then his argument really is that the newspapers should be influenced by the people, that they should endorse ideas because of their popularity. Yet this is the reverse of the argument that Mr. Stevenson pretends to make.

But I am not concerned so much with inconsistencies that glitter through Mr. Stevenson's shining phrases. What interests me is the underlying assumptions in all this talk about the duty of a newspaper and the "public responsibility" of an editor commenting upon the passing scene.

The primary function of a newspaper is to tell people what is happening in the world, be it good, bad, or neither. In our own field we on *The Wall Street Journal* report bankruptcies as well as successes, "bad government actions" as well as "good government actions." We do it not to perform a duty but to fulfill a function. We have no duty to print a newspaper at all, but if we do and fail to carry out the function of one we would quickly find the readers going elsewhere.

A newspaper editor who becomes overwhelmed with his sense of duty and decides that some news ought not be printed because it would be bad for the public to know about it will quite likely find one day that he has no newspaper to be an editor cf. The graveyards are littered with the wreckage of newspapers that tried to censor news instead of printing it.

A secondary function of a newspaper is to offer judgments and opinions on the passing events. And it is here that the critics of newspapers most often bring up such phrases as "duty" and "public responsibility." The thought seems to be that an editor has a responsibility for what his readers think, that he has a duty to mold public opinion, and that if the editor and his readers get out of step, then the newspaper has failed in its duty. As a corollary it is said too that the editor has a duty only to utter "responsible" thoughts—an irresponsible thought being generally one that runs counter to the great public policies of the day.

I do not think that an editor has any duty to mold public

opinion. Indeed, when he conceives this to be his duty and to think that he can do it, he is in the greatest danger of ceasing to perform his editorial function. It is only in totalitarian countries, in the realms where there is dogma, that such a "duty" is accepted and attempted. The function of an editor is to express an opinion which the reader can judge. And that function is properly performed only if the opinion is an honest one. The minute an editor withholds an opinion for fear that someone may think it "irresponsible" or that he may be "out of step with the times," he ceases to perform his function.

If an editor believes, say, that a policy of government deficits is bad, he should say so, and continue to say so, though for twenty years the government with the acquiescence of the people continues to depreciate the money with government deficits.

A newspaper editor who becomes overwhelmed with his sense of duty to uphold, say, the foreign policy of his government and suppresses his thought that it is bad out of fear of "irresponsibility" has ceased to perform his function. So has he too if he yields up his opinion because somebody tells him editors are getting too "one-sided" and he thinks it his duty to redress the balance.

The reason he has ceased to perform his function is that he has ceased to give an honest opinion. And in due time his readers will find him out, and his editorial page, for all his sense of duty, will join the graveyard of the discredited.

September 10, 1952

130

V

PURELY PERSONAL

SOME HAPPY PREJUDICES

THE late W. C. Fields once opined that any man who hated children couldn't be wholly bad. Doubtless the sentiment outraged a good many people, especially mothers. All the same, everybody laughed uproariously. The humor lay in its unbelievable absurdity. It's only when you have arrived at grandfatherly estate, a happening of some moment, that you can afford to admit publicly that there's a kernel of truth amid the Fields corn.

There's truth, if you'll just admit it, not only in the general adage that children should be seen but not heard; at times it's better to have them well out of sight. The proof lies in a mere two weeks' visit with the grandchildren. A little wisp of heather, aged sixteen months, is a delight to the heart. Warm, cuddly, and loving, she has all the virtues of her sex, with the added boon that not yet having achieved the gift of speech her affection is not mixed with admonitions to comb your hair, shave before breakfast, and please change those dirty denims. For so much love, you give most humble thanks. Nonetheless, let all confess it, the ages of man are well defined.

Happy chortling at 6 a.m. can disturb the repose of the slippered pantaloon. The less happy cries of a worn-out toddler can mar the quiet cocktail hour. And too much quiet, suddenly noticed, demands an agile scamper up the long stairs to rescue the bedspread before grandmother's face lotion is too thoroughly smeared into it in a worthy exercise at artistic self-expression. As for an afternoon nap, that's an impossibility in a friendly neighborhood where joyous seesaws give loud evidence of the population explosion. Thus two weeks confirm the wisdom of confining the blessings of children to the young. And make the silence of that dull, staid, impersonal city apartment appear, for the nonce, a blessed sanctum.

But it's not a sanctum long for this world—not, that is, if the House of Representatives has its way. The House approved a provision in the civil rights housing bill that would make it unlawful to refuse to sell or rent housing to people with children. A landlord couldn't even count them and say there were too many children for the space being rented. In short, no more sanctums from the pitter-patter of little feet, under penalty of the law. The aged, the childless, and the just plain Fieldsian curmudgeons will jolly well honor the Biblical injunction, and suffer the little children to come unto them, or get whacked by the judge.

It would all be funny if it weren't so sad. This bill, as you might suppose, was sponsored by two Congressmen who enjoy twenty-four children between them. That they are to be commended for their vigor and virtue surely goes without saying. But their mentality, unfortunately, is another matter.

That mentality is one which begins with its own clear concept of what is virtuous—and usually indeed a concept which can be shared by men of good will—and then proceeds to the conclusion that if it be virtuous that alone is justification for forcing it upon the frailties of men. To such a mind it is not enough that one should refrain from robbing one's neighbor; one must love him, since that is the injunction, and if not we'll hang the malefactor for this transgression. Or at the very least, he must not be allowed to escape his neighbor, since any desire to do so is itself confession of unvirtuous prejudice. Thus this particularly silly bit of lawmaking (what's to become now of those special developments for Senior Citizens?) symbolizes one thing that has gone awry with what is called civil rights legislating.

134

It began as an endeavor, both wise and virtuous, to see to it that all our citizens had equally their rights as citizens; this required some changes in the law, and the changes have been made. Beyond that it was an endeavor to educate and persuade the white community to alter customs and practices which were, in their own way, as hurtful to the Negroes as the flaws in the law. These alterations have not been completed; they have been, however, more than begun.

Not enough, said the virtuous. So we were soon bussing children miles from their neighborhoods not for equality of rights but for equality of numbers. If some of the Negro parents and their children themselves objected; no matter. They too must enjoy enforced neighborliness, like it or not. From this it was an easy step to some "civil rights" laws patently absurd, because so totally irrelevant. Not only are you not supposed to choose a secretary with whom you may be congenial through shared race, religion, or background; moreover the law says you may not choose a quiet male secretary over a chattering female. Misogyny, in the land of the free, is now a federal offense.

Thus by some alchemy the civil rights laws are becoming not laws to free people but laws to take away their freedom of association, on the grounds that any preference for living in close association with one group is a prejudice against others.

I will admit to a bare minimum of prejudices. In a long life I have been neighbor to and broken bread with Methodists, Negroes, Texans, Jews, Hoosiers, Catholics, several Communists, and at least one Nazi. I have been roommates with members of both sexes and passed a number of years in a houseful of children. But some prejudices cannot be denied. One is a prejudice for those of like habits and interests, and for that matter, of like age. The young and the stimulating can be fun, but fun can be exhausting. At times a man even wants a place to escape the charming sex.

Most pronounced is a prejudice against those who would

135

compel all men not merely to be just in their dealings but to live by a single prescription, however virtuous it appear to those who prescribe it. Not only is the legislation of virtue impractical, as Cardinal Gibbons remarked; it sinfully suggests that the lawgivers are duty bound to correct the oversights of the Lord in failing to cast us all in the same mold.

But that's the way it is. Congress goes to work to protect all men's inalienable rights, and the next thing you know nobody's grandfather has any right to peace and quiet.

August 11, 1966

THE IDLER'S RETURN

THE trouble with vacations, as philosophers long ago discovered, is their transience. Few of us get to test the apothegm of which once brave Homer sang, that too much idleness is unendurable. That privilege is reserved for millionaires and paupers.

To add to our woes, the world thus fleetingly fled remains perdurable. If the calendar didn't insist upon those vanished weeks, you'd swear you'd never been away. The airline strike you thought to escape upon a small boat awaits your return. The only difference in the headlines about riots in the streets is a shift in locale. The bulletins from Vietnam read nowise different from before. Your stay-at-home neighbor's brow is just as furrowed by the sluggish stock market. His wife, speaking of rising prices at the supermarket, sounds a familiar refrain. Even the aberrations of men are monotonous. You flee the shock of wanton murder in Chicago, and, returning, are greeted by wanton murder in Texas.

The few changes you do note are neither surprising nor cheering. The subway fare is notched another nickel. New York's mayor plans to make it the city of opportunity by taxing outlanders who come to labor there. In merrie England, where political events so often foreshadow our own, the government has decided to eschew voluntary guidelines for mandatory economic controls. It's all very discouraging, for in a trice the respite is undone.

Well, perhaps not entirely. It's true enough that the perturbed

137

spirit, like the weary body, is by rest made better able to endure the perturbations. Or more accurately, after a few weeks of not worrying about anything but primeval woes like wind, rain, and lightning it takes a few days to work up a fret about what's happening in the Congo or whether the TFX contract was McNamara's blunder.

During this period of adjustment, of course, you are totally incapacitated for being a good citizen, since everybody these days is required to worry about world events. It's especially hard on those of us who are paid to be perturbed about everything, inflation one day and Indonesia the next. The difficulty is that idleness has altered your perceptions, which incidentally is one of the warning signs of mental illness. For one thing, the idleness has been so pleasant as to tempt you into seeing virtues in useless activity and an empty mind, both viewpoints being un-American.

The current literary lion, for example, is James Boswell, a busybody if there ever was one, while his mentor, Samuel Johnson, has fallen into neglect. The reason is plain: the good Dr. Sam was the patron of all idlers, and even wrote a book for them, in which he laid down such sound dicta as that we would all be idle if we could, and that to be idle ought to be the ultimate purpose of the busy.

For the same reason Artemus Ward, who wrote lying down and delighted generations with his humor, is today unread; the fad is for stand-up comics. It was Art who confessed he could live for months without any kind of labor, and would then feel refreshed enough to go on the same way for many more months.

Such men, though we forget, are Daniels come to judgment. The virtue of idleness is that it gives you time to perceive that while many of the world's woes are perhaps worth worrying about, worrying about them doesn't get you anywhere. This typewriter has lost track of the number of fretful words it has mothered about inflation. Yet inflation is here, just as hale and hearty as if all that worried wisdom had never been uttered.

Moreover, in the slough of idleness you also begin to suspect that the world's woes number some that aren't worth worrying about at all. It may be true that smoking gives you cancer, but considering the number of hazards to health—such as walking across the street—there's a disproportion of emotional energy in getting hysterical about it.

Much the same thing could be said about the amount of worry extravagantly wasted on pop art, atonal music, the John Birch Society, beatniks, the packaging of cornflakes, or the meretricious quality of soap operas. When you are idle it's really no trouble to turn off the TV, put Beethoven on the phonograph, and pick up a book to savor the drawings of Leonardo or the politics of John Stuart Mill. Or, if you prefer, just close your eyes and meditate.

Meditation leads to the recollection that wars, riots, upheavals, and worrisome matters of all sorts are not new to the world. What's new is the constant dinning of them into our brains. It wasn't so long ago, as history flies, that we won a great battle after the war was already over. That unnecessary fighting around New Orleans in 1815 may have been regrettable, but how comforting the lack of news must have been to those who didn't even know battle impended until they already knew it wasn't very fateful anyway. Saved a lot of suspense on the nerves.

You can get the same effect on a vacation. Just shut off the din. The world will go right on having riots, wars, crises, none of them either mitigated or acerbated by your ignorance. Meanwhile the world's work—things like running airplanes—won't not get done any less for your idleness. Did the office really collapse while you were away? The pleasurable effect of all this on yourself may be slightly demoralizing, offering the same sort of temporary escape provided by alcohol, opium, or LSD. But at least there's no hangover.

There is, of course, a catch. When you come back, as even the opium smoker must, the world will be exactly as you left it, which means full of toil and trouble. If this is depressing, it's also enlightening. It makes you realize the permanence of woe, which is in fact very cheerful.

Thus if you must consider the state of the world, your despair over the facts will be lightened by the insight that if woe is permanent then tomorrow it could be worse, and may well be, so why not enjoy the surcease from toil and worry while you have it? The enlightenment can also reconcile you to vacation's end. For as some other philosopher remarked, I forget who, you can't really enjoy idleness unless you have lots of work and worry to escape from.

August 5, 1966

BAD HABITS AND GOOD MEN

IN an ordinary lifetime most men accumulate a nice collection of bad habits. Among the mentionable ones on my own list are smoking, whiskey drinking, gluttony, and sloth.

Sloth—now there's a word with an awe-inspiring sound to roll off a ministerial tongue—simply means that you have a disinclination to labor. Gluttony, its companion in the catechism, means that you eat too much. Gluttony and sloth, besides being uncommendable to the righteous, are definitely health hazards. The one gives you a paunch in the lower abdomen, which means that you are lugging around several extra pounds to burden the machinery. Sloth gives you those flabby muscles, reducing both your energy and your resistance.

The two together, as almost any doctor will tell you while he is feeling your arteries, can combine to pack a lot of dangerous fat in the arterial system, especially around the heart. There's a noticeable correlation between heart attacks and the fat and the flabby.

Yet many a good man who eschews the more notorious bad habits, like tobacco and whiskey, is hardly aware that for all his clean living he is a prisoner of these other two companions. He may pride himself on enjoying a good meal, or think it wise not to overexert himself at his age. His disapproving glance is saved for his neighbor relaxing in a cloud of smoke whilst sipping a highball. And nothing can be more furious than the disapproving glance of good men at the failings of other men. Especially when they decide it's their duty to save other men from their foolish habits.

Well, if you don't watch out, the good men are going to save you once more from your bad habits. This time it's tobacco. If you're honest with yourself you'll have to admit it's a commendable endeavor. To try to refute the indictments of tobacco by the Surgeon General is as futile as trying to rebut Carrie Nation on the evils of drink. Like that lady, the worthy is right. To be sure, the Surgeon General is as weak in his scientific arguments as Miss Carrie. Teetotalers have died of collapsing livers and topers have died of old age; cancer antedates Columbus, and if its determinant was smoking then Winston Churchill would never have been Prime Minister.

The idea that "no reasonable man" can dispute his proofs of causation is simply poppycock. You would have to suppose that madness had simultaneously overtaken some thirty thoracic surgeons, cardiovascular specialists, professors of bronchoesophagology, pathologists, bacteriologists, professors of biostatistics, and doctors of mathematics, all of whom disputed the official at the recent hearings.

No matter. None of these gentlemen, or ladies, argued that smoking is a healthy habit, only that the causes of cancer, heart attacks, and other ills of the flesh aren't to be so simply pinned on one villain. The Surgeon General is right in general that you add to life's hazards when you inhale cigarette smoke, the noxious fumes of street traffic, the pungent aroma of burning leaves, or the deadly gases pouring out of factory chimneys. Cigarettes were rightly called coffin nails when we were young—only then they caused TB and the vapors. You certainly ought to kick the habit before you get any older.

So what's wrong then with doing what the Surgeon General really wants to do, prohibit you from smoking them? Or at least doing what he suggests as a first step, putting a skull-and-bones warning on every pack? Or maybe doing what the good governor of New York is doing, tax them out of the poor man's pocket?

There's no use trying to rebut the questions by logic. Once a person is convinced he knows what's good for other people and sees it as his duty to save them from perdition, then logic permits only one action. Miss Carrie was as honorable as the witch hunters of Salem when she went about chopping up saloons. Of course you can point out the futility of laws to save foolish people. At one time or another good men have tried to halt face painting, betel nut chewing, sloth (remember Captain John Smith), late carousing, Sabbath fishing, gluttony (the Caliph had a point), mixed dancing, and mushroom eating—not to mention that noble experiment with whiskey drinking. Even the laws against more serious things, like narcotics, haven't been a howling success and have bred evils of crime and corruption as terrible as the evils they would correct.

The practical difficulty with sumptuary laws is that if men can't indulge in human frailty one way, they'll do it another. They'll go over, under, and around the law. Take away good whiskey, they'll make home-brew. Take away cured tobacco, they'll smoke raw weeds from the back yard. Or find a new bad habit that might be worse.

And, pray, why should they not?

A dollop of whiskey may not be good for your liver. Perhaps it doesn't relax the arteries. It can relax the spirit, and only in part because of its chemistry. Its true satisfaction is the moment's feeling of defying duty and the upright life, a thing taxing even to saints, and of enjoying the pleasure of being a human being.

An old gentleman of fond remembrance could teach the Surgeon General a thing or two. Confronted in middle age by the admonition to stop both smoking and drinking at peril to his health, he tried it for six months and then remarked to his wife: "Hallie, if this is the way I have to live, it isn't worth it." He died of cancer at seventy-two, but who's to say he was foolish?

Other men, other choices. But what is really left out of the equation by the good people who would make all men behave themselves for their health's sake is the human necessity for human failings. Our life here below is brief enough, and harried enough, that men must have some way to make it tolerable—especially so against the uprighteous who would smash saloons and padlock the tobacconist. So here, make of it what you will, is a good word for bad habits. And a pox upon those who think governments were instituted among men to save us from our follies.

April 12, 1965

OCTOBER, 1932

O NE of the pains of growing older, so it's said, is a growing feeling that the world is going to pot. Maybe so. But what can be just as trying is the repetitive monotony of the way the world gets there. After a certain number of decades have passed you can't pick up the morning newspaper or a current magazine, all chock-full of laments on the decline of just about everything, without feeling that you've been there before. The word is not so much despair as boredom.

The immediate cause of this lugubrious thought is a somewhat faded and muchly tattered copy of a campus literary magazine that arrived in the morning mail. Unearthed by some sardonic scholar it bears the date October, 1932. The masthead of *The Carolina Magazine,* published these years ago at the University of North Carolina, has itself a certain antiquarian interest. Foreign service colleagues of Robert W. Barnett may be interested to know that he was a literary editor before he became an Old China Hand and took to writing books on Asiatic economics. His associate editors were one Don Shoemaker, now known to the citizens of Florida as editor of the Miami *Herald*, and an E. C. Daniel, better known to New Yorkers as Clifton Daniel, managing editor of their local *Times,* the "Elbert" which hid behind the initials now having disappeared altogether.

But it's the magazine's content that fascinates. There is, for example, an article by a Joseph Sugarman commenting on the New York theater and the state of its drama critics. In 1932, it seems, the New York stage could be described as stagnant and ineffectual. Producers could be condemned for offering what "appeals solely to the box office" and playwrights for lack of originality. Even the audiences were pummelled because they were "moronic, sex-struck and incapable of artistic appreciation." Sound familiar? Young Mr. Sugarman also took dead aim at the drama critics, who it appears wrote more in haste than in thought. None escaped unscathed, Brooks Atkinson, Percy Hammond, George Jean Nathan, or Burns Mantle. But Mr. Sugarman had a thought of his own. Why not, he asked, have the critics review from the dress rehearsal to give them more time for reflection?

Thirty years later his idea was given a try—under Clifton Daniel at *The Times*, no less—only to come a cropper. And today Yale professors make headlines with comments on the stagnant state of the theater and the sins of the drama critic.

In those days, incidentally, Mr. Daniel wrote Swiftian satire. In the guise of fiction ("Steve sat in his room, laboriously knocking out on the typewriter one of Senator White's stock interviews") he flayed politics as a dirty business and journalism as a grubby one. The magazine had poetry too, including one by Vermont Royster that begins "For forty cents I bought the soul of Keats." Its meter is impeccable, and that young man could turn a phrase. Its sentiment moreover is durable, for here the poet slays the Philistines for their bourgeois getting and spending instead of more properly tending their souls.

So it goes. The young writers of 1932 lay about them at just about every aspect of American life, its culture, politics, sexual mores, and its aspirations. Hardly an icon is left unsmashed. From the vantage point of thirty years it's plain they didn't always know what they were writing about; you can't help but be amused at a nineteen-year-old's dramatic rendering of middle-aged adultery. Yet some of the shafts thrust home, and any of them might have been fired day before yesterday. The campus writers of 1966

146

are as fresh as ever; the weariness is in the reader who's read it all before.

This is the dreadful part of having a long memory. Thirty years ago the elders were upset because a university sociologist, famed in his day, was advocating premarital sexual relations and there was some suspicion some students were taking the advice. The campus peace movement, later to flower into the League Against War and Fascism, was equally upsetting, especially since the leaders who hung around the bookshop wore dirty corduroy trousers and didn't bother to shave. Off campus the situation wasn't any better. The stock market—remember?—was in a slump and the elders, if not the students, were wondering when it would bottom out.

In October 1932, a younger Franklin Roosevelt was belaboring the reckless fiscal policies of the government and vowing that if he were elected President all that would be changed. President Hoover, for his part, was vowing a war against poverty and promising that the government would spend whatever was necessary to keep the country prosperous.

Around the country there were paralyzing strikes and disorder in the streets; a mob of a thousand people descended on Washington to demand a $2 billion handout from Congress. Across the seas there was unrest in Europe, aggression in Asia. An international conference was being called to deal with the problem of world currencies. What lesson lies in all this nostalgia is difficult to fathom. But the burden of it is boredom. The trouble with the "new economics" is not that it's new and untried but that it's wearyingly old. What troubles the peace of the world is not new madness but one bent with the weight of age.

Or make your pick at random: the decline of the arts or the decline of the Supreme Court, race riots or labor riots, go-go girls or economic nostrums, bourgeois mores or avant-garde revolt. Stick around long enough and you'll meet yourself coming back. Pretty soon you begin to wonder if anybody learns anything. And begin to wish you could pick up next month's campus magazine to find that the new campus rebels had thought up some fresh foibles, just for the novelty. But then you realize that this is one area in which the young can hardly improve on their fathers.

October 18, 1966

RESERVE CALL-UP

YOU get to a certain age and the first thing you know everything that happens today makes you think of the long ago. So it was the other day when President Johnson acknowledged he was considering a "limited call-up" of military reserves. While the vulnerable young fellows around the shop were fretting about it, you could hardly listen for the thinking back. President Roosevelt, that distant autumn, was careful to explain that it was only a "limited call-up" of the National Guard and the organized Naval Reserve units. The idea was that the first units to go would serve a year on active duty and then be replaced by other units in their turn.

There was, then, considerable excitement among the young fellows when the First Battalion of the District of Columbia Naval Reserve, as befitted a Capital crew, was among the first to get orders, especially when they learned they'd be assigned to a destroyer. It sounded a bit like a year's adventurous vacation. Since the orders were for January 1, 1941, there was a dash of extra spice to the Christmas holidays. Old uniforms were refurbished, new ones bought; leaves of absence obtained from drab workaday jobs; plans made for wives—and in some cases children—to come a-visiting down to Panama, where the ship would be based. And the battalion commander drew up an operational plan for a grand reunion party on New Year's Eve, 1941.

The departure was festive, with the band playing and the flags waving, even if the first leg was only overnight passage on the Potomac river passenger boat to Norfolk. From there there'd be a leisurely cruise through the Caribbean on the U.S.S. *Nitro,* a slow and comfortable supply ship even if it was loaded with ammunition. Everybody would have a chance to get his sea legs.

The U.S.S. *J. Fred Talbott,* which awaited at Panama, wasn't exactly the pride of the fleet. An old "four piper" of World War I vintage, she was equipped with antiquated guns, no fire control system, not even echo-ranging equipment for searching out submarines. The captain was supposed to take a look at the empty ocean and scatter his depth charges by guess and by God. All the same, the sailors were better off than the soldiers who went marching off that January. Many of them had to skirmish with wooden sticks for guns, or drill with pick-up trucks on which a paper sign read "tank." At least the old *J. Fred* could whip up an easy twenty knots, maybe thirty knots with a little careful nursing of her tired boilers.

The reception of the reservists, incidentally, wasn't exactly the same as they'll get today. From captain to bos'n the old-timers left aboard looked with jaundiced eyes at the civilian sailors with whom they'd have to make do. With such a ship and such a crew, their sighs said plainly, the good old Navy was down to the dregs.

The Old Man—he must have been all of thirty-five—took one look at this landlubberly crew and assigned officers with engineering backgrounds to topside and stuck deck-trained officers in sweaty boiler rooms, which naturally struck everybody at the time as a typical muddleheaded Navy way of doing things. Only afterwards, when the young grew quickly old, did this madness reveal its wise method.

In a novel all this might make a tale of bitter feuds, bungling, and unhappy men. To the young men today it must seem crazy, man. In real life it was a lark. After all, everybody knew the President hated war, and although there was a lot of it in distant parts of the world, places like Europe and Asia, he had just won re-election with a pledge not to send American boys to fight in those foreign wars. True, a couple of sister destroyers had caught torpedoes in the Atlantic, but the wardroom chatter blamed them for getting careless.

Meanwhile, there were bustling dashes back and forth through the Canal; the rattling *J. Fred* probably holds the world's record for Panama transits. There were lazy rum collinses on the hotel verandas, visits to Caribbean isles, and delightful cruises through the lovely Gulf of Panama into the Pacific southward beyond the equator. If there was a bit of loneliness too—most of the wives never made it, and those who did stayed briefly—the comfort was in that phrase "limited call-up" and the approach of Christmas. The detachment orders began arriving around December 1.

The Sunday morning that stands out most in memory found the ancient destroyer division moored in Balboa. The day was sunny but cool for the tropics, and most of the crews—including the captains—were ashore enjoying (or recuperating from) a pleasant weekend. The duty officer on the *J. Fred,* a journalist turned citizen sailor, was writing a letter home when the radio operator reported some chatter about Pearl Harbor. After a bit of gunwale gossip with the lone young officer on the next ship the cold boilers were heated up, while a long wait began for some orders and the straggling return of officers and crew.

As a minor footnote to history it might be recorded that the Japanese therein missed a great opportunity for a surprise attack. As it was, neither newspapers nor history paid much attention to the belated bustle that stirred the Panama Sea Frontier, with tired tin cans making like greyhounds chasing nonexistent rabbits through two long nights and days over an unruffled sea.

The Bureau of Navigation—or Bureau of Personnel, as they call it now—didn't pay much attention to us either. The weeks passed and no word ever came cancelling those nice orders to go home, kiss the wife, and return to the quiet of the Senate press gallery.

On Christmas Eve the captain was reminded of the orders. He

read them through slowly, and then with a chuckle tore them up and dropped them in the wastebasket. Which leads us to one word of cheer for any caught in the next temporary call-up. Don't believe the old saw about the bureaucracy-ridden military squelching independence and initiative in local commanders. Technically that captain deserved a courtmartial. He never even got a reprimand.

July 15, 1965

THE FULLER LIFE

T HE lure of escape from a world too much with us is probably as old as the first middle-aged man. But it's had an especial appeal ever since that French stockbroker decided to chuck it all, flee to the South Seas, and play artist hero for a Somerset Maugham novel. Hardly anyone notices that Paul Gauguin's Tahitian paradise proved not all cakes and ale. If he sickened miserably it was at least amid sunshine and nubile maidens, and he expired as romantically as Keats or Byron.

For lesser mortals, no less romantic dreams. The farmer muses on distant seas and the sailor longs for a home on the prairie. The housewife in Sauk Center wants to swap the P.T.A. for Manhattan *soirées*, while the busy and glamorous model in time grows pensive over vine-covered cottages. That staid-looking commuter's bulging briefcase hides a copy of *Flying Magazine*.

But we more prosaic mortals tailor our dreams to smaller ambitions. A few extra hours on the golf course, perhaps, where whacking a ball can substitute for hacking our way through jungles. Or, if we're lucky, a centerboard sloop that imagination rigs as a barkentine rounding the Horn. Not many of us actually chuck it all, at least not until the years have left the flesh less resilient than the spirit.

Hence our fascination with those who do, and live to tell about it. Not just those who dare a single adventure, like crossing the Atlantic in a tiny *Tinkerbelle*, but also those who boldly uproot settled lives and family, abandon in midstream a certain livelihood to chase a dream before it's lost.

153

One who did is Edmund Fuller, whose essays on books grace the pages of *The Wall Street Journal* and sundry other publications. Now he tells about it in a book of his own, *Successful Calamity*. It's a pleasant tale and he tells it well, but best of all it's a tonic for those who are heavy-laden. Mr. Fuller, to be sure, took a rather shopworn journey. What he chucked was the "rat race" of New York City, where he was then a young man of promise in a publisher's office. What he swapped it for was a Vermont farm. What happened was just what you'd expect.

There are all the stereotyped tribulations—the hazards of Vermont snows, busted plumbing, recalcitrant pigs, sickness, bone-wearying labor, the frustrations of an outlander amid alien neighbors. Their freshness comes from his skill as a raconteur; the chapter on his adventures with the cow and the artificial inseminator is sheer delight. But the real rewards in the tale come from his gift of self-perception. Without benefit of LSD, Mr. Fuller can stand off and watch himself being naïve, romantic, impractical, and even foolish, all with wry amusement. The reader can watch a man as he grows in wisdom about life, dreams, and self.

One thing he learned is that paradise is an illusion. In the countryside to which he escaped he found a different rat race. More, as in the big city, he found adultery, incest, murder, fraud, brutality, stupidity, sloth, greed, hatred, and bigotry. He also found what he had also found sometimes in the city, honor and integrity, diligence, common sense, compassion, kindness, faith, and perseverance in adversity.

Perhaps a wise man might have told him beforehand that this is the elemental human face. But it's a discovery each of us must make anew, and some of us never do. Anyway, it was not his most important discovery. That, as it turned out, was his discovery of Edmund Fuller. For one thing, he learned not to blink facts; his venture did fail. Yet his paradise lost, he did not retreat to the

154

place from which he had fled. He turned a gallant mistake into an onward-leading mistake.

For Mr. Fuller this self-discovery led on to the quiet class-room and writing room. Since then a good many young men have profited from his company at the Kent School; the rest of us have enjoyed his small shelf of books. Other men, other ways. But whatever your way, you will be rewarded by sharing this modest Odyssey.

And marvel at the durability of the adventurous spirit. At this moment Mr. Fuller, the family all uprooted, is teaching in Rome, exploring the ruins of antiquity and no doubt taking copious notes. Which reminds me that our own new boat is launched and ready for the distant shores of Maine. Pray don't tell me this is a waste of time and money for a grandfather. Tread softly, as the poet begs, because you tread on my dreams.

April 12, 1966

PAINFUL PERCENTAGES

RELENTLESSLY once a year comes the season of chills and fever, especially for those of us who enjoy the rarefied air of New York City. And it's astonishing how little it takes to give you big miseries. With the mouth thermometer registering no more than 100 degrees, your nose runs, your eyes water, your bones ache, and every muscle feels like you just finished the Super Bowl game. What makes the reaction seem incommensurate with the provocation is that the normal body temperature is 98.6 degrees. Thus 100 degrees on the Fahrenheit scale is barely a 1 per cent increase. Let the rise top 2 per cent and you're apt to face not only miseries but a big doctor's bill.

In such a state it's hard enough anyway to read the morning headlines, and you're certainly not in the best mood to react with proper gratefulness to the latest word from the Bureau of Labor Statistics. Right there on page one it says that food prices this year should go up by "only" about 2 per cent, and even this would be due mainly to price increases on beef and dairy products. Forgo the milk and shift to pork chops, and you might even shave off a percentage point.

Moreover, according to the Commissioner of Labor Statistics, the whole Consumer Price Index (which includes the price of clothes and such as well as food) may not rise any more than a mere 2.5 per cent. The especial cheer in this good news stems from the fact that in 1966, a lamentable year on several counts, the same Consumer Price Index shot up 3.3 per cent, for the

156

largest single year's rise since 1957. This chunk out of the household budget, so it says here, was offset somewhat by wage increases. But they in turn were offset by increased social security taxes. On a net balance the drop in real purchasing power amounted to $1.35 a week for the average worker, or a decline of "only" 1.6 per cent.

The difficulty with trying to keep all this straight in your mind is the aspirin. It makes your head ring. The lady of the house can tell you that the cost of living has been going up every year, almost since the memory of man runneth not to the contrary, but it's a struggle to explain to her that each year, most years, the rise was "only" a percentage point or so.

She gets out the *World Almanac*, which you can hardly read through puffy eyes, and points out that since 1959 the cost of living has gone up 15 per cent everywhere, almost 18 per cent in Mayor Lindsay's Fun City. It mounts up, she says.

That, of course, is one trouble with percentages. Just the other evening, for example, the man in Washington explained that he was going to have to raise our taxes, what with the war on and everything, but that it would be "only" 6 per cent. Take a married man with about $6,000 of taxable income. He'd only pay about $5 a month more, or $60 a year, the man said. It didn't sound like much; what can you buy these days with $60 anyway? But that doesn't count the $1,000 he is already paying, which is something else and no small percentage.

Then if he's lucky enough to get a raise this year, he'll pay 19 per cent of the extra money to Uncle Sam right off, plus an extra 6 per cent of that if the little old tax bill goes through. Nor is that all. This week the man suggested raising social security taxes by a small amount; that is, "only" about 1 per cent more than they would rise anyway. By 1969 that means a total social security and medicare tax of 5 per cent on the employee's wages covered plus an equal amount to be paid by the employer, or a total rate of 10 per cent on a dollar's worth of wages.

And in case you've lost count, that 10 per cent is in addition to the hereinbefore mentioned 19 per cent and 6 per cent of that. At which point, if you've got a headache, your arithmetic breaks down. All you can remember is that somehow you've forgotten the governor and the mayor. The governor in this case likes to remind everybody that he takes "only" 10 per cent of their earnings at the most, and for most people it's hardly more than 6 per cent, which by this time seems like a pittance indeed. Something, we suppose, must be left for the mayor of Fun City, who takes away no more than 2 per cent of net taxable income and only 5 per cent of what you spend of what you have left.

Somehow you do have something left, and in the process you've taught the lady of the house a valuable lesson in the difference between gross and net. So perhaps there is some comfort in being told that this year what you have left will be worth only 2.5 per cent less in the market place than what it would have been worth last year. In any event, it's plain enough that the rise in the cost of shoes and groceries, even if it amounts to 3 per cent all over again, still won't boost your cost of living as much as the cost of government. The B.L.S., incidentally and quite shrewdly, doesn't count the cost of government as part of the cost of living. You can always escape the cost of government by not earning anything, going on relief, and living off the government. Which is something you can't do with the butcher.

To be sure it can get confusing when you're lying there in the half-dark listening to the telly explain about the government's new budget. On an administrative budget of $135 billion for fiscal 1968 the deficit is "only" 6 per cent (that is, if you count in the 6 per cent tax increase the President asked for), which doesn't seem so terribly much when you figure the lady of the house ran a bigger percentage deficit than that just last month.

But then the smiling TV reporter says that in this case 6 per

158

cent amounts to $8.1 billion and that between now and the end of 1968 the accumulated deficit will add up to nearly $20 billion. Like the lady says, percentages do mount up. Or down. For if the cost of living rises 2.5 per cent each year, that is just another way of saying that the dollar each year is depreciated by that amount in purchasing power. Now if each year the dollar shrinks by only 2.5 per cent, and if you can work the calculus out in your head, how many years will it be before you can use dollar bills like Kleenex to blow your nose?

But the mental effort is exhausting, and besides, why bother if each year the government is going to let you keep fewer and fewer dollars anyway? So you just stick the thermometer in your mouth and wonder why the devil you feel so lousy with only a 1 per cent fever. Hardly seems reasonable.

January 26, 1967

REFLECTIONS ON A
GREAT-GRANDFATHER

T HE picture on our living room wall is a bit formal for these
times. The old gentleman wears a high wing collar, a soft
white beard, and steel-rimmed spectacles over eyes watery with
age. Although I remember him as a warm and kindly man, he
seems now strange and distant to his great-grandchildren. That's
a pity, I think, for this fall one of those great-grandchildren goes
off to college, and that journey will be a gift from this man of
Puritan ethics who, in a way no longer fashionable, gave thought
to those unborn who would come after him.

Nor was that thoughtfulness all there was to mark him as a
man of a different time. He came to manhood in the aftermath of
a great civil war which had cost him a father, a brother, a home,
and the education which is today thought every man's due. He
could not take himself a wife until he neared his fortieth birthday
since it never occurred to him that the responsibility for a family
lay upon anyone's shoulders but his own.

In due time, laboring with his hands by day and his mind by
night, he became a merchant, a musician, something of an artist,
and enough of a scholar to discuss Latin subjunctives with his
more learned sons. Before it was over he had built a house with
tall columns, dreaming that someday his grandchildren would
dwell therein with their own children in turn.

The dream is gone, of course, just as the house is, where now
dwells a filling station. Times have scattered the family, and new

ideas about society and the role of a family have dispersed the legacy he so carefully husbanded. Taxed and taxed again, it cannot much longer pay a child's education. Hereafter each generation begins anew. There are many, we know, who think this is the way it ought to be. With the welfare state we seek to make outmoded this self-reliance of a bygone time. And with our laws we make it difficult for any man to dream in such a fashion of his great-grandchildren.

At first the aim of heavy death taxes was only to break up the concentrations of great wealth, such things being thought bad for society. But really great wealth has its own defenses; the fortunes of the Rockefellers, Fords, and Kennedys survive. Today the true penalties fall upon those who, like the old man in the picture, accumulate a little in hopes for the next generation but not enough to build bulwarks against the erosion of taxes. And this is by design. No one pretends these taxes are for revenue, for they bring in little. By intent they put a levy upon the savings of every family that gives thought to its own tomorrow.

If the government had its way, these penalties would be even higher. The President wants Congress to tax every estate twice; to charge first for any alleged "capital gain"—real or imaginary, realized or not—that may have accrued in dollars on a lifetime's property, and then to pile the estate tax upon top of that. Thus a house bought thirty years ago and made "worth" more in paper money cheapened by thirty years of inflation could be a taxable gain just because a father died. Then the heirs could pay another tax for the privilege of living in it still. The same principle would apply to all other family savings.

Fortunately a House committee has, for the time being, rejected this vicious injustice. Yet curiously hardly anyone seems to have looked beyond that plain injustice and asked about the injury this philosophy also does to society itself. For beneath all the spoken arguments for this kind of taxation, however phrased, is in fact a hostility to the very concept of family as a continuing institution, progressing from generation to generation and handing on a better heritage to each succeeding one.

It is true, of course, that not everyone has a father, or great-grandfathers, able to accumulate material things or willing to do so by sacrificing for what may be when they are dead. Nor is it only a question of material things. Some men are at home with books, and they pass this familiarity on to their children, which may give them an advantage in a world where education is capital. Indeed, in almost every aspect of life there are some who begin with better fortunes than their fellows, if in nothing more than that some fathers bestow good health and others a sickly life. All this, so it is said, is unfair. It is wrong that the child of one family should begin with more than those of another; that some, for example, should go to school on the earnings of the past while others must earn their own way. So society, by it laws, must eliminate such advantages.

Perhaps so. But why, then, should any man deprive himself of present pleasure to save something for those who come after? He need only spend what he has while he lives and there will be nothing left for the taxgatherer. Why, indeed, should a father trouble himself at all with his young, if none should have the patrimony gained by generations?

Yet if this had been the view of the man on our living room wall, who should be the loser but society itself? For laws can only level downward, not upward. They can take from one child the birthright of a great-grandfather; they cannot give to all what one has lost, and the sum of this must be a subtraction from the whole. But it's hard to explain all this, these days, to a great-grandchild. Even older, and supposedly wiser, men seem to have forgotten that society itself is nothing but a large family which has also built its present on the accumulations of yesterday.

September 5, 1963

VI

FACE OF THE LAND

WAR: 1950

LAWRENCE, KANS.

T HE farmers who come into the Underwood brothers' feed and grain store, which is most of them in Douglas county, don't show much interest in the things that go to make up politics— the Communists, gambling scandals, war and inflation, crop prospects, and what's going to happen after the election. And what's true of the farmers seems also true in varying degrees of the groups that make up this small Kansas community. Everybody's convinced that Republican Frank Carlson is going to get elected Senator next month, so why waste talk about it. On any other subject, Lawrence is one of the easiest places in the world to start an argument.

That's largely due to the way the town is made. It's compartmentalized, composed of farmers, of townsmen who service the community, and of a large educational group at Kansas University and Haskell Institute for the Indians. So you can always find someone who is vitally interested in any matter you pick, whether it be American Indians or Indochina. The town's groups are separate but they do react on one another in a kind of cross-fertilization process. What emerges is perhaps a hybrid, but if so an instructive hybrid. It gives the stranger a good chance to get a nodding acquaintance with many facets of Kansas.

When all the community gets together, as it did recently for a "Haskell Day" barbecue picnic, you can stand in one spot and touch a wheat farmer, a student from Dodge City, an insurance broker, a professor of economics, or a Pawnee from Wichita. And all of them are Kansas, met together. Nobody in the group will ask any more: "What's the matter with Kansas?" but a good many of them will ask: "What's the matter with the world?" There's no more isolation in the sense of ignorance or disinterest in world problems. Everybody's interested and few are ignorant.

As brother Bob Underwood says: "The farmers around here listen to the radio, read the papers and know what's going on. They're willing to listen about Korea or any other place. But that doesn't mean they believe everything folks tell 'em."

Farmer Stevens, whose first name got lost by a careless reporter, put it like this: "Out my way we're pretty conservative. We don't like a lot of things we hear about Washington and politicians. Mostly they get us into a lot of trouble running all over the world. But who's going to get us out?"

But if all this shows an end of ignorance and disinterest in world affairs, it does not—or so it seems to a stranger—reflect the death of isolationism (if Kansas will pardon the word) in the sense that the word implies a reluctance to accept the idea that an international policy means a global interventionist policy. It certainly doesn't reflect unrestrained enthusiasm for foreign policy as recently conducted.

W. C. Simons, editor of the local paper, views Korea as "a rather unsatisfactory" war. "I think old Stalin outmaneuvered us," he says. "But now that we are in there's only one way out, the long way." J. W. Murray expresses the view: "One time or other we made a terrible mistake. Either we should not have gotten out of Korea or we should not have gone back."

This dualism of progressive interest in world affairs and of traditional caution against mixing in the world's ills is also shared by the cap-and-gown. The interest sparked a new seminar this fall at Kansas University on the broad subject, "The World in Crisis"; it offers to students and others fifteen lectures on foreign affairs, embracing every point of view. Yet Kansas University Chancellor Deane W. Mallot, an intense observer of foreign affairs, urges some caution toward the whole policy of "fighting Communism everywhere."

"With containment of Communism—or the protection of free countries—as our purpose, we must keep constantly on the alert and constantly prepared on all fronts," he says. "This is a burden I do not believe we can bear."

The cost of the burden burdens the thoughts of others, too. Professor John Ise—who has the distinction of having been Alf Landon's economic adviser and also a target for charges of "radicalism"—preaches pessimism on the domestic economy. Talk of price controls set him rumbling. "They'll just hide the inflation and make matters worse. They won't stop pumping out money and so we're going to have a bad inflation. Even an economics professor doesn't know what to do with his small savings."

Yet if one can judge by casual talk, Truman's decision to fight in Korea is not seriously criticized. "Korea?" asks truck-driver Hank Moss. "Hell, yes, we were in such a fix we couldn't do anything else." The younger men are particularly anxious to carry through. "If we back down now," according to one draft-age K. U. sophomore with youthful vigor, "it would be disastrous for civilization."

Perhaps that explains why Maurice Knott, farm supervisor at Haskell and National Guard captain, has been able to keep up with recruits for Company "H." "The vets aren't so keen about it," says veteran Knott, "but the younger fellows are more eager." And he adds wryly, "Maybe they don't know what they're getting into." The older folks who know—like Mr. and Mrs. E. J. Lambert and Mrs. Helen Price, who have lost boys already—speak softly.

But determined or frightened, few people here give a stranger the impression they have gained more respect for our foreign policy. President Truman, whose home town is not so far away, has not sold himself to Kansas. That, of course, is not so important, for this is a traditionally conservative and Republican state. But—and this is important—he has not sold this part of Kansas confidence in his government's conduct of foreign affairs.

Perhaps the reason for this is, as insurance man C. B. Holmes humorously observes, that "people around here, like people everywhere, just rearrange their prejudices and go ahead." But neither Mr. Truman nor anyone else can any longer blame it on ignorance or disinterest in the world. Lawrence takes many sons of Kansas and gives them a long look at the world. Perhaps, instead, it's just that Kansas doesn't like what it sees.

October 25, 1950

WAR: 1966

ORDINARILY nothing so lifts the spirits of a provincial New Yorker as a journey west of the Alleghenies. There people are usually too busy building the future to be preoccupied with the floating anxieties of the present. You can renew not only your own spirit but your pride and confidence in the country. But in the midwinter of 1966 the mood is different. Wherever he goes the visitor is more questioned than questioning, and the questions betray an unaccustomed unease. You return with the feeling that in the wide country too people are troubled not just about the problems of the moment, of which there are always a sufficient number, but with the kind of vague forebodings that no man can quite put a name to.

It's true that nearly everybody mentions a name: Vietnam. That war crops up in conversation as ubiquitously as King Charles's head. It matters not what you start out talking about— the outlooks for auto sales, the fate of Taft-Hartley's 14-B, urban renewal, or career opportunities for college graduates—you end up talking about that war on the distant shores of Asia.

Yet war, as war, is nothing novel to present generations. Many of us are now living through our fourth pretty good-sized one. Some have fought in two or three of them. The young may hope, but hardly expect, to avoid war in the future. Fighting and dying are ever a cause for sadness, but up to now at any rate they've never made Americans feel the chill of despair.

No, in the brooding there is something else. The word Vietnam covers a multitude of anxieties. Begin the journey in Washington. That city may sometimes seem to stand apart from the country, but this is mostly illusion. For here more than anywhere else all the strands come together. Men shuffling papers in the White House or making speeches on Capitol Hill do not escape the crosscurrents of the cities or the mood of the prairies. If they are sensitive they can even anticipate.

Right now it's no place to go to lift despondency. There is not an admiral or a general who really knows what to do to win the war. Or, perhaps more accurately, none agrees with the others. The Chiefs of Staff can reject the ideas of their old colleagues, Generals Gavin and Ridgway; they have nothing hopeful to offer in their stead.

Thus Secretary McNamara, who in any other time would have been long since discredited, can offer one plan today and another tomorrow with none to dispute him, simply because he is at least self-confident. Everybody else is just too benumbed. Thus the State Department, for the first time in American history, can rush frantically about the world begging for somebody, anybody, to rescue us from battle, and everybody tries to pretend they don't feel ashamed. Even so, it's hard to find anybody who really thinks that the United Nations can, or will, extricate us from our troubles.

But it's not only the military problem abroad. The economic advisers at home lay out their charts without confidence; they have to confess that an uncertainty beyond calculation lies over everything. The abstract name for the anxiety is inflation; the concrete fear is of shortages of those nails for want of which kingdoms are lost. If no one predicts, no one would be surprised to see higher taxes, price and wage controls, and all the other desperate measures of desperate nations.

And there's little political comfort to be found in any of it. President Johnson, so they say, carries about the clippings of the polls that show his Vietnamese policy still has the people's support, as if to reassure himself. And he talks as boldly as ever about building the Great Society from the riches of the land. All the same, a visitor in the gallery the other day could hear Senators arise, one after the other, to attack the renewal of the war, with none rising to answer them. Altogether very nearly a quarter of the Senate has opposed the bombings, a not very cheerful prospect for a President who leads a nation in war.

End your journey on a campus, and by then you will know that Washington is not alone in its anxieties. The unease is reflected not only by the students at Michigan State, who are just beginning their lives, but by their elders assembled from all over the state who, as editors of the weeklies and small-town dailies, are close to their neighbors. You may want to talk about the future of journalism; they want to talk about the future of the country. Quickly you discover it's not a fear of fighting that discourages the young or the old. It's the thought of fighting for an uncertain purpose and with no prospect of a victory to end it. Suppose we did beat the Vietcong, so the question runs, what then? A man who fought in the jungles of Guadalcanal, and thought he knew why, asks if his son dies in the jungle of Vietnam for what purpose will he have died?

Among the old, if not among the young, there is another thought that lies heavy on the mind. For these people inflation is not an abstract word; nor are war taxes and war controls unfamiliar blights. If this little war threatens all of these things, they wonder, what is there ahead but bleakness in endless, and perhaps bigger, war? Over all the conversation there's another thought, less spoken than suggested. What has happened to the United States, once the greatest power in the world, that it should now find itself paralyzed and pleading for help, not knowing which way to turn and finding few friends to turn to?

This, or so anyway it seemed to me listening, is very likely the root of the nameless anxiety. Very few of those encountered along the way want to run away from the fighting. Some in fact are made more belligerent by their very unease; let us unleash our might, clobber the enemy and get it over with. But hawks or doves, young or old, statesmen in the capital or politicians at a city hall, union men or industry leaders—talk to whom you will, people are uncertain what their country ought to do and anxious of what will happen to it. Even for men who have lived through three wars and a great depression it's a new mood.

The temperature was 12 below zero in East Lansing. But that was the least chilling part of the journey.

February 8, 1966

THE AMERICAN WAY

N OWADAYS it's hard to travel the wide countryside without dodging college students—or their professors—parading in a demonstration. Back East the subject was philosophy. At Yale the students marched to the defense of a professor charged with the heinous sin of not writing, only teaching, a failing of Gautama Buddha and Socrates. At Rutgers the students were vocal for and against a professor whose professed philosophy is that of Karl Marx, a man who wrote much and taught little, and the row soon swept up the governor and would-be governor of New Jersey. On the West Coast, at Berkeley campus, the students stood up four-square for pornography and the right to speak to the coeds in whatever terms came to mind.

But without doubt the most exciting demonstrations have been the classroom sit-ins, street corner stand-ups, and marching parades protesting Vietnam and the military draft. In this area the Middle West has snatched the place of pre-eminence.

The command headquarters for one of the biggest demonstrations was at the University of Wisconsin. Headline-making cooperation came from students at the University of Michigan, Colorado University, and the two largest universities here in Chicago, to name a few.

If you find all this collegiate excitement about public ques-

173

tions a bit puzzling yourself, consider the journalist's problem explaining it to Latin American colleagues at the San Diego meeting of the Inter-American Press Association or to Canadian friends here for the meeting of the Inland Press Association. The Canadians seem to consider it all a bit untidy; indeed, unseemly. The Latin Americans wonder out loud if it means that student action, as in some of their own countries, is becoming a force capable of toppling governments. To everybody it seems uncharacteristic of the American way.

The difficulty in explaining is that there are so many partial answers, each of which is true but any one of which, taken alone, is misleading. By now the evidence is pretty plain that most of these spontaneous demonstrations are carefully contrived and centrally directed. The placarded slogans are the same from campus to campus; demonstrators get their marching orders from walkie-talkies which materialize from nowhere.

Even without documentation from the FBI you can recognize the trail of Communist or other left-wing groups, whether they originated or merely latched onto the movement. They would infiltrate any movement out to cause public disturbance, and in this case they have the added incentive of aiding a specific Communist cause, creating an appearance of dissatisfaction with the anti-Communist military effort in Vietnam.

So the view that it is all a part of an organized "plot" is correct enough as far as it goes; certainly correct enough to justify some inquiries by the authorities. You can't watch one of these demonstrations, however, without realizing that many of the participants are no more Communist than the proverbial little old lady in tennis shoes. Quite apart from the conscious agitators and the just plain kooks, a number of students get involved simply because they are at the age where they want to get involved in public questions and protest "whatever is." Yesterday they revolted against the policies of the university, today against the policies of the government. You could make a good case, then, for the thesis that college students today are more aware and more interested in the problems of the world than in days gone by.

But to leap from the vehemence of the protests to the conclusion that the present generation of students has lost its ever-loving mind, or that we are faced with a Latin-American type revolt on the campus, just doesn't square with the facts. The *National Observer* recently did a little arithmetic that is instructive. At Roosevelt University here 40 students showed up on the anti-Vietnam picket line from a total student body of 5,000. At Michigan the ratio was 300 demonstrators from 32,000 students; at Wayne State University 400 from 29,000. These are hardly the proportions of a mass uprising.

Finally, the perspective is helped a bit by the historical record. Noisy protests of this kind may be un-American but they are not uncharacteristic of America. Almost every war we ever got in has brought them forth. Even the idealism of the original revolution wasn't unmarred by protesting riots; neither was Mr. Madison's war with England nor the Civil War amongst ourselves.

Our entry into World War I brought riotous protests, and anyone around a campus on the eve of World War II will recall the militant pacifist organizations, many of them Communist dominated until Mr. Hitler took after Mr. Stalin. If the students seem more noisy about it now than then—well, they are just aping their elders, who have given them the example of taking to the streets for their causes. It's rather much to expect the young to discriminate among riots, just as it may be hard to teach them not to use four-letter words in speech when the elders think them all right in books and on the screen.

And it's devilish hard to explain all this to a visiting journalist from abroad. The difficulty is that you have to agree that these campus demonstrations are troubling things for thoughtful men,

175

the more so because their inspiration comes often from those hired to teach the young and their organization comes from professional enemies of society. Yet you must also remind the visitor that this is a huge country, numbering now nearly 200 million, and that it's still a free country where a man who doesn't like what the government's doing can wave a placard. A thousand or so people, all yelling at once, can make an awful racket, especially when they can get on a coast-to-coast network. But for all the headlines they make in foreign places they are still just a tiny handful.

Besides, how do you explain to a stranger that the same young men who today jump and scream and shout will tomorrow, if need be, land on a distant beachhead and put on the demonstration that counts? That both are the American way?

October 22, 1965

GANGWAY FOR DE LAWD

THE youngsters being grown and gone, we've lately been squeezing down from a largish house in the country to a smallish apartment in the city. And as you might expect, we've found both pleasure and sadness in rummaging through a lifetime's accumulations. It's hard to keep packing when you come across a third-grade essay in girlish scrawl entitled "My Daddy." Or when you take down from the study walls dusty photographs of long ago. So it was I paused before the autographed picture of Richard B. Harrison, the original de Lawd in *The Green Pastures,* that magnificent play Marc Connelly made from the Negro biblical stories of Roark Bradford.

It was more than thirty years ago when *The Green Pastures* came to the North Carolina campus theater and Mr. Harrison spent the afternoon of the performance visiting with some of us of theatrical interests. Over cakes and ale in our student rooms we tired the sun with talking and sent him down to bed.

Richard Harrison was born in Canada, but before the days of his fame he had become an adopted North Carolinian and he had always a deep feeling for the past of his people. Along with Countee Cullen and James Weldon Johnson, both of whom touched our college days, he took pride in the music that filled his people's poetry and the poetry that colored their music. Mr. Harrison was a big man, of craggy features and leonine locks, who could fill a whole stage with his presence. His first entrance as de Lawd, on Broadway's opening night, has become legend. The play begins, you'll remember, with a fish fry. Then when all the angels and cherubim are in happy picnicking mood, Gabriel enters crying: "Gangway! Gangway for de Lawd, God, Jehovah!"

Because the audience was still in happy mood, when Mr. Harrison first made his entrance he was met with waves of unexpected laughter. As he recounted it afterwards, he was stunned. But he was determined that no one should laugh at de Lawd. So he stood, immobile and silent, until as the minutes ticked by the audience quieted and there was not a rustle of a program. Then he said in commanding tones: "Let de fish fry proceed." He said it in a way which, I fear, will never be heard again. For though in ordinary speech Mr. Harrison spoke in precise accents, the accents of de Lawd were the soft ones of the Negro preacher of a bygone time.

Richard B. Harrison's whole life was devoted to the progress of the Negro people—in 1930 he won the Spingarn medal—but it never occurred to him that in the dialect of the Southern Negro, in his folk songs and his folk tales there was anything to be ashamed of. On the contrary, he was wise enough not to let the struggles of the present becloud his pride in that heritage.

All that is changed now. By the time *The Green Pastures* became a movie most of the dialect was gone, just as it somehow vanished from *Porgy and Bess.* On the television and radio, even when the program says Stephen Foster, all them darkies are no longer in the cornfield. The music may be the same but the words and the spirit are gone.

In literature the casualties—innocent victims in the Negro's struggle for his civil rights and for a rightful place in the sun— have been almost as great. You can still buy a copy of the *Tales of Uncle Remus,* but Brer Rabbit and Brer Fox no longer have a home on the schoolroom shelf. And we can't help feeling, deep in our heart, that the loss is not only to the children growing up without the Tar Baby but to the whole country.

How sadly misguided all this can be is nowhere better illustrated than in the quiet attack on Huck Finn. In some places Mark Twain's novel has been removed from libraries; in a great many high schools the teacher of English literature who assigns it risks criticism, or even a reprimand. The reason for this, of course, is that Huck's companion on his picaresque journey is called Nigger Jim, and Jim is not only a slave but ignorant and illiterate. At first meeting, perhaps, he seems in language, in bearing, and in his treatment by the white people the epitome of all the past which the Negro today is trying to escape from and to forget. Yet the effort to banish the novel is a mistake not simply because it is one of the greatest, if not the greatest, American novel. The fact is that *The Adventures of Huckleberry Finn* makes one of the most powerful attacks extant on the institution of slavery and a superb sermon on the dignity of man.

Time and again it's the "white folks" who come off as cheap, shoddy, prejudiced, cruel, and foolish, and the black slave who shows dignity, courage, compassion, and wisdom. Huck's soliloquy on why he's "wicked" to help Jim escape is a paean to human freedom. Jim's account of his wife and children is testimony to man's inhumanity to man.

When the tale is told, Jim towers over all the others like a colossus. Among the white folk only Tom and Huck, in their poignant and hilarious struggle to help their friend on his Odyssey, trail any clouds of glory. Here, surely, is a poetic epic for our time.

But there's more that's misguided in the current Negro attitude, I think, than not recognizing Nigger Jim as a towering hero. The real point, or so it seems to me, is that for the Negro people there should be only pride, not shame, in being up from slavery, as an Englishman takes pride in being up from medieval cruelty and squalor. Most of all, it seems to me, the American Negro ought to glory in all that his people contributed in the past to

179

enriching the poetry, the music, the literature, and the language of his country. And be grateful to all those, white or Negro, who have tried to record this past before it too is gone with the wind. For without that heritage, this would be a poorer country. Just as we ourselves would be poorer if we had not spent an afternoon long ago in the company of de Lawd.

February 27, 1964

THE MORAL ISSUE IN
MISSISSIPPI

W HILE statesmen were issuing statements and soldiers were marching to and fro, the mob before the gates of the University of Mississippi was singing a song. Its title was *Never, No Never.* And the lyrics made no pretense that the mob, in resisting a federal court order admitting a Negro to the school, was pleading time and patience before overturning customs generations old. To the Negro people, and to the whole country, the song chanted one word over and over—Never.

Governor Barnett, in all his legal maneuverings, had taken the same position as the battle song of the mob. Even as he yielded officially to the inevitable, he told the people of Mississippi that they should "never" accept a black skin in the halls of their university. So now two men are dead, a score or more are in the hospital, and no man knows what will be the end of mob violence.

I am no less conscious than others that many questions have been involved in the recent events in Mississippi, including a grave constitutional issue. But it seems to me that nothing has put quite so starkly the central moral question as this word "never." It exposes clearly what is fundamentally wrong with Governor Barnett and the mob which he incites.

The constitutional question of state and federal responsibilities is one on which moral men may differ, even though the outcome of that struggle was from the beginning foreordained. President Kennedy, like President Eisenhower before him, did the only thing he could do, assert the supremacy of federal authority against that of any state if the two are forced into collision.

The question of speed or slowness in changing old ways is also one upon which moral men may differ. Honest men must admit to themselves that there is some truth in the cry that immediate, wholesale integration, South or North, would do an injury to society because it would level down and not up. In any event, it is not so simple as many outside the South suppose to change a social order by a court order. But the mob did not make these the issues in Mississippi. The mob, led by the governor of the state, tried to say that never shall there be any change.

This is indefensible. For what it says to the Negro people of Mississippi is that it no longer matters what they do with their lives. No matter what effort they make to lift themselves by character and intelligence, the state of Mississippi will not accord them the dignity of manhood. It would strip from them even the patient hope of time. So it strips from all who utter it not only the support of reason but of morality. It leaves empty all the arguments about states' rights, about the constitutional division of powers, about the wisdom of leaving the people of a community free to work out in their own way their age-old problems.

These are weighty questions of long ancestry in our political history; wise men have stood upon both sides. But there is another doctrine of equally deep roots in our tradition. It is that men must come into court with clean hands, and it is an immutable doctrine when men come before the bar of public opinion.

For the most part, this has been the way of the South. Some states have yielded slowly on their custom of absolute segregation of the two races; doubtless all of them have been reluctant to meet changes of unknown consequence. Yet throughout the South, from Virginia to Texas, men of good will have nonetheless accepted the necessity of change because in their hearts they knew it was right; they debated only about how and when. It has been the pace, not the direction, that has divided them.

182

This being the case, people all over the country—including the men of good will among the Negro people—have offered patient understanding. Neither courts nor Presidents have tried to replace evolution with revolution. But there can be neither patience nor understanding when a mob arises to say to other men that their future is only hopelessness. For any man to say this to another man is immoral. For an institution of government to elevate it to a policy of state is something that good men cannot tolerate. And the true lesson of Mississippi, whatever the constitutional lawyers may say, is that they will not.

October 2, 1962

BACKLASH

ONE of the little extra dividends of a political party convention is that it collects in one place all sorts of people from all sorts of places. Couple this with two transcontinental journeys, around and back to New York City, and a traveler catches the sound of many voices.

One phrase occurs over and over this political summer of 1964—"the white backlash." It crops up in the conversation of politicians, other journalists, taxicab drivers, and assorted acquaintances met in brief encounters. Most especially these days in New York City it is heard in corner taverns and at neighborhood teas. Everybody agrees it is something important, and quite a few think it will play some unknown role in the fall election. But the curious thing is that most people think of it one way in their own minds and yet imagine it as something different in their neighbor's. All of which suggests that this thing we call the white backlash could well be misunderstood, perhaps dangerously so, by the very people—the white and Negro leaders—who ought most clearly to see what it is. And what it is not.

One thing it is not, or so anyway it seems to one patient listener, is "anti-Negro." That is, it does not represent any rising hostility to the Negroes as people or to their aspirations to continue to improve their position in the American society. Even in New York City, which has lately been rent by the most terrible kind of violence, there is as yet no serious backlash against the movement to improve opportunities for Negroes in housing, in education, in jobs, or in better acceptance within the community.

Thus far, the reaction against the city's violence has not spilled over into a reaction against the Negro's general striving for betterment.

Yet many people interpret the backlash just that way. A common occurrence is to hear someone lament the arousal of "racial hatred" in others while showing in his actions and words that his own reaction to disorder and violence, while strong, is not of this kind at all. The same process will be repeated with another, each thinking himself unique in his ability to make distinctions.

This doesn't mean there hasn't been a strong backlash against the demonstrations, the upheavals, and the violence. There has been, and it's a force to reckon with. It simply means that up to now it is of a different order from "racial hatred" or anything so frightening. The nature of it is not easy to explain, for few people are articulate enough to express their own feelings. But perhaps it is best explained in that old phrase "too much, too soon," especially if you will now add the words "too frenzied."

The impression is that the white community has come to feel just too overpowered by the rush of events. Except perhaps in deepest Mississippi, these are people who approved of the Supreme Court's desegregation decision, who approve now of the intent if not always the form of the Civil Rights Act; people who believe that a Negro is entitled to what his endowments entitle him to and do not believe that society should wall him off simply because he is a Negro.

But all of a sudden the idea changed—or so anyway it seemed to many people—from the simple one of admitting any qualified Negro to any neighborhood school. Suddenly the middle-class white population found itself faced with demands for a wholesale and totally indiscriminate mixing of schoolchildren of disparate background—the good and the bad together—in the name of an abstraction called integration.

Before long a white person of good will found it not enough

185

to be open-minded about the arrival of a middle-class Negro family in his middle-class neighborhood. He found himself faced with the active recruitment of Negroes—any Negroes—in what appeared to be a campaign to overturn whole neighborhoods overnight. In the job area, too, the open-door policy changed to one of forced entry.

The civil rights demonstrations, it might as well be admitted, have played their part in intensifying the feeling of many white people that they are being pressured not for evolution but for revolution. A year ago a traveler in Wisconsin could have found little sympathy for white resistance in the South. Today he will hear many people in such a Northern state criticize those they think are "going down there stirring up trouble." In short, the "white backlash" does not strike at the Negro as a Negro. It does strike, and sharply now, at the society-shaking events which no one seems able, or willing, to control. The feeling is the desperate one of being overwhelmed.

There is another thing. A white journalist, no matter how quiet a listener, cannot be sure that he hears Negro voices aright; not the least of the sadness is that it is harder now for men to talk to one another. Yet a few conversations suggest that among many Negroes too there grows a sort of backlash—not against the struggle of their people but against the means of the struggle. Certainly it is true that there are many good people in Harlem more frightened of the violence than their white neighbors in New York; they live in the midst of it. It is not uncommon for those who meet Negroes in their daily lives to find thoughtful ones who are worried and even ashamed.

So there is no denying the reality of the backlash against events, and futile to pretend that it is not portentous. But it is vital that it not be misunderstood. Anyone, politician or otherwise, does his countrymen a great disservice to think of it as a new growth of "racial hatred." He mistakes the mark who thinks it can be either capitalized politically on such a ground or exorcised by denunciations hurled at "hate groups" or "bigots." Bigots we will always have, but in small numbers.

What is happening is that with blood and death running in the streets it is no longer rare to hear people, white and Negro both, asking each other the question, Where will it all end? And a traveler recollecting in tranquility the emotions encountered on a journey cannot help but fear that those who would ignore that heartfelt question do risk whipping a backlash into what it now is not.

July 28, 1964

NATIVE'S RETURN

O NE thing about taking a trip abroad, it's surprising how much things can change while you're away and how different familiar things look when you get back home. You need a bit of time to catch up on who married whom. And you may notice for the first time how much young Bill has begun to sprout in the legs. Or perhaps with some shocked surprise that Aunt Martha really is beginning to show her age.

These days things can move pretty fast indeed. A few weeks abroad, concentrating on the separatist issue in Canada or the British balance of payments, and you return to find that Bob Wagner is no longer running for mayor, Congressman Lindsay is no longer running as a Republican, and Barry Goldwater is thinking of starting a whole new party.

Then there's the stock market. You left Kennedy Airport amid the continuing Kennedy boom, returning to find people worried about a possible Johnson slump. The Johnson people, of course, seem to be blaming this on William McChesney Martin, who works at the Federal Reserve Board, and is therefore not the President's responsibility. As best you can untangle the tale, Mr. Martin recently gave a little lecture on safe driving, and is now being held responsible for all the accidents on the highway.

The situation in the Dominican Republic seems to be different, too. When you packed your bags it was perfectly clear that the whole trouble had been caused by some nasty rebels, many of them Communists, and that the Marines had landed to put down the rebellion. As you unpack, you're told we're talking in friendly fashion with some of the rebels and trying to get the junta to make peace.

Vietnam is just as puzzling. On departure, the U. S. was bombing North Vietnam to clear the way for negotiations and to avoid getting U.S. troops involved in the fighting in South Vietnam. Walter Lippmann was saying this was a dreadful thing and might get us into a war. On return, U.S. troops are in the thick of the battle, there's very little talk about the prospects for negotiation, and Mr. Lippmann sounds like he's urging us to be resolute.

There are a few other minor changes. Connecticut doesn't have a birth control law any more, thanks to the Supreme Court. Dimes and quarters aren't going to have any more silver, thanks to Secretary Fowler. And our own balance-of-payments problem, which everybody once said had gone away, seems to have come back, thanks—so they say—to the British. The explanation for this last bit of intelligence is that the dollar would be getting along all right, thank you, except for the fact that the pound sterling is under new pressure. If the pound falls Heaven knows what this will do to the dollar. This seems a bit odd since in London only a few days ago you were told that the pound was getting healthier until the U. S. started taking action to support the dollar.

Finally, there's the Great Society. It was going great guns when you left and everywhere President Johnson, as its author, was hailed as a master politician and a peerless leader. Home again, all you hear is grumbling about the President. Even *The New York Times* almost sounds like it's sorry it supported him against Senator Goldwater.

But perhaps what strikes you the hardest, coming home, is something less susceptible to summary in a newspaper headline because it's less tangible, less measurable. It's a feeling that a sort of malaise has settled over the country. This indefinite feeling of uneasiness is strongest, and most understandable, about Vietnam. No rational man can be cheered by the possibility of drifting into a real war in that distant place. Nobody was cheered by World War II, either, or Korea, or the Cuban confrontation. But when President Truman suddenly took on the Korean War the worry was mingled with a determination, a sense of purpose. So it was when President Kennedy put warships in the Cuban straits. Today neither those who want to stay in nor those who want to get out of Vietnam seem confident of why they advocate what they advocate. Everybody expects a disaster to which none can put a name.

The hullaballoo over the stock market also seems to mask a nameless fear. In Wall Street and in Washington everybody— well, almost everybody—assures everybody else how prosperous we are, how fundamentally sound everything is, and how the boom will be bigger tomorrow. Yet all the same people are constantly sticking the thermometer in the mouth of this vauntedly healthy patient, and shuddering when the mercury fluctuates a trifle.

The unease is more vague, but no less felt, when the home-coming traveler hears about more homely matters. You cheerfully inquire how things are down at the store, around the town, or up at the state house. Or maybe just ask what Johnny's going to do now that he's graduated from college. Johnny's won a year's more study on some foundation grant, and isn't that nice? The shop's been pretty busy, there's going to be a new deal at city hall, and at the state house they haven't done much of anything, thank goodness. All good news, you might suppose, but none of it comes with great enthusiasm, and you think you see some new worried furrows on your neighbor's face.

Americans are nice people and their very niceness makes them instinctively optimistic. Yet after a day at home you begin to wonder if they really think the new mayor can grapple with the sprawl and disorder of the city streets, if they really see great leadership for the country, if they really believe the durable virtues they grew by—thrift, energy, honesty, pride, duty, purpose— are enduring among the people.

It's a curious feeling. You know perfectly well that the mood of the country can't have changed that much in a couple of weeks. Perhaps it's just your own imagination. Tomorrow, it's possible, young Bill will seem just a kid again, and Aunt Martha will look as young as ever. All the same, such a homecoming is enough to give a middle-aged man involutional melancholia. Makes you wonder if what you need isn't a nice vacation trip.

June 23, 1965

CITY OF WONDER

Not planned with a thought of beauty!
    Built by a lawless breed;
Builded of lust for power,
    Builded of gold and greed.

Risen out of the trader's
    Brutal and sordid ways—
And yet, behold! A city
    Wonderful under the stars!

—Don Marquis

WHERE London, Paris, Rome, or Vienna are hubs of a wheel, New York juts out from a sprawling nation, both in geography and in spirit. In government it yields to Washington, in muscle to Pittsburgh, in heart to Chicago or Dubuque. Even in the lively arts it is not so much the bountiful creator as the bustling market place, drawing its hewers from the hills of Catawba or the wastes of Minnesota.

Yet, for all of that, Manhattan is our city of wonder. A parasite, it is nonetheless a pinnacle. The well-stomached banker, the well-bosomed beauty, and the haggard poet are none so proud until they have conquered New York and been conquered by it. It is the city of the great, the city of the mean, the city of the oppressed, the city of comets, and the city of faceless masses.

No wonder then that its fascination is endless. And no wonder that no one has ever seen it whole; it can only be glimpsed in bits and pieces. But even the smallest glimpse, if it be sharp and true, is a delight. Sometimes it can be deeply moving.

The stranger beyond the Hudson can find this out for himself in an anthology of words about New York compiled by Esther Morgan McCullough under the title *As I Pass, O Manhattan*. So, too, can the New Yorker himself; and in so doing, he will find in sadness or delight that beyond his own small corner he too is a stranger to his island. For the impressive thing about this collection of words is its staggering variety, not merely in authors or in modes of expression but in the varieties of experience. As in the parable of the elephant and the three blind men, Manhattan shows to every man a different shape and texture. Are you one drawn by the dramas of everyday life? Here you will find O. Henry visiting a furnished room, Thomas Wolfe driving on a May morning through Central Park, Theodore Dreiser walking the waterfront, or Willa Cather probing the adolescence of the dispossessed, drawn to and destroyed by the city.

Or are you more moved by the impressions of poets? Here is Walt Whitman singing O Manhattan as he strides the city of docks, Edna St. Vincent Millay watching Washington Square in the hours before morning, and Langston Hughes listening to the jazz trumpets on 52nd Street. Perhaps instead you are in a mood for laughter. Then you can hardly do better than go to church with Clarence Day's father or stop off at a Third Avenue saloon with John McNulty. Or perhaps your fascination is for the city itself, how it got here, how it grew, and what manner of men turned a small island into a colossus. Miss McCullough has not forgotten the giants.

You may begin, if you wish, with Giovanni da Verrazzano, who discovered the bay in 1524, or Henry Hudson, who sailed up its river in 1609. But for me Manhattan really came to life when it became Little Old New York. The shape of the city can already be seen by the time Fulton's *Clermont* tied up at the quay. Then came the men who left their indelible impressions on it. Horace Greeley, Peter Cooper, the Roeblings of Brooklyn Bridge, Edison, Roscoe Conkling, Boss Tweed, Edgar Allan Poe, the elder Morgan, Carnegie, Henry James, Adolph Ochs, Lindbergh, and La Guardia.

They are all here, many in their own words. Here also are many others who passed by as spectators recording the wondrous love of the growing city. Dexter Fellows chronicling the days of Barnum and the old Madison Square Garden, George Templeton Strong putting down in his diary the city at the end of the century, Brander Matthews on Edwin Booth and the birth of Broadway. Indeed, Miss McCullough has provided almost too rich a diet. Like so many who fall in love, she finds it hard to put aside anything about her beloved island. The result is a memento almost too heavy for handling, and only a person equally enthralled would try to read all its 1,236 pages. It is not for the reader who likes to swallow his meal in a gulp. But for the sipper it is a heady wine. It is sure to brew in the reader a pleasant intoxication with the town that is all at once apart from America and yet one of its greater parts.

December 20, 1956

VII

WINDOWS ON
THE WORLD

MOTHER RUSSIA

SOCHI, U.S.S.R.

T HE night train from Tbilisi to Sochi is a local which follows a westerly line for 150 miles through the Georgian countryside until it touches the Black Sea, where it bends to the north. The first few hours of the run are in daylight, or soft twilight, and from the car window the visitor gets new glimpses of the land and its people. On the right side, not too far away, is the ridge of the Caucasus Mountains. To the left the land is flatter, showing at first the outskirts of the city, then a row of villages close together, until finally you reach more open country.

There the dreary apartments of the cities give way to separate houses, small, often unpainted, sometimes rather tumbling, but usually surrounded by a plot of land which supports a garden. More often both house and garden have a well-tended look, with flowers around the doorway. The passing train, as everywhere in the world, draws the gaze of curious children, and a friendly wave is always answered.

The depot platforms, like the train itself, are crowded. There are soldiers, more often carrying babies than guns. Young girls in blouses and skirts. Older women, kerchiefed and shawled. Farmers in boots and tunics. Here and there a Western-style suit. And always boxes, bundles, and the ubiquitous bulging net bags in which shoppers and travelers stuff their belongings. From the car window a "Hello" in halting Russian will bring delighted laughter and a hail of friendly chatter. If an interpreter is handy (and quite often one of the younger people on the platform will know a score of English words) you will soon have a little crowd gathered with whom to pass a pleasant time.

It is a leisurely journey from Tbilisi to Sochi—all Soviet trains go slowly—and it permits you to reflect upon all you have seen, the beauties of land and simple niceness of the people. Physically the Soviet Union is an impressive country. Its cities are well laid out; its villages full of rural charm. In a few hours by jet you can sweep over farmlands like Southern Illinois, wheat fields as in Kansas, plains that look like Texas, deserts with the desolation of Death Valley, and mountains with the bleak grandeur of the High Sierras. It is an unforgettable experience to fly across the great plain of Turkestan, east of the Caspian Sea, crossing great gorges in the earth for all the world like the craters of the moon, over the edge of the Tien Shan Mountains, and then drop down into the green and abundant valley by the city of Tashkent.

It is a land rich in resources. Much is said of Soviet wastelands, but its arable land is fertile indeed; in former times the country was an exporter of wheat and other agricultural crops. Mineral resources, including oil, abound. There are plentiful forests and great rivers. As a land the Soviet Union is as fully endowed as the United States, and fully as beautiful. A visitor has no trouble understanding the mystic feeling of the people for Mother Russia. But the people themselves are perhaps the greatest resource. These are able people; patient, long-suffering, intelligent, wonderfully hospitable, and full of vitality. The manager of the ball-bearing plant in Moscow, the director of the cooperative farm in Uzbekistan, the shop foreman in *Pravda's* printing plant, the electrical technician at Volgograd's great power plant— these are people who know their business. It is not their fault that the horizons of what they know are so narrow or that their abilities are confined by the system under which they live.

198

The same is true of the nimble-fingered girls who run the looms in the textile mill that is the Soviet's pride, or even of the husky women who have to dig a sewer line with pick and shovel; they too labor with energy. Everywhere you turn the air is full of vitality and eagerness—and a frustrated curiosity to know more. These are outgoing people. Whenever the American editors in our group could slip away from our traveling Soviet hosts, we had no difficulty in starting conversations, and found no effort to hide inquisitive minds. True, the conversation would begin with some such question as "Why did President Kennedy shoot off the atom bomb?" or "Why do you enslave Negroes in the South?" and it was futile to argue back; the people were not insincere, merely ignorant of what goes on in the world. Still these were passing questions. Inevitably, our Soviet acquaintances would get around to asking about America, its techniques and its way of living. One evening in the square at Tashkent there were eight such talkative groups going simultaneously, each with its American editor surrounded by a score of local people. Do you have a car? What is a schoolteacher paid? How many rooms in your apartment? How much did that suit of clothes cost? Is it true that the masses have washing machines? How does a young person go to college if his father is not rich?

Sometimes, unfortunately, the questions would get too technical for poor journalists. A farmer asking questions about nitrogen fertilizer, a machine shop foreman wanting to compare lathes, or an airline pilot asking about pounds of thrust in jet engines. But always an insatiable curiosity about America, and sooner or later the questions about wages, prices, employment, and the whole standard of living. These, of course, are the same questions the visitor also asks about the Soviet Union. And the answers always seemed (as no doubt ours did to our Soviet friends) complex and often paradoxical.

The minimum wage here is about 30 to 40 rubles per month, little more than the lowest relief pension. At the official rate of exchange, $1.10 to the ruble, this seems incredibly low. The average for fairly skilled workers is estimated at only 90 to 100 rubles. But wherever possible Soviet wages are on a piecework basis and there is a complicated bonus and penalty system. Thus a linotype operator at *Pravda* is paid by the lines of type set; there the average printer will get over 100 rubles and some more than 150 a month. Collective farmers are paid by "working day units," each of which is worth (in Uzbekistan) 2.70 rubles plus 200 grams of rice and a half kilo of potatoes; the average is 300 working day units per year, an income of less than $1,000.

The intangibles confuse matters further. The farmers, of course, have their housing and their garden plots which give them both extra food and some cash crops. The city workers also get their housing at a nominal "rent" (it's cheap but minimal housing) and side benefits depending upon their rank and status. Rank and status are the most important things. Second-tier managerial people may get 250 to 500 rubles per month, top management up to 1,000 rubles. But their main reward is in the "perquisites," priorities on cars, housing, recreation facilities, and so on. If you are far enough up the ladder—party leader, manager, scientist, or government functionary—you may have a car and chauffeur furnished, the privileges of household help, and a host of things that money cannot buy.

For money here does not buy much except labor, the cheapest thing in the Soviet Union. A poor-quality suit of clothes runs 70–80 rubles; a halfway decent one 150 rubles. The cheapest street shoes we saw were 25 rubles, many were 35–40 rubles and up. Yet it's not unusual among the new upper classes to see Italian and British tailored suits or imported broadcloth shirts. New York's "Bond" clothes (with two pairs of pants) are not uncommon among journalists and others who have had the privilege of visiting America.

It is different with the masses, and you only need to look at their clothes, their housing, and their food to see that they live not only below the standard of the working-class Americans but also below their counterparts in most of western Europe. Still, prosperity and austerity are relative things. The people tell you happily about the improvement in their living standards over a decade ago, and still more proudly speak about what they hope for from tomorrow. Tomorrow is a big word here. The government's propaganda, blared from every newspaper, billboard, and radio, is not about what is but about what is going to be. Ask how many apartments were built last year in such-and-such a place and you will be told how many square meters of living space are called for in the current Seven-Year Plan. Ask about the number of tractors on a farm, or how many people have telephones, and you will be told what it is supposed to be a few years hence.

The Seven-Year Plan replaced the last Five-Year Plan in midstream because the latter had gone askew. No matter; it keeps everybody's attention focused on the future. Thus, while much of what a Western visitor sees here seems so backward that after a few weeks he begins to feel sad for the Soviet people, still he cannot recall any sadness in the people themselves that is not matched by their faith in tomorrow. And while they obviously have their share of lazy and shiftless comrades, most Russians work for that future as ably as they are allowed to. A plant manager's eyes brighten as he tells you of the new equipment he is going to get under the Plan. The young girl at the spindle who has set a production record displays her bright red pennant proudly, even if she is somewhat flustered at being fussed over before all these foreigners. Make no mistake about it. These people have vigor, a sense of purpose, and an unabashed love of country.

Looking about that country it's not hard to see why. When morning comes a train attendant brings you a glass of steaming tea, brewed at the end of the car in an old-fashioned boiler heated by an open charcoal fire. You open the window curtain and sit idly watching a countryside that might have been America fifty years ago. A man digging in the earth, a woman washing clothes in a big wooden tub, two boys herding some cows on a dusty road. But the air is warm, and here and there between the houses you catch glimpses in the distance of early morning bathers relaxing on the beach. And beyond, a jewel in any land, the Black Sea glitters in the summer sun.

August 10, 1962

COMMUNISM—OR FEUDALISM?

MOSCOW

Anyone who has traveled some 8,000 miles inside the Soviet Union—visiting schools, farms, factories, homes, talking with hundreds of its citizens in village streets and Kremlin corridors—is bound to leave stuffed with many little impressions that add up to a few main thoughts about this strange and paradoxical land.

For this visitor, returning from a summer's journey, they are these.

First, the Soviet Union is a feudal society, in the true sense of that word, and measured against any of the advanced nations of the West it is a backward country, whether the test be industry, agriculture, technology, labor skills, or the standard of living of the people.

Second, it is a land of immense potential, rich in physical resources with many able and vigorous leaders who have an evangelical fervor to lift their country to the top in every field.

Third, it has an economic system—Communist in name but a weird mixture of socialism and capitalism in fact—which "works," but which does so only by brute strength and awkwardness and therefore by its inefficiencies constitutes a drag on the nation's progress.

Fourth, it has a political system that does exactly what it was designed to do, to bend 200 million people to a single will and purpose, that of the handful of men in the Central Committee of the Communist Party. In no foreseeable future is this system likely to be overthrown from within.

Fifth, one purpose of the nation's political leaders is the ascendancy of Soviet power in the world and they pursue that undeviating aim both inside and outside their country with skill, intelligence, and single-minded devotion. To think otherwise is a delusion.

Finally, the deepest part of the paradox is that the great obstacle to this ambition for world power is the very economic and political system on which that ambition rests. The source of Soviet power is such that it is weakened by the very thing it feeds on.

All these things pose an equal paradox for the United States and the West. For the sum of them is to make the Soviet Union a formidable military and political threat—capable at any time of playing hob with the world, even plunging it into a terrible war —but at the same time to make its threat less formidable than it seems.

A returning visitor, setting down these impressions, is well aware that some of them seem to contradict others. But the problem here is not to be misled by the differing aspect of the parts examined separately. For example, it may seem misleading to speak of the Soviet Union as a backward country at a moment when it leads the world in space, or weak when it displays such a vast military force. In fact there is a temptation to remove the contradictions by explaining away one part or the other, either to "run down" the space effort or to take that success in space as evidence of a highly advanced and strong state. But the truth is something else.

First off, it is necessary to understand that "backward" is a relative word; it requires a point of reference. The Soviet Union is advanced compared to, say, India or Burma or many parts of

Latin America. But compared with the great industrial nations of the West, the only honest word is "backward."

Pass over the fact that the standard of living of the Soviet people is below not only that of the United States but also below most of the countries of western Europe—shabby clothes, poor and crowded housing, monotonous food, and a relative poverty of what might be called the material amenities of life such as cars, telephones, washing machines, and the rest. While these are one measure of a nation's progress, they are not necessarily a vital part of its power, as the Communists will remind any tourist who gets smug about the comforts back home. Barbarian hordes are always poorer than the people they overrun.

Look instead at the economic sinews, the farms and factories. You can find somewhere in America or Europe farms as antiquated as those they show you in Russia, or plants with less modern equipment than the Soviet best; just as at home you find crowded housing and people with shabby clothes. But you can safely assume that when your Soviet hosts have taken you to a farm or a ball-bearing plant they are showing the best they have; the Communists have an almost pathological desire to have their works admired. What you see then is never quite first class. The brand-new milking shed is surrounded by an antique dairy. The modern Japanese looms are patched with makeshift rubber bands because of a shortage of parts. A good automated assembly-line process in that ball-bearing plant is a modern island surrounded by outmoded methods. Symbolically, the point is driven home when you walk out of the Moscow Exhibition of Progress, where Soviet citizens glimpse the technological wonders of tomorrow, and see an old woman with a peasant straw broom sweeping the street.

The resulting product of industry is also nearly always poor in quality. The buildings crumble, the tractors break down, the shoes quickly wear out. Prototypes, or equipment that is individually made, are sometimes excellent although usually imitative.

This suggests that there is nothing wrong with their technology; the breakdown occurs when the item moves to mass production. But good mass production is the hallmark of a really advanced industrial society; it is an essential support, as the Japanese discovered, for any nation aspiring to modern military power. And a great deal of the Soviet trouble in this area is fundamental, imbedded in the nature of the economic system.

One factor is that labor is the cheapest commodity in the Soviet Union and there must always be "full employment." This results in wasteful practices, a kind of featherbedding that makes American union rules look amateurish. But probably the biggest factor is the absense of competition and any real market system, the presence of rigid central planning incapable of adjusting itself rapidly to changing conditions.

A simple example: two plants make refrigerators, one more efficiently and of better quality than the other. The better plant is ahead of schedule and sells all it makes; the second lags, and its wares move slowly. But the production schedules and the supply of materials are fixed in the year's plan, and it is a laborious and time-consuming process to get the plan changed. So there is an excess of steel in one plant, a shortage in the other. This kind of dislocation is endemic.

This is not to say that the system doesn't "work." It does; farms grow wheat, apartments get built, and autos come off the assembly line. The expectation that a socialist system must grind to a halt is on a par with the Communist idea that capitalism must collapse. It is simply to say that it works inefficiently and that to anyone familiar with the farms of France or the industry of West Germany—never mind the U. S.—the Soviet economy is many years behind.

Paradoxically, this system which is such a drag on their general program helps the Soviets to give the appearance of great power. As an autocracy the government can commandeer the very best brains, together with the best available materials and equipment, and put them under forced draft for limited purposes —developing space rockets, for example. Yet it does so at a tremendous cost, some of it half-hidden and immeasurable, some of it plain to any visitor's eye.

The cost would be worse, except for two things. One is simply the size of the Soviet Union's physical resources. For instance, the agriculture crisis which Mr. Khrushchev talks about results in a poor diet; but there is no starvation because the arable land is so productive it can produce much in spite of all the foul-ups and inefficiencies. In a country less well endowed by nature things would be much worse. The other reason why the economy "works" at all lies in the talents, energy, and determination of the small minority of people who make it work in spite of everything. The Soviet Union has its full quota of the lazy, the shiftless, the apathetic; you can see more boondoggling there on a construction project than in New York City. It also has its quota of superior people, scientists, technicians, managers. Concentrated on a special project, such as the space program, they can make it hum. Elsewhere they use energy and symbolic bailing wire to keep the creaky economic system working.

For instance: in spite of the theoretical rules there is a lot of wheeling and dealing for materials by plant managers who, out of ambition or just plain pride, are determined to get their own job done. Living in a Communist society doesn't keep an astronomer with brains from being an astronomer with brains; and since Stalin he's allowed to use them even if he isn't a Communist.

The motivation of these people is complex. In part it is the natural desire of any able man to succeed at whatever he is doing; the scientist wants his rockets to go, the manager wants his shoe plant to make shoes, for his own personal satisfaction. Part of it is sheer nationalistic pride; a Russian, Communist or not, loves Russia and wants it to "catch up." But part of the motivation comes from the very ruthlessness of the system. As in the U. S., a man gets ahead, and reaps the rewards of success, by succeeding; he is punished for failure. But there is a major difference in the Soviet Union. There "success" is doing exactly what the government orders; there punishment for failure can be total. The manager manages what he is told to manage; the scientist works where he is told. There are no ifs, ands, and buts about it. Personal survival is at stake.

This seems to be a source of strength. It accounts for the Soviet achievements. Yet it is also a source of weaknesses because the political leaders are so devoted to military power, to scientific work that contributes to military power, that the whole country—its brains, energy, materials—is wrenched out of shape. It pays an unknown price in brains, energy, and materials misdirected.

Is the loss worth the gain? The political leaders think so, because their intention is to win not by absolute superiority but by the power of appearances. If they can frighten the West out of, say, Berlin then their weaknesses do not matter. If they have atom bombs and an atomic war is so frightful no one will stand up to its threat, then brandishing the bombs may be enough. It is less important that the steel industry, the auto industry, the transportation system are wire taut and have no excess capacity with which to meet the strains of war.

At any rate, viewed thus the contrast between the Soviet achievements in certain scientific fields and its visible backwardness in general ceases to be inexplicable. Still, this leaves for the visitor other intriguing questions. Why are the Communist leaders so bent on world domination? How do they succeed in mobilizing basically nice and friendly people to this ambition?

The first question could be answered by saying that they are moved by the same motives as, say, Jimmy Hoffa; he keeps reaching out for more power simply because it is there. But a visitor who travels much here comes slowly to the thought that there is another reason. Put simply, it is that the Soviet leaders must try to extend their power to protect and consolidate the power they have. The Communist system simply cannot stand comparison; there is a wall in Berlin because some way, somehow the Communists must shut out comparison with the free world. The Soviet Union itself has a wall around it. No one is allowed to go touring abroad unless there is a practical necessity for it and then only if the person is absolutely trustworthy. The wall bars not only foreign newspapers but a Sears, Roebuck catalogue, or so nonpolitical a magazine as *Good Housekeeping.*

But walls are inefficient things, in Berlin and elsewhere. People leap them and ideas seep through them. If West Berlin can be grabbed, the wall becomes unnecessary. If Communism conquers all, then there is nowhere any yardstick to judge Communism and its power is secure. The West must be destroyed for the same reason that Trotsky must be axed or Beria shot.

And how do they mobilize people—people basically no different from ourselves—to do this task? Most of the ways are too well known to need laboring—the propaganda, the skillful use of rewards, the force when necessary. What needs to be reported is that these ways are successful in bending the people's will if not their desires. Illusion on that point is dangerous. If the Soviet Union tomorrow opened its borders for people to leave, there might well be an exodus to equal the biblical flight from Egypt. But that possibility is a wholly different thing from an open revolt stemming from deep discontent matched with action. That, or so I think, is not in the cards. And the reason is that the Communists have taken the feudal system of old Russia with which the people are long familiar, restyled it, stabilized its pressures, and brought skilled political techniques to its management.

If a serf is a man tied to the earth or to a machine, able to leave it only by death or permission of the authorities, then the Soviet citizen is a serf. If the feudal relationship is that of service to an overlord, it is not altered by changing the overlord from a duke to a farm cooperative or a state-owned plant. If the feudal economic system is the fixing of wages or prices by authority, the system is unchanged when the authority changes from tradition, or the Church, to an autocratic group of planners in Moscow. And if the obligation of the feudal overlord was to feed, clothe, and give military protection to the masses, that too you will find in the Soviet Union. The feudal overlords of the czars forgot their obligations, thinking only of their privileges, and so they fell. The Communists have not forgotten this—they do "take care of" the masses—and they are not likely to fall until they do forget.

A feudal society is a "workable" method of organizing society; when the people so organizing it are not ignorant Africans or primitive Asians but highly intelligent men the result will seem like a great leap forward to those Africans or Asians. Therein lies the Communist success, such as it is, in those parts of the world. Nonetheless, feudalism is a backward system, and after traveling through it for 8,000 miles the visitor from the Western world leaves convinced that this is so.

A small incident may show that even in the Soviet Union there are some who sometimes wonder themselves. The night before my departure from Moscow I was talking to one of my new friends and making the usual courteous remarks about how much I enjoyed my trip and how interested I was in what I saw. Then my friend asked me with a smile if I was now convinced that in time the Soviet Union would catch up with the Western world.

My Soviet friend was an intelligent and sensitive man whom I had come to like, and the temptation was to avoid hurt feelings and an angry rebuttal by speaking some vague politeness. Instead, I replied as softly as I could: "Never in your lifetime or in mine." The expected explosion didn't come. A shadow passed over his face, we shook hands silently, and he left me. The next morning I got on the plane for Paris and never saw him again.

August 22, 1962

TARNISHED IMAGE

LONDON

D ROP into any British pub, and once you've broken through the reticence of the dart players—it doesn't hurt to try your fumbling hand at a toss or two—you'll find a warm welcome and a hot argument. The welcome will be warm because the English aren't quite as reticent as they seem and, by and large, they rather like Americans. The argument will be hot because right now, "you bloody Yanks are at it again." What we are "at," it seems, is stirring up trouble.

The immediate cause of the outburst is our little expedition in the Dominican Republic, the pub attitude toward which is best summed up by the cliché about "Yankee imperialism." But the criticism also reflects a jaundiced view of our deepening involvement in Vietnam, which is thought of hereabouts as having the makings of a general war in Southeast Asia. And before the conversation has drifted on to more pressing subjects, like the sporting pools, you discover that we are even being blamed for some of the British troubles over the Common Market. At any rate, you'll be told that if we hadn't irritated General de Gaulle so much maybe he wouldn't act so prickly toward the other half of the Anglo-Saxon axis.

In short, just at the moment the image of the United States as the foreign policy leader of the West is somewhat tarnished. Not surprisingly, a good bit of this verdigris has rubbed off on the image of Lyndon Johnson. Nor are these tart opinions about

U.S. foreign policy confined to those made genially outspoken by a pint of mild and bitter. In gatherings where the preferred beverage is whiskey and water (without ice) the critics are equally vocal. And in the public press, which both reflects and helps inspire these views, the criticisms are painfully blunt.

"Where Will the Marines Go Next?" reads a headline in the influential *Economist* magazine, and the article goes on to argue that if we are going to jump into every Latin-American country on the excuse we offered for the Dominican Republic we'll soon have Marines scattered all over the Southern Hemisphere. A less staid London paper devoted a full page to an article entitled "Emperor Lyndon," likening him to untrammeled sovereigns of yesteryear.

In this reaction to the displays of U.S. muscle our English cousins are apparently not alone. At a meeting of the International Press Institute, which gathered together here journalists from fifty countries, the Americans present found themselves caught in a fall-out of criticism about their country's course.

The French press, not too surprisingly, have had a field day with our troubles in Vietnam. Somewhat more surprisingly the leading Swiss papers seem to have lost, at least momentarily, their normal calm about foreign affairs and severely criticized our actions in Santo Domingo. Though in varying degrees, much the same can be said of the press in other European countries. But judging by after-meeting conversations with journalistic colleagues, the most aroused criticism of American policy is to be found in Asian and African countries.

An African journalist, himself friendly and professing sympathy for U.S. "problems," thinks we have played "right into the hands of the Communists" in that it is impossible for us to explain to Africans any difference between our Dominican intervention and the imperialism of the last century. A Japanese colleague notes that no issue since World War II has so aroused hostility toward the U.S. as our bombings in North Vietnam.

212

Much of this, when you reflect upon it, is probably inevitable. It hasn't been easy, or at least wasn't up to the time we left home, to explain U.S. foreign policy even to Americans in such a way as to still criticism. So it isn't easy, as you'll find if you try it, to explain U.S. policy to foreigners even when you talk in friendly face-to-face encounter. How, for example, does a touring American explain one day why his country is on the side of the junta in Santo Domingo and the next day explain why we are supporting the rebels? You do need a sense of humor to steady you in your forays as an amateur diplomat. All the same, the sharpness of the criticism of the U.S. actions in England and Europe, if not perhaps in Asia or Africa, is both surprising and puzzling. You may not expect Africans to see the difference between nineteenth-century interventions in China and our efforts to keep modern China from swallowing Vietnam; you do expect it from the Englishmen, Frenchmen, or Swiss.

Yet much of the criticism from the Europeans, if casual conversations offer any guide, is not limited to practical questions of whether we have handled things badly or whether, say in Vietnam, we have bitten off more than we can chew. That kind of criticism, however severe, would be understandable enough, and perhaps right. What defies answering is the assumption, several times expressed in varying forms, that the U.S. is throwing its weight around just to be doing it; that is, out of a sort of slapdash adventurism. This makes it pretty hard indeed to have a rational discussion on the merits, or lack of them, of what we are doing. It also gives a visitor the feeling that he is dealing with unanswerable emotions. Africans and Asians are reacting from long memories. The Europeans are getting along very well, thank you. The British aren't getting along very well at all. For different reasons, nobody wants anybody to come along and rock the boat, whatever the provocation or the reasons.

Whatever the explanation, however, there's no question but

213

what President Johnson's boldness in Vietnam and the Dominican Republic has pushed U.S. prestige, if that's the word for it, to a low ebb. And the parting conclusion of at least one visitor is that the complaints can't really be argued away even by the most skillful Presidential statements. We'll just have to get used to it. If all this sounds like a gloomy report for summer tourists, it isn't quite. It's American policy not its people that is in disfavor. General de Gaulle's courtesy campaign moves on apace, the pub dart players will throw with you not at you, and even after the most heated discussion nobody will mind if the Yank picks up the bar check.

June 14, 1965

LE GRAND CHARLES:
GENERAL DE GAULLE

I T was summer in Vienna. The new President of the U. S. and the old premier of the USSR had been meeting in the ancient palaces of the Hapsburgs, and the newsmen, as is their wont, were trying to get "reactions" to the great confrontation. The West Germans were uneasy, the Italians indifferent, and the British bland. But from the French observer there came a Gallic shrug and the comment, "*Les deux grands ne sont plus maîtres du monde.*"

In saying that the two "grands"—Kennedy and Khrushchev —were no longer the masters of the world our French friend was making a profound comment on the new order of world power; no longer could Russia and the United States arrange everything as they chose. He was also, if we but had the wit to realize it, making a prophetic comment on the foreign policy of France. Hereafter France would go its own way.

We may perhaps be forgiven our obtuseness, for it sometimes seems that two and a half years later our State Department still hasn't the wit to understand the changing order, much less the foreign policy of General de Gaulle. When the General dismisses the British from the Common Market, refuses to accept our view of the Western Alliance, or embraces Peking without so much as a by-your-leave, it is all put down to some irrational whimsy. In Washington—and in London, too— "Le Grand Charles" is treated much like a mysterious force of nature, inexplicable, illogical, and uncontrollable.

It's quite true, of course, that it's hard to approve of all that General de Gaulle does. The prospects for a true Common Market in Europe would seem to be enhanced by including the British Isles, and so his rejection of Britain appears to be a long-run injury both to Europe and to France. And personally I find it hard to see what he hopes to gain for France—much less for the Western cause—by recognizing the Chinese Communists at this time. Up to now, the most visible result of the General's gesture toward Peking has been the diplomatic confusion noted in the corridors of the State Department.

But this is not the same thing as saying that his actions are irrational. They proceed, or so it seems to us, from the clear objective of restoring the "glory" of France, which is simply another way of saying to make France again a power in the world. This may be chauvinistic; there is nothing about it that's incomprehensible. The policies for this objective are formed from an effort to see the world, and France's place in it, free from illusions. The General tries to see with a clear eye what he cannot do and refrain from doing it. This alone makes him an unusual statesman. But he also tries to see what he can do to shape the realities more to his liking, and then do it. General de Gaulle, like all of us, may mistake the realities of the world, but he does not make the mistake of denying their existence.

Algeria illustrates this well. It's nonsense to suppose that the General wanted to dismantle France's North African empire. If he could have kept it for the glory of France, he surely would have, and when he came to power that's what many thought he would do. Yet whatever he desired, he saw clearly that in the real world France could not keep its empire, that it would be stronger when it had cut out this draining cancer. So he cut it out, never once deterred by riots, bombs, and near revolution from what seemed to him the only realistic course.

If you grant his premises, there is a like logic in his other policies. If it is true that the United States cannot be depended upon forever to defend Europe, then there is logic in building a separate force in Europe, including necessarily an atomic power. If it is true that Britain with its far-flung interests would never really accept full-fledged membership in the Common Market, then there's logic in calling a halt now. And if it seems likely that the United States in time will be forced out of Asia and that the Chinese Communists will become wholly dominant there, then there is a certain logic in trying to establish some sort of relationship with the power that will be the real power in Asia.

Be these things as they may, there is truth in General de Gaulle's broadest premise—that the two great powers, Russia and the United States, are no longer alone. They could not, even if they would, settle the affairs of the world by agreement between themselves. They must reckon with others. And General de Gaulle intends that one of these others shall be France.

That being so, it's problematical whether the U. S. could "handle" the General no matter what it did. Consultations and discussions would not necessarily assure agreement. But surely the U. S. has aggravated the problem by neglecting consultations and discussions, by its treatment of this proud leader of a proud nation. Given General de Gaulle's view of the world, and of France, what could we expect when the American President and the British Prime Minister sit down in Bermuda to recast the nuclear defense of Europe without so much as a by-your-leave from the central power in Europe? Or when in Southeast Asia, where France had a century of experience, the U. S. makes all the decisions without seeking the counsel of that experience?

It's pointless to dismiss General de Gaulle's reaction to this treatment as mere pique. Even if he has that human failing, he's never displayed it when we truly had need of his support; in the successive Berlin crises and the great Cuban blockade crisis, France was first to rally around. Beyond that, one duty of diplomacy is to recognize the human factors as a part of the realities of the world. And it is of course always possible that General de Gaulle, who has now been on the world scene longer than any other statesman of the free world, might have something useful to offer. Yet all the indications are that Washington has little interest in talking even to the General's representatives.

Anyway, it seems silly to treat General de Gaulle like the weather. You know, always complaining but never doing anything about him.

February 14, 1964

THE GENTLE PEOPLE

VARANASI, INDIA

THE train winds slowly southward from Nangal, high in the Punjab, through New Delhi and Agra down to Harpalapur. There it turns eastward and works its way across country to this ancient city beside the Ganges, once known as Benares in the gazetteer of the British Raj. Along the way it cuts through the other provinces of Rajasthan, Uttar, and Madhya Pradesh to give the curious visitor a glimpse of varied terrain. There are mountains, plains, lakes, lowlands, neat fields, baked and deserted lands, thousand-year-old temples, and the chimneys of modern industry.

The people are as varied. At Chandigarh's new university or the Punjab agricultural college the students seem as informal in dress and manner as their Western counterparts, but just as youthful and far more serious and determined. At a hydroelectric plant or a diesel locomotive shop, both of them immaculate, the managers and foremen are articulate, able, and knowledgeable; the lathe operator, while seeming perhaps quaint in his Gandhi cap or colorful turban, goes about his job with quiet competence.

In remote villages, an hour or so's drive from the nearest railway stop, you feel the centuries peel away. The power that turns the water wheel comes from a patient bullock and a resigned boy; in the fields the plow too is bullock-powered, the farmer at the reins with his wife following after, scattering seeds from a homemade basket. At every station platform, town or village, the crowds gather to peer with inquisitive eyes at the luxuries of the dining car; barefooted, dusty, ill-nourished, and clothed in no more than that homespun dhoti or simple loincloth.

Here in Varanasi the people are packed so densely along the banks of the Ganges—washing, praying, preaching, burning the dead, or simply squatting motionless in meditation on the infinite —that the visitor can only pick his way slowly, zigzag fashion, up the banks from the boat landing. At the top, save for an occasional automobile creeping and honking through the tangle of people and cows, the scene would probably not startle the eyes of Gautama Buddha, who in a nearby deer park preached his first sermon more than two thousand years ago.

Thus are all the clichés about India embodied in a thousand-mile journey. Progress and primitiveness; well-being and poverty; knowledge and ignorance; rationality and mysticism; hopefulness and despair. Yet there is one impression that remains constant throughout the journey. That impression is of the gentleness of the people. It's a quality that cuts across the lines that divide the castes, the rich from the poor, the educated from the illiterate. It's one thing that seems to be universal amid all the diversity.

The population spectrum in India is extremely wide. There is a small class which for generations has been to the manner born, and a somewhat larger group rather inadequately described as "upper middle class" in terms of both education and economics. Taken together they form an elite of unknown numbers, Western oriented in many ways but with an old-world sense of *noblesse oblige*. Below them is a still larger group of the partially educated. These are the government clerks, the business book-keepers, the more advanced farmers, or the skilled mechanics. That they are able people is plain enough from watching them at their farming or running a rolling mill, and they are helping their children take a further step into the modern world.

The difficulty is that even if all these number in the millions, the number is minuscule in 480 millions. Below them is a vast sea of the ignorant and the illiterate, of such poverty as to make a paradise of a New York Harlem. In both city and country are the millions who are born, live, breed, and die but a tiny step above the dogs and cattle who share their lives. Yet everywhere you turn there is a dignity that is astounding. The hospitality of an Indian home is courtly; the affairs of the world are discussed thoughtfully and, even in disagreement, with such gentleness as to force an unaccustomed quiet upon the visitor.

And the quality is not exclusive to the homes of the cultivated. At every station along the journey the curious crowds gather on the platform to gaze at these well-fed strangers from afar. Of sullenness there is not a trace. The old man sits perched on the station railing, his feet neatly tucked under him, and watches you with friendly eyes staring out of a handsomely chiseled face, and you feel that if you and he could speak yours would be the profit. Along the streets the beggars gather, as everywhere in Asia; old women with shriveled breasts, young men with misshapen arms, and children by the hordes holding up their empty bowls. But the faces smile, the eyes dart, and the noise is not of angry birds but chattering magpies. Unlike other places in Asia, the stranger feels no barbed pricks of resentment.

Being emotional, the Indians can be aroused, even to violence, but considering the crowdedness of their lives, mobs are remarkably rare. Gandhi knew what he was doing when he chose gentleness as the weapon for his people to wield against the British. The roots of this lie deep in history, for India is a land that has been endlessly overrun by foreigners; deep in their religion, too, for Hinduism values every living thing and Buddha was the gentlest of men. Gentleness is also for them a practical requirement of living. When people by the scores must dwell in a one-room hut, or sleep nightly cheek by jowl on the pavements of the city, a softness of spirit is the only safeguard against chaos in the society.

This gentleness, to be sure, moves all too easily into resignation, and the resignation into apathy. The virtue, true enough, saps the energy that must feed on ambition, and this has held back the progress of India. Among people resigned to expect nothing you can't have a revolution of rising expectations. All the same, it's an endearing quality. And if a Western visitor, impatient for the Indians to get on with the task, is sometimes stirred by frustration, he is also moved to a wistful hope that progress will not mar the gentle people.

December 19, 1966

HOPE FOR INDIA

EVERY Westerner who comes to India and tarries more than a tourist's time passes through a cycle of moods as ordered as the seasons—and as endlessly repeated. It begins with despair, born of shock. This is especially true if his introduction comes in one of the sprawling cities, such as Calcutta, where the human degradation of poverty assaults his eyes, nose, and ears on the briefest walk from his hotel's haven. Mind and spirit recoil from the night streets of Calcutta, paved over with the sleeping homeless.

Next the despair gives way to hope as the visitor encounters able men, rich in both heart and mind, and as he travels the country seeing with his own eyes what they have accomplished and yet can do. To this are added the beauties of the land, the evidence of its potential in minerals and grain, and everywhere the signs—the ruins of temples, palaces, waterworks, and cities—that once these people accomplished prodigious things. Then once more depression falls as a brief journey from the new model city, farm, or factory brings you again to the primitiveness of a millennium past. And always the cycle repeats itself, as relentlessly as Buddha's wheel of life, and sometimes thrice over in the space of a single day.

Caught up in such bewilderment even those who have lived here long vacillate as to whether India can establish a viable economy capable of supporting the people and providing an underpinning for political stability. The passing traveler can at best make only hesitant judgments. Yet there are some things that can be confidently said, in which both despair and hope intermingle. The first is that nothing—nothing whatever; neither money, effort, will, nor brilliant scheme—can perform an instant miracle in India. This is not only the first certainty but the one that must never be forgotten, for pretending otherwise is the fatal trap for the unwary, whether Indians or those who would help them. That pretense has already cost India dearly.

The second is that there is no inherent reason why India cannot be what it hopes to be. It possesses all the resources, physical and human, to build a strong and prosperous nation. The obstacles to be overcome were not put there by nature.

The third is that a prerequisite for progress, much less for the distant miracle, is an assault on the problem of food and people. This solved, all else can follow after. A failure here, only disaster follows. For this no magic is required; the remedies are at hand and there remains but for men to apply them.

A fourth thing that can be said with confidence is that, in this land above all, one of the major obstacles to economic progress is political policy. Obviously the political policies of twenty years of independence did not create the problems of a thousand years; they have compounded them. Moreover, if India cannot solve its political problem there may soon be no India at all but only a subcontinent further fragmented.

Plainly these things, however confidently asserted, leave the central question in as much uncertainty as before. They do no more than outline its dimensions. And whether India can succeed as a unified, politically stable, and economically viable nation is no trivial question for the West. A glance at the globe shows how it lies astride the pathway between East and West. A glance at history reminds how it has been ever a turbulent stage for the clash of peoples. A glance at a gazetteer suggests that an area of more than a million square miles, populated by 480 million people, could not collapse and leave only a passing ripple on the world's political seas.

But if the uncertainties must remain on that question, it is still possible to cast a balance sheet and to find at the bottom of the line some grounds for hope. The liabilities, to be sure, are depressing. The bulk of these 480 million people live not only in poverty, for some of them a poverty beyond comprehension, but also in ignorance. Barely a quarter of them could be called literate in any language, and are therefore beyond teaching except for the simplest things. They live off a land which for centuries has been ravaged by armies, abused by men, and washed by floods, droughts, and plagues of crop-destroying pests. For equally long the people have been ravaged by disease, from malaria to leprosy, and though less so now they are still ever conscious of the fragility of life.

Even where they have had the blessings of medicine, the blessing has compounded the woe. Every year their numbers increase by some 10 million to 12 million people, putting more impossible burdens upon the produce of the field. Moreover, millions of them cannot even speak to other millions through the babel of fourteen languages and countless dialects.

So much for the broad strokes. There is no need to labor the point that nothing man can devise can bring swift remedy to such ills. But it is not unrelieved bleakness. In the treasury of modern technology there is the knowledge of how to multiply the fertility of the land manyfold. Nothing new is required, only the doing of it. A remedy is also at hand for controlling the fertility of the people. The cervical loop, which can be inserted once and for all, promises for India what no other form of birth control could possibly accomplish.

Neither of these measures—for the underproductivity of the

225

land or the overproductivity of the people—can alter much soon. There is no quick way to insert some 200 million cervical loops, or to irrigate, fertilize, and chemically treat more than 300 million acres of farmlands. The main effects, even when done, are for the future not the present. The task of public policy is to encourage, or at least to permit, the doing of them. The political task is to keep such order in society, and to provide a mechanism for people to express themselves, so that the right public policies can evolve and grow.

Unfortunately past public policies have hindered, not helped. Spurred by visions of instant grandeur, the political leaders poured too much of the nation's scarce resources into mills and factories, leaving agriculture as a stepchild. Frightened by tradition, they dodged the population problem. Bemused by socialism, they wrapped both agriculture and industry in the tentacles of strangulating controls. The result has been a fiscal and industrial crisis and an agricultural famine.

A tragic example is displayed in Bihar. The drought in that province was not caused by ministers in New Delhi. But because those ministers left undone for twenty years the simple, practical, and technically understood means of storing the waters of the rainy season, the consequence of nature's drought is a man-made disaster.

Unfortunately also the political development of India has not been such as to develop political alternatives to the ruling Congress party, or to provide the means for absorbing the political pressures within the country. Thus when there are elections dissatisfaction with Congress party leadership, which is quite widespread, has no way to express itself except to give protest votes to regional or small factional parties. There is no other party of national standing. This poses some political dangers. As a nation India never existed prior to the British; even the Moguls never ruled it all. At the moment of independence, in 1947, it split again in violence, spinning off the two sections of Pakistan. What remains is not fully stable. The south is divided from the north in language, culture, geography, resources, and to some extent in religious outlook. It is not unusual to hear talk of a "southern secession," and only half in jest.

The politically conscious part of the population, a minority in numbers but large in influence, is also split on philosophic grounds. There is a very articulate group that differs with the neutralist foreign policy and the socialist economic policies of the present government. This adds to the tinderbox of discord.

Against such an array of liabilities, what are the grounds for hope? For one, much has been accomplished in India for all the mistakes. If the production of industry and agriculture has not kept pace with either hopes or needs, it has increased. Enough has been done in farm and factory to show the capabilities of the Indian people to learn new methods of agriculture and to acquire the skills of modern industry. Education has dented the literacy problem; in twenty years the primary-school population has risen from 17 million to 45 million, the college population from 300,-000 to more than a million. Per capita income, now $56 a year, has grown from $45 a year. The number of doctors graduated each year has increased from 700 to 5,000. All is not unmitigated gloom, even in the statistics.

The intangibles are equally impressive. If the party system offers little opportunity for meaningful debate, there is at least a good deal of it in the press and other parts of the public forum. Much of it is thoughtful and well informed; relatively little of it is demagoguery. This has had its impress within the ministerial councils. Within the government there are changing views about the economic policies.

The emerging middle class—the journalists, the factory managers, the professional men, and the university professors—number men of obvious intelligence and ability. They remain a small

227

group among the 480 millions but their numbers are growing. In the final analysis they constitute the best resource for the future. Perhaps when you add it all up the result is still an uncertainty. But at least an uncertainty forecloses no possibilities, and is therefore no cause for despair in a departing visitor.

December 21, 1966

VIII

AMERICA:
A PLACE IN THE SUN

THE DREAM AND THE REALITY

WHEN Americans of that generation went off to fight World War I, there were few who doubted that they were fighting to save the world for democracy. It all seemed quite simple to us then. All we needed was total victory over the enemy. Not merely to halt the Kaiser but to destroy entirely the enemy governments, to break up forever the hateful political institutions of the Old World and to create a New World of little democracies after our own image.

When Americans again went off to fight World War II there were few who did not know that its seeds lay in the very totality of that victory twenty years earlier. The achievement of our 1916 war aims in Germany left its people in chaos and finally prey to a demagogue preaching vengeance. By destroying the Austro-Hungarian Empire we created a new power vacuum in Eastern Europe that plagues us yet. And in the Far East we left a disorder from which the Japanese grew their new empire.

There are few so blind today as not to see from what blunders comes the threat of World War III. Again, we destroyed the enemy entirely only to create a new and greater one. It is not President Kennedy—nor Eisenhower nor Truman—who is to blame for the dangers of the hour. It is our own fatal fascination, which President Roosevelt embodied, with the idea that if we can just win total victory over our enemies, then all will be resolved—that out of the ashes of evil destroyed there will spring the brave new world.

It is a fascination which lingers. For once more there are voices, of which perhaps Senator Goldwater's has been the strongest, telling us that our only aim must be "total victory" over the forces of Communism. It is not sufficient that we check Soviet aggressions. Nor that we achieve a balance of power which makes real coexistence a necessity for the Russians. We must destroy Soviet Communism utterly.

Of course those who thus dream of a total victory over Communism do not advocate global war; they would achieve their ends by other means. Yet it is, inexorably, a policy admitting only one instrument for its achievement. No man in the Kremlin will acquiesce in the liquidation of the Russian empire, in the surrender of East Germany or Poland or Czechoslovakia or Hungary. If we are to achieve that kind of victory, the only way is by war—nuclear war. And if we gained that total victory, what then? Let us suppose that there were a nuclear war between the United States and Russia, suppose even that its end were absolute and complete annihilation of the institutions of Communist Russia. In short, the total victory of which these men speak.

To begin with, we would be confronted with the problem of what to do with the ashes of Russia itself, the vast land mass stretching from the Black Sea to the Pacific. Nor could we expect such a war to come and pass and not leave all Europe as well in destruction. Even in the unlikely event that this country emerged relatively unscathed we should have to take upon our shoulders the staggering burden of occupying, policing, managing, and—in time—even rebuilding much of the world.

And what of Red China? Destroying the power of Russia would indeed rid us of one enemy, as we were rid of Hitler and Tojo; but the destruction of one power would again leave an enormous vacuum into which would pour no man knows what forces. Or must we destroy all Asia as well, and take for ourselves hegemony over the whole?

232

So much of the problem any man can imagine. Yet there is more. For we delude ourselves if we think that by the mere disappearance of Communist Russia we thereby put an end to the ferments of Africa, of South America, of the Middle East, of Southeast Asia. The truth is, or so it seems to me, that the chaos which would confront the world after such a holocaust defies even those imaginations trained by the failure of our last two efforts to obliterate all the forces of evil in one blow.

This blind faith in the magic of "total victory" is worse than an illusion. It can be fatal because it assumes that evil exists in the world only by sufferance, that all it takes to destroy it is a godlike power. A nuclear war we may have, precisely because evil exists in the world. If such a war comes, we must have the courage to face it just as before men have faced wars and death rather than surrender to barbarism. Indeed, if we show that courage to the barbarians we offer the best hope that we will spare the world that tragedy.

But this courage is something else than the delusion that if, somehow, we can just slay the enemy in front of us then we shall put all aright and the world will live happily ever after in peace. Good men always dream, but wise men never confuse their dream with reality.

October 16, 1961

233

THE WEST AND ASIA

F OR more than five hundred years, from the Norman Conquest until the time of Charles II, maritime England tried by diplomacy, money, and force of arms to keep a fulcrum of power on the continent of Europe. In the end the English failed, and thereafter had to play their European role—which continues a considerable one to this day—by bringing their outside influence to bear on the balance of power of the continental land mass.

For more than four hundred years, dating at least from the Portuguese conquests in Malaya at the beginning of the sixteenth century, the Western maritime powers have been trying to maintain a foothold on the eastern slopes of the Asian continent. So, until very recently, has the island nation of Japan. Today, hard though the question be, we are all being forced to ask ourselves whether this task will prove as impossible as the English efforts in Europe centuries ago. That's what the argument over Vietnam is all about.

If it's not impossible, how and where is it to be done? If it is, what other role can Western power play in Asia, and how? And what, in terms of our own interests and those of the peace of the world, are the costs of the alternatives?

Right off, we must face the fact that neither history nor the map offers much encouragement that any non-Asiatic power can indefinitely maintain a physical power base on the continent itself. Certainly the struggle to do so has been long, arduous, and confused. The Western position in Asia was at its strongest just prior to World War I when the U. S. together with the other leading European powers could, and did, enforce the "open door" policy on a weak and divided China.

Japanese power in Asia, which ultimately brought her into conflict with the U. S., reached its peak during World War II, when at one point Japan controlled much of the Chinese seaboard and all of Southeast Asia to the borders of India, as well as the offshore islands. From these peaks everything has been downhill. The Japanese, of course, lost out by losing their American war. But even victory or a "negotiated settlement" with the U.S. might not have profited them much. They never succeeded in conquering China even when they were fighting only makeshift and strife-torn Chinese armies; there's reasonable doubt they ever could have conquered so vast a land.

Be that as it may, the consequence of the American victory in the Pacific war was the loss of Western power in China. Whether that loss was the result of betrayal, foolishness, or ill luck makes an interesting intellectual exercise; it alters not the fact. Nor is this all. The French lost Indochina, including what are now the two Vietnams. The British lost Burma. The Dutch lost Indonesia. Aside from the enclave of Hong Kong, allowed by sufferance, the toeholds of Western power are reduced to the two peninsulas of Korea and Malaya and to the American presence in Saigon.

The map isn't very cheerful about the prospects of retaining all this. Malaya and South Korea, perhaps; the very fact that they are peninsulas makes them susceptible to the influences of sea power, in which for the time being the West is supreme. But looking at the great land mass of Asia, and the distances that stretch between from Europe or America, it's hard to be sanguine about the chances of keeping a physical military fulcrum on that continent if the millions of Asians are determined to throw us out. If that be the case, the cost of staying would be staggering.

Finally, both history and the map suggest that in time all the

Asian people—Malays, Thais, or what-have-you—will want us to be gone. Men do not like to have their destinies distantly controlled, even when it is to their own benefit. This, then, is a harsh aspect of reality which we ignore at our peril. But it is not the only aspect of the Asian world, and we would be foolish to overlook these others.

Asia is not unlike Europe in one respect. It is populated by people of different histories, races, and cultures; its homogeneity is deceptive. China is the dominant power, both in history and on the map. But the Thais, Malays, Koreans—even the Vietnamese —are no more anxious to be subjugated by the Chinese than we are to have them so, although they differ, as other nations do, in their ability and will to resist domination.

For this reason the "domino theory"—the idea that if one nation topples the others will follow—may also be deceptive. If perchance Vietnam is lost, it doesn't follow automatically that the Thais with their thousand-year history of independence will simply fold up from despair. As a matter of fact, it doesn't necessarily follow that even if Vietnam becomes "Communist" its interests and desires become identical with those of China because China too is "Communist." Never in history have like religions or like forms of government assured that two nations of different people and different national interests forget their differences. Witness the Sino-Soviet clashes, the defection of Yugoslavia, the restlessness of the Eastern European "Communist" nations under the Russian yoke.

Therein lies considerable hope for Western interests in Asia, the essence of which is not to control Asia but rather to prevent any one Asian power (China) from subjugating the whole of the continent. This is, interestingly enough, exactly the same as the American interest in Europe, as it was England's before us. For the moment the effort there is to restore a balance of power against Russia. But in the past, let's not forget, the same effort was aimed at the France of Napoleon and the Germany of the

Kaiser and Hitler. The names change; the principle remains the same.

All this is quite pertinent to the present problem. The best thing, of course, would be to maintain the independence of South Vietnam because in so doing we strengthen that bastion against the Chinese ambitions. We must not suppose that the effort was wrong even if it fails. But we have to recognize that it may fail. History and geography pose enough obstacles. The crux of the matter, however, is that no outside power can save a nation whose people, for one reason or another, are not united in their own determination. Not all the power of the United States could have liberated Europe from the Nazis if the people of Europe had not themselves wanted to be liberated and were willing to suffer that it might be done.

Many of the Vietnamese, or so the evidence suggests, are weary of this war. The country is also torn by internal rivalries of religion and politics. Perhaps too our own country has been inept in its role as intervener. Certainly we are left with very few supporters for more militant action among the other Western nations.

So, like England once with regard to Europe, we may have to yield the illusion that we can make Asia fit our specifications; that illusion will serve us as badly now as it did in our China policy after World War II. Yet what we need not do is fall into the opposite delusion that because we cannot control events we are left powerless to influence them. In fact, once we begin to look more realistically at our position in Asia, clearly perceiving its limitations, we may actually improve that position because we will see more clearly what we can do. There is still much we can do to influence the future of Vietnam. Conceivably the situation within South Vietnam could stabilize to the point where we could be there not as interveners but as allies in the real sense. This could alter much.

Whether or not that happens, our power rightly used can

affect the relationships between Hanoi and Peking, between Peking and Moscow. Vietnam poses problems for others besides ourselves, and the Russians are no more pleased than we at the prospect of Chinese domination over all Southeast Asia. Beyond that, we are not bereft of power to influence events in Burma, Thailand, and elsewhere; the lesson that the U.S. will help those who help themselves will not be lost. And in all the offshore waters from Singapore to Tokyo we remain, as before, the dominant power, politically and militarily.

Admittedly none of this will be easy. What is in this troubled world? We may even fail in all, although here we have history and geography on our side against the ambitions of one nation, China, to have hegemony over so huge a continent. But there is no defeat that comes to a great nation so complete as the defeat that comes because it refuses to measure realistically its own power against the realities of the globe.

March 3, 1965

AGONY WITHOUT ECSTASY

O NE of the most striking things to any eavesdropper on the great debate over Vietnam is the awareness that it really isn't about Vietnam at all. Or at any rate, only partly so. What is being thought about, talked about, and quarreled about is something more transcendental than that messy war on a distant shore. To borrow some shopworn phrases, it's a debate about manifest destiny and the nation's place in the sun. This is as true, or so it seems, whether the disputants are unshorn activists waving placards against war, emotional hawks seeing no substitute for victory, articulate Senators decrying the arrogance of power, or a brooding President who deals less with philosophy than with daily decisions that sometimes make philosophy academic.

Of course the Vietnam war itself makes much philosophy academic. We are there, whether or not we got there wisely. Whatever the consequences of our abstention in the first place, the consequences of our withdrawal now would obviously be profound, possibly catastrophic, and certainly immeasurable. The world would take it as a signal not only that nothing stood between Red China and Southeast Asia but that the great and mighty U.S. was no longer so. The trauma to our national confidence would be as deep. It is one thing to abstain from a fight and another thing to be bested. That being so, the generalities about power and responsibility or about the U.S. role as a world power are bound to seem often irrelevant. They help no one decide what to do about the Buddhists or General Ky. All the same, these general questions are entwined in every argument about Vietnam, consciously or otherwise. Every debater, hawk or dove, argues a view about the manifest destiny of the nation as a world power. Vietnam has forced us to think again of these things, and the process is an agony.

When some future historian comes to write of the decline of the United States as a world power, hopefully yet many years away, he will perforce deal with many complexities. He should have no trouble putting a date to its zenith. That day was September 2, 1945. At that moment of history, when the surrender of the Japanese Empire was accepted on the decks of the U.S.S. *Missouri,* the United States stood alone on a pinnacle of power. No nation anywhere in the world could say us nay.

It was not merely that our enemies had been vanquished. The other big powers that stood with us as allies—Great Britain, France, Russia—were exhausted victors. As a world power China was then only a figment of men's minds. We and we alone wielded the atomic bomb. Nor was this all. Victors and vanquished alike had to turn to us for enonomic succor. Russia could not have saved herself without our arsenal. Europe could not rebuild itself without our wealth. Everywhere smaller nations were beholden to our largess. From that day onward everything has been downhill for U.S. power, at first imperceptibly and then with increasing speed.

Other nations became atomic powers. Europe recovered both its economy and its spirit. Russia, freed from the worst deadening effects of Stalinism, spurted forward. The Red Chinese, for good or ill, awoke that sleeping giant to make the beginnings of a nation. All over the world revolutions erupted, and new nations emerged, often in a violence to tax the forces of order. Twenty years later no one can pretend that the United States, though possibly still the greatest of world powers, can any longer act without reckoning with the power of others. Today we must cut our cloth to fit a smaller bolt. You may weep or sigh at the change, but it is a simple statement of fact.

Yet the self-image of VJ Day bit deep into our consciousness, and has affected every foreign policy attitude since then. There have been times when we had arguments about whether, or how, we ought to use power, as with Truman in Korea or Eisenhower in the Middle East. Even in Korea hardly anyone doubted that we could do what we wanted to do if only we decided to do it; Truman and MacArthur quarreled over the use of the power, not its existence. This attitude was dramatically in evidence in Vietnam. At each stage of the involvement, from Eisenhower to Johnson, there were disagreements over how much we ought to intervene. But right up to the moment when President Johnson decided on an all-out military effort hardly anyone doubted that the mighty U. S. could, once it decided to throw its weight in the balance, do what it wanted to.

Today not even the hawks are quite so confident. The military men speak less boldly of victory. The political experts are not so cocky as they were when they acquiesced in the Diem overthrow. And all around us the diplomats have become more conscious of our isolation in this affair; we stand in Vietnam almost alone. All this accounts for the nation's great sense of frustration. Senator Fulbright depresses people with his gloom; former Senator Goldwater frightens them with rashness. In general the nation has little enthusiasm for any of the proposed courses. This is what sets Vietnam apart from the agonies of other wartime debates. As late as Korea, certainly in the two world wars, the agony of war was at least made bearable by an enthusiasm for what we were doing and a confidence that there was an ecstatic day of victory to be claimed. All we had to do was rise up and fight.

No more that confidence. Somehow we all realize that the reality of 1945 is a mirage today; we have lost our illusions of omnipotence. This brings the painful task of self-reappraisal, which is in truth what the Vietnam debate is all about. There is, no doubt, some danger here. It is very easy, being suddenly disillusioned, to succumb to despair; just to throw in the sponge and think once more that manifest destiny is withdrawal into a Fortress America. That is the opposite illusion. The world cannot ignore our power, nor we its responsibilities.

But after Vietnam—however that ends—we are not likely again to succumb to overweening pride. And that, as the ancient gods knew, is a lesson worth learning.

June 7, 1966

BITTER TEA

THE army is determined to stand up to and continue the national revolution, to answer the whole people's wishes. . . . The army is determined, together with our fellow citizens, to restore security and order, bringing about happiness and welfare for the whole people."

Expressive words, these. In a couple of sentences they sum up what has happened to one American dream, the dream of twenty years ago that if only the United States would use its power in the world it would set the world aright. All that was necessary to remake it in our own image of freedom and democracy was to crush the fascist powers, lift the colonial yoke, and reach out a helping hand to the nations newly made. Yet here is a proclamation in one of these nations that only bayonets are the answer to the people's wishes, that the people must look to soldiers for happiness and welfare. And the words of the proclamation are, sadly, symbolic of a time.

The particular words quoted happen to have been spoken by Major General Nguyen Khanh after the army of the Republic of South Vietnam toppled the government of Major General Duong Van Minh, who had toppled the government of President Ngo Dinh Diem, who had toppled the government of Emperor Bao Dai. Earlier, under the government of France, there had been for a century surely no less order and welfare than the Vietnamese now enjoy.

It's enough, I should think, to make President Johnson's cup overflow with frustration. As much as any of our postwar Presidents, Mr. Johnson would like to turn his attention primarily to domestic affairs, to the welfare and happiness of his own country's citizens in their own country. But whether he will or no, he cannot. One day it's Panama. The next Cyprus. The next Berlin, or Indochina. And if Mr. Johnson is ever given to brooding in those wakeful nights of his, he must have some sardonic thoughts on how the cup was brewed.

In Vietnam the irony is clear. We gave neither help nor sympathy to the French; if anything, we encouraged them to get out. Then we lent our support to the division of the country. We were happy to see Diem replace Bao Dai, stepped in to support him and to fill ourselves the vacuum we discovered after the French had left. Finally, grown unhappy with Diem, we encouraged the coup that killed him. If there is chaos now, it is no less for our own handiwork. The irony, of course, is even more bitter in Cuba. We as much as anyone put Castro where he is because we did not think Batista a very nice fellow. Here, on our own shores, is a monster of our own creation.

But it is not alone in Cuba or in Vietnam that the present troubles are flavored by our own meddling. Turn to almost any troubled part of the world and you will find it touched by some past action of our own. The United States is responsible almost alone for the situation which permitted the Russians to divide Germany and Berlin. Not only did our own officials dream up the idea of separating the defeated Germany into separate occupation zones, but they also had the incredible thought of plunking down a divided city in the midst of the Russian zone. With this we made an insoluble problem. In other places we have aggravated problems even if we didn't create them. We aren't responsible for the crumbling of colonialism which, being so precipitant, has left so many lands in disarray. But we did repeatedly urge on the pace at which the once colonial areas gained independence. And if others pointed out to us danger in such haste, we looked the other way.

How naïve all this was—well, Mr. Johnson needs only to spin his office globe and look at the pretty colored pins that mark his problem spots. Even in Panama old American words come back to haunt him. Personally I think it would be a mistake to blame all this past naïveté on those who happened to be the leaders of the moment. Anyone whose memory reaches back to World War I is aware that the country has long had a streak of self-conscious righteousness. As a nation we have been moved by the idea that our way is best, and that if the rest of the world would do things our way then the world would soon straighten itself out.

Yet to this native naïveté, with its overtones of evangelism, it seems to me that something else has been added, for which those who have led us must take the chief responsibility. For lack of a better phrase, it might be called an overweening pride in our own power. When World War II ended the United States seemed clearly the most powerful nation on earth. With the atom bomb and its immense economic strength, it towered over everyone, including the Russians. So it was easy to think that the United States could arrange things as it would, and therefore that it should.

This illusion, rather than any confusion about the Soviet Union's intentions, was probably the real root of the mistakes at Yalta and Potsdam. Caution was buried under the confidence—a feeling very strong in Mr. Roosevelt—that the rest of the world, including Russia, could be made to behave. Along with this illusion of omnipotence, unfortunately, came the delusion of omniscience. In practice the realities of power asserted themselves very quickly; from Truman on, every President has been acutely aware of the limitations of American power. Yet there persisted the delusion that we knew what should be done in almost every spot in the world. We knew what was good for Cuba, for the Congo, for the Suez Canal, for Dutch New Guinea, for Vietnam. And look what we've got.

Mr. Johnson, to be sure, may not find these very helpful thoughts, for he must deal with the present. But there is some merit, as he says, in viewing that present from "the perspective of history." The way to brew a better cup of tea is to learn what made the last one bitter.

February 6, 1964

THE ENEMY

I N Norman Mailer's *The Naked and the Dead*, that best-selling
novel of World War II, part of the drama of the finale is the
way the big battle ends in a whimper. Up until the very last day,
you'll recall, the American forces on this imaginary Pacific isle
appeared to face a strong, resolute, and unconquerable enemy.
Suddenly the break-through; and then the American forces discovered to their astonishment that much of the enemy's strength
was a brilliantly erected façade to hide weakness. The American
attacks had punished the enemy far more than anyone realized.
This is a phenomenon as familiar in real war as in fiction. In
battle each side knows all too well its own failures, defeats, casualties, and weaknesses. The great unknown is what lies behind
the façade the enemy presents to its foe.

The classic case of this in American history was in the Civil
War battles from the Wilderness to Appomattox. In retrospect it's
clear that Grant was marching ever onward toward victory; the
surprising thing is that it took so long. Yet it did not appear so
at the time to Union soldiers fighting the bloody battles; and to
the stay-at-homes it seemed the struggle would be interminable.
A good many veterans of more recent wars will recognize the
feeling. There were generals as well as GIs who didn't recognize
the Battle of the Bulge for the last gasp that it was. And many
a seaman on VJ Day, looking at the tattered remnants of the
Japanese fleet, found it almost incredible that such a hollow shell
could have appeared so mighty for so long.

This phenomenon is one that ought not to be forgotten today. For among the many uncertainties and confusions in the
Vietnam war the greatest unknown is how the Vietcong fares
behind the façade of battle. Our own troubles are hidden from no
one. Every newspaper reader knows of our soldiers' difficulties in
the jungles. Every reverse, every disappointment, is catalogued.
Our casualties are driven home not only by the reporting of gross
figures but by the arrival of the telegrams at a neighbor's house,
or perhaps our own. If we are short of helicopters at a jungle
clearing, or if a company at the front has to husband its ammunition, the matter is not long secret. The mistakes in planning, the
snafus in operations, the immense difficulties of a long supply
line, all these things are recounted for all to know.

Nor is it any secret from anybody that we have divided
councils not only about the way to fight this war but, indeed, a
division over the war itself. The various views are debated in
Congress, aired on the TV screens, and endlessly discussed wherever men gather. In short, we know full well our own woes.

Few would have it otherwise. In this country troubles con-
cealed, or differences of opinion plastered over, would be far
more dangerous. All the same, the situation poses two special
risks we must ever keep in mind. One, of course, is that troubles
known and divisions publicized may beguile the enemy. It has
happened before that those who would do battle with us have
been misled by apparent weaknesses of both power and resolution. But there is an equal danger that we may mislead ourselves
into unjustified discouragement. We may suppose that because we
do not see the enemy's mistakes, snafus, and difficulties they do
not exist. All the woes will appear to be upon our side. The
enemy will appear to be untroubled.

Some of this attitude can be detected now in the talk about
Vietnam. Much is said about the insuperable advantages of the
guerrillas in jungle warfare, as if we had never fought—and won

248

—in the jungles of Guadalcanal or on the mountain tops of Korea. The problems of our supply line are much talked of. Little remarked is the enormous quantity of weapons and machines we have successfully poured into the battle. Hardly appreciated are the enormous difficulties of the jungle supply line which the enemy must cope with; for them a weapon lost is much more difficult to replace than for us. Perhaps most important of all is the apparently monolithic nature of the enemy's resolution. There are no public hearings in Hanoi where critics can speak their piece. From where we sit, all seems serene in the enemy's councils.

This may be the greatest deception of all. North Vietnam is almost totally dependent on others for every sinew of war except bodies. If it has ambitions in South Vietnam it also has fears of China. If it is willing to pay a large price for victory, it too must reckon that some price will come too high. And Hanoi too, be it remembered, has had to bear ten years of frustration and defeat while its "hawks" were promising quick victory. As a matter of fact, there are some signs that the enemy in South Vietnam is having more troubles than appear on the surface. They've lately taken a few lumps on the battlefield. Their supply apparently isn't functioning as smoothly as before. And from Hong Kong come reports of division in Hanoi's councils.

Apart from these specific signs, ordinary common sense ought to suggest that we could hardly pour as much fire-power into battle as we have and not punish the enemy. And the very swiftness with which the Vietcong melts away from a head-on fight, while it may mark cleverness at maneuvering, suggests not strength but weakness. But the point is that we can't really know. And because we can't know, we need to be on guard not only against overoptimism when, for a space of time, we seem to be having successes but also against that discouragement that comes when, for a space of time, our own troubles pile up and few are discernible in the enemy camp.

We Americans are of mercurial mood. Last fall, with the first quick build-up, our spirits rose almost to euphoria. This winter, when it became clear that the Marines weren't going to have it all wrapped up by Easter, the whole country fell into a fit of depression. The moral of all this is not that Americans should ever underestimate an enemy. It's simply that in battle we shouldn't be too hasty in underestimating ourselves.

March 2, 1966

ANATOMY OF MELANCHOLY

THEY gave a farewell dinner party in New York the other evening for Herve Alphand, who has rounded out a decade as the ambassador from France. It was a festive affair, with the men beribboned and the ladies bejeweled. But it was also, as the French say, a bit *triste*. This melancholy was not entirely due to the departure of the ambassador, although Mr. Alphand is a charming gentleman and his wife a lovely lady who have acquired many friends to miss them. What nobody could quite forget was that this is not the happiest moment in the relations between France and the United States.

Everybody knew that matters stand on a quite different footing than when Ambassador Alphand first came to Washington, which was before the days of General de Gaulle and during the days when the United States could, and did, dominate the politics of Europe. The fact that the Alphands saw all the changes, wrestled with the resulting problems, inevitably made their farewell party an occasion for reflecting on it all.

The easy temptation is to blame the change in relations on the special mystique of General de Gaulle. Before him everything seemed friendly; after him the difficulties; ergo, the one is cause and the other effect. Besides, he's a strong-minded man, given to uttering dogmatic pronouncements like thunderbolts fired from Mount Olympus. There's just enough truth in this to make it appear an adequate answer. But it doesn't suffice, for if much else hadn't changed, the thunderbolts would be ineffectual firecrackers.

We would do better to measure more carefully what's been happening in Europe, and to alter our own attitude and policies to the alterations found.

Many of the alterations are, by now, self-evident—the economic revitalization everywhere, the return of political stability (especially in France), and consequently the renewed confidence of the people in the future. This has been paralleled by a diminished fear of overt aggression from Russia or its European satellites. Some of the consequences of this are, if not self-evident, at least much remarked upon. The NATO arrangement, which was founded on the premise that the U.S. would play not only a major but the dominant role, is not and cannot be what it was. If General de Gaulle irritates us by saying so, the irritation is what he says out loud that everybody knows but doesn't quite want to admit. But perhaps what is underestimated is the extent to which this revitalization of Europe, politically and economically, alters every political relation among the European nations themselves, and therefore affects every relation between Europe and the U.S.

The history of the Common Market may serve as an illustration. The impetus for it, which so confounded skeptics ten years ago, came because it seemed to nearly every country almost the only hope for the economic regeneration of the continent. Today the economies are rejuvenated. If the drive for economic unification continues, there is nonetheless no longer that sense of driving urgency. The same thing has happened in the political arena. Each country today feels more free to pursue its "normal" political interests than when they were submerged in common fears.

This is beginning to be reflected especially in the relations between France and West Germany. Ten years ago they were driven as by devils not merely to effect a diplomatic rapprochement but to walk hand in hand. Today rapprochement is still important in each's foreign policy. But neither Erhard nor de

Gaulle feels impelled to sacrifice everything to absolute unity. Each feels free to walk a little bit on his own. And their interests, though we forget it, do diverge. The "German problem"—the East-West division and the matter of the Polish borders—is the preoccupation of the Bonn Foreign Office. This is of small concern to the French. They are more apt to be concerned lest the West Germans grow too venturesome in their efforts to rearrange things in the East.

It follows then that West Germany and France have different ideas about the U.S. role in Europe and consequently different U.S. policies. The West German objective is to keep the U.S. involved in Europe, specifically in West Germany itself. Not only do they therefore support us in our view of NATO; they refrain from monetary or other economic measures that might irritate us, and speak softly about U.S. actions in the Dominican Republic or Vietnam. The French feel no such constraint because they would just as soon we withdrew from Europe, leaving Europe to manage its own affairs—doubtless with France itself as the leader. This reflects itself in a relatively outspoken independence on everything from balance-of-payment problems to the multilateral force. General de Gaulle has surely played an author's role in this alteration, but not the one usually ascribed to him. It took de Gaulle to liberate France from its Algerian problem, to restore its political stability, and prepare the way for its economic resurgence. This done, the rest followed.

That is, given a rejuvenated Europe and a prosperous and stable France, French foreign policy would almost inevitably have moved in the direction it has, de Gaulle or no. Likewise, given a rejuvenated Europe and a West Germany recovering its confidence, it was almost inevitable that the latter's foreign policy would look more boldly at the "German problem," whether the government was headed by Adenauer, Erhard, or Willy Brandt. In sum, what is commonly called a "deterioration" in French-

U.S. relations is not merely a general's whim or a surge of "anti-Americanism." It is, rather, a manifestation of the fact that the basic political situation in Europe has changed while we continue to think of Europe as it was a decade ago, and base our European policy on an attitude ten years out of date. In any event, it's no fault of our departing guest, nor likely to be cured by exchanging one charming Frenchman for another.

October 27, 1965

ROMANTIC DIPLOMACY

WHEN Henry VIII, that English monarch who looked something like Charles Laughton, took to wife Catherine of Aragon he was following a rather romantic tradition, though one of diplomacy, not of love. The idea was that family ties between sovereigns would make for peace and amity between England and Spain. When the marriage broke up in 1533, as every schoolboy remembers, it also broke up English ties with the Roman Catholic Pope. This in turn proved one of the causes of the century of religious wars which followed shortly after and of which no schoolboy remembers anything except the stirring sea action of the Spanish Armada.

The romantic idea—the word here is used in its pristine sense of something fanciful or unreal—in both this diplomacy by marriage and the wars by religious alliances was that the comity or hostility of nations could be controlled by such things as kinship or worship. In fact, the proposition didn't seem as unrealistic then as it does in retrospect. After all, the crusades had been built on an alliance of all Christendom against the infidels, and the religious wars of Europe, Catholic against Protestant, did drag on until the Treaty of Westphalia in 1648.

All the same, history has shown that the binder of shared family, shared religion, or even shared language and culture has sooner or later come unglued when submitted to the political stresses of different national needs, interests, or desires. Yet curiously enough the same idea has sprung up in a different guise in the twentieth century. In its simplest form you see it in the fanciful hope that frictions between Russia and the U.S. can be smoothed over by a pleasant visit, complete with a ballet, between President Kennedy and Premier Khrushchev. In a more dangerous form—dangerous when it becomes an unquestioned assumption for policy—it embodies the idea that a shared economic or political ideology makes for monolithic partnership among nations, and that differences insure intractable enmity.

So persistent is this assumption that when former Ambassador George Kennan recently suggested to the Senate Foreign Relations Committee that in the case of the Communist bloc it ain't necessarily so, his remarks hit page one across the country.

Said he: "To attribute today to the various parties, regimes and factions that make up the world Communist movement any sort of unified political personality—to speak of them as though they represented a single disciplined force, operating under the control of a single political will . . . is to fly in the face of an overwhelming body of evidence, to move intellectually in the realm of patent absurdity, to deny by implication the relevance of external evidence to the considerations and decisions of foreign affairs."

Mr. Kennan's thought is more incisive than his rhetoric. He is simply reminding us that the Soviet Union and Red China, though both carmine in political coloration, have different needs, interests, and desires which cannot be permanently glued together by ideology alone. The same is true to a less noticeable degree of the Communist countries of eastern Europe. There is, of course, a reverse side to the thought. The "Free World" is also not a monolith. As we can now observe, not every nation which is anti-Communist in politics and economics thereby shares automatically the same foreign policy. For one example, we have not been able to rally western Europe to our cause in Vietnam just because its purpose is to halt Communist aggression and expansion.

So far, then, so good. Mr. Kennan has done a service by stating what actually ought to be self-evident: Cracks in the Communist monolith are hopeful auguries for our side, especially so if imaginative diplomacy can find ways to exploit them. But there is also a risk, and one not without precedent, that the burying of one romantic notion may give rise to another one.

The precedent and the warning can be found in the memories of World War II. There was nothing wrong from our point of view in the U.S. alliance with the Soviet Union against Nazi Germany. At that moment in history Russia's interests coincided with our own; to have rejected mutual military aid on the grounds of "ideology" would have been plain foolish. The error, and a costly one it proved to be, was the widespread notion that because the Soviet Union was for the moment our great and good ally it would continue to be so afterwards.

This idea captured President Roosevelt and most of the intellectual community, and it led directly to the blunders that haunt us to this day—the partition of Germany, the disappearance of half of Europe behind the Iron Curtain, and the swift Communist victory in China. The brutal reality of Vietnam is one aftermath of that romantic dream.

The new dream, if it takes hold of us, would run something like this. See, world Communism is not a great monolith after all. The Chinese variety is more dangerous than the Russian. It behooves us then to seek a rapprochement with the Soviet Union against the Chinese menace. And finally, that community of interest founded on this cause, to convert it once again into the same euphoric feeling that all U.S.–Russian interests are glued together by this common bind.

The reality this overlooks is that then, as before, other interests would remain divergent. Ideology would be one; Russian Communists still want to convert or subvert the rest of the world if they can. But quite apart from that the interests of the Soviet

Union in Eastern Europe (and their "needs" if you look at it from their point of view) will not be the same as our own. Nor will their interests in Asia, aside from the shared antagonism to Chinese expansion.

These differences still have to be dealt with, hopefully by diplomacy. Since one of the Soviet interests is also to avoid war if at all possible, they can in fact be dealt with by diplomacy. But only by a diplomacy that is clear-eyed. That means recognizing that the interests of nations abide through ideological marriages and divorces. Foreign policy is not the place for romance.

February 2, 1967

IX

A FEW ASIDES

LITERATURE AND LIFE

ONE of life's little puzzles, on which I have been brooding for nigh onto twenty years, is how in the world we won World War II. Since I had some personal interest in it at the time, I've read most of the novels about it, seen numerous war plays and movies, and come away with the impression that most of the generals and admirals were a pretty sorry lot. Indeed, that pretty much goes for all officers.

Occasionally there's a young lieutenant, leading a platoon, who pluckily wins through in spite of the mismanagement at head-quarters. More often it's the sergeants who have to step in and take charge, unless maybe it's a comic novel, in which case there's no time for them either. The higher the rank the more likely the character is to be venal, cruel, dull-witted, bungling, and just plain incompetent, perhaps with a bit of sex mania and alcoholism thrown in for good measure. You really wonder how MacArthur, Patton, Nimitz, and Halsey ever got through the American pro-motion system, or even how they managed to get to Berlin or Tokyo. Must have been sheer luck.

And judging by the novels, movies, and TV it must be sheer luck that DuPont, AT&T, General Motors, and IBM, not to men-tion Macy's and Gimbels, haven't collapsed under the backbiting, blindness, and blundering that apparently is the daily diet of ex-ecutive suites. No wonder the University of Minnesota was moved to call a "Conference on Understanding Profits" and ask Walter Heller to explain it.

Just the other evening I flipped on a TV playlet billed as a comedy about business. Since it starred my old favorite, Groucho Marx, I looked forward to some fresh and knowing satire; all I got was an exhausting cliché of the stupid boss grinding down his patient, able underlings. It was implied that this oaf had built from scratch a world-wide washing machine business, but this appeared more marvelous than the miracle on 34th Street.

It was a week when "The Week That Was" wasn't sharp either. A little ditty in honor of National Secretary Week got off to a good start and then collapsed into nothing more than boring insults flung at The American Businessman. Heavens knows, there are enough foibles and human foolishness in business offices to stock a comic novel twice the length of *Tom Jones*, and my own secretary ought to write a book about them, but this script writer was just too ignorant to know where the humor lies.

Ignorance, of course, is a possible explanation for the curious picture of generals and business offices painted in literature. Mr. Fielding, the man responsible for all that hilarity in the *Tom Jones* movie, remarked that a writer had to know his people well and respect them before he could see where they were ridiculous. You have to know the world of Squire Alworthy to laugh at Squire Western. And very few writers know what they are talking about when they set a novel in GHQ or the executive suite. Lew Wallace is the only general I can recall who wrote a novel, and he wrote about Ben Hur in ancient Rome.

Still, I wonder if ignorance is the whole explanation. Shakespeare, whose birthday everybody is now celebrating, never walked with kings and only saw a queen from a distance. Yet four centuries later his kings, queens, generals are as full of flesh as the Falstaffs and the Mistress Quicklys with whom he must have shared many a tankard. One difference is that Shakespeare had the wit to know that kings and generals, like the rest of us, are made up of ambition, greed, generosity, cruelty, and kindness;

that a man upon whom a battle's decision hangs can be as wise, as stupid, as tormented, as exhilarated or depressed, as cowardly or courageous, as any poor bugler caught between here and eternity.

But another difference is that from Shakespeare's time until our own there was no thought that in order to glorify the common man it was necessary to denigrate uncommon men. Tolstoy could paint a fumbling, frightened General Kutuzov and still leave his merits unsullied. Galsworthy could make old Soames Forsyte a narrow man of business and still leave him a warm human being with capacities beyond the ordinary.

Today we are impelled, everywhere, to level down men with such capacities. We all really know that the President of the United States must deal with extraordinary problems and that any man who achieves the Presidency—even the poorest of them—must have some extraordinary abilities that make him, at least in these particulars, an uncommon man. Yet people are pleased when he is cut down to size, if only by turning the White House into a cozy cottage and the President into the next-door neighbor.

This outlook is reflected in much of our literature. A widespread social attitude is that all heroes must be "just ordinary folks" caught up in machinery they don't understand and against which they are helpless. It follows, then, that the machinery itself must be villainous, and the people who run it can't be themselves heroic. Hence a literary convention that the general got to be a general only because he was lucky, or knew how to play politics in the Pentagon; he mustn't really be more able than the sergeant or the draftee fresh from a Harvard course in creative writing. Politics must be venal, politicians shady. Businessmen must be silly, fatuous, ruthless, greedy, or at best dull people in a grubby business—the mixture depending on whether the script is comedy or melodrama.

Still, the writers are to be more pitied than scorned. The debate in the boardroom, believe me, can be hilarious, but in the

263

boardroom as in the trenches, the humor arises because the affairs are serious and they are dealt with seriously. But the debate in a boardroom can also be high adventure. Somewhere, be assured, there must be uncommon men in any IBM or General Motors. And since these captains command more men than Henry V at Agincourt, and on their decisions hang matters of no small moment, here surely is the stuff of high drama, though you'd never know it from all you read or see. Someday, maybe. All it takes is that some other grubby playwright, hacking out his scripts to order, have a touch of uncommon imagination.

April 30, 1964

EGGHEADS IN ACTION

W HEN Charles André Joseph Marie de Gaulle began to crop up in the news again, the background articles made much of the fact that he had written a book. He was described variously as poet, mystic, philosopher, historian, political theorist, and visionary. So no wonder we were startled when de Gaulle went into action. Here, surely, was an intellectual, an egghead. How could he so skillfully outmaneuver the practical politicians in the Assembly and outflank the dashing generals in Algeria? For it's deeply imbedded in our culture that when it comes to practical affairs eggheads aren't very smart. We are proud of our poets, painters, scholars, writers. They are useful, even necessary; a poet makes people happier and a scientist sometimes invents things.

But, so the tradition runs, it took "practical men" to clear the prairies and build the factories out of the wilderness while historians wrote about it and philosophers thought about it. And after Adlai Stevenson it will be a long time before an American political leader lets on he's literate. Even the eggheads think of themselves as a group apart. The avant-garde in Greenwich Village were as puzzled by the phenomenon of a poet in the insurance business as Wallace Stevens's fellow executives were to find he thought of something besides actuarial statistics. Americans think it an exception to the rule if ever the twain shall meet.

This is certainly one aspect of our culture that is strictly modern and largely indigenous to America. It's an idea that hardly occurred to the ancients, or even to our own forefathers. To the

Greeks, of course, a man wasn't a man unless he was a whole man, both doer and egghead. Nobody thought it strange that Alexander was a star pupil of Aristotle or that Archimedes should be invited into a council of war. It was a journalist, Xenophon, who was called on to save ten thousand Greeks from the Persian army, and a dictator, Pericles, who made Athens the city beautiful. Caesar wrote history while he made it and Marcus Aurelius wrote philosophy while, as emperor, he applied it.

Nor was this just ancient history. Frederick the Great debated philosophy with Voltaire. Napoleon was a man who saw visions and argued the philosophy of the law. The British Empire was built and preserved by men who were novelists, essayists, poets, artists, scholars, or philosophers—men of action like Bacon, Disraeli, Gladstone, Balfour, and Churchill.

So with America. It would be hard to gather in one place more eggheads than in a reunion of our founding revolutionists: Franklin, Jefferson, Hamilton, Madison, and Adams. This dichotomy between eggheads and "practical men" is partly a result of our history and, one suspects, partly due to a confusion of intellectualism with education. Pushing westward and building factories left little time for the kind of education we call cultural; a covered wagon has room for few books. The prideful builders in time acquired a scorn for the scholar who couldn't plow a furrow, and the few with leisure for education came to look down their noses at the builders' ignorance of Homer and Beethoven.

This separation by cultural exposure, a wider gulf than in the Old World, obscured the fact that "intellectual" describes not education but a quality of mind. The man who thinks from particular problems to general ideas and back again, who has curiosity for all within his purview, who has sensibility for beauty in music or in mountains—such a man is an intellectual whether he digs in ditches or in libraries.

Thus Andy Jackson, roughhewn soldier, was a first-class egg-

266

head; we are still influenced by his political theories. So, unquestionably, was Lincoln. So too were the plainsmen who saw more in the West than adventure or the tycoon who saw visions as well as money in the railroads. America would never be if its men of action hadn't included a high percentage of men of speculative mind. Yet the dichotomy persists. Scholars disdain "practical affairs" and executives hope nobody will notice if they read philosophy at home. Casey Stengel, the Yankee philosopher, is barred from the fraternity of eggheads just because he garbles his grammar. And radio and record crooner Pat Boone dumbfounds teenagers when he graduates from Columbia University *magna cum laude*.

We don't know whether in the final analysis de Gaulle can do for France what Churchill did for England. But maybe both of them can do something for America. They can remind us that action doesn't require a silencing of the mind. Perhaps they can even lift the impression left by the many drudges educated beyond their capacity—that all eggheads are incompetent to do anything.

June 24, 1958

267

SEX AND THE ROBED
JUDGES

T HE nine old men on the Supreme Court—well, not young, anyway—have been having some stimulating hours of winter reading. Chief Justice Warren, snuggling up to the fireplace, can break the monotony of involved patent briefs by reading one of the few extant copies of a little volume called *The Housewife's Handbook on Selective Promiscuity*. Mr. Justice Black, the oldest of his confreres, can take his slippered ease by browsing through such periodical literature as *Eros* or something caller *Liaison*, a sort of a newsletter for tired businessmen, even if it bears scant resemblance to such prosaic prototypes as the Kiplinger *Washington Letter*.

Mr. Justice Stewart, the baby of the bench, can potter around with some 140 volumes on one publisher's list which includes among the fetching titles *Sex Switch* and *The House of Torture,* all of them imaginatively illustrated. Mr. Justice White, as befits a Rhodes scholar, may have a taste that turns more to classical English literature of the eighteenth century, the era that spawned the epigrams of Sam Johnson and the lyric poetry of Blake and Burns. He might thus feel more comfortable with *The Memoirs of a Woman of Pleasure*, the succulent biography of a lady known as Fanny Hill. On the other hand Mr. Justice Douglas, the most vigorous of the judges, might find himself with a neoteric book succinctly titled *Raw Dames*.

But be assured, straightaway, that all this winter reading marks no renascent surge of prurient interest among the learned judges. Possibly they will all find it a dreary chore, since hearsay testimony has it that such a steady reading diet becomes more boring than delectable to men arrived at a certain age. For this reading matter, *inter alia*, comes before the court for solemn judgment as to which of it, if any, is obscene enough to be barred from street-corner bookstalls by some village fathers. So tangled is the legal thicket, no lesser court can find its way through the brambles, moving the Chief Justice to mourn that "we're in for trouble."

The trouble began back in 1933 when District Judge Woolsey lifted the ban on James Joyce's *Ulysses*. The good judge burrowed his way through its 968 pages and decided, with justice, that a few four-letter words therein didn't make it obscene. But not content with judgment on the merits, Judge Woolsey added a few woolly phrases about the book's literary merits and the judgment that Joyce was "a real artist with words." This tempted judges to be literary critics. Then in 1957 the Supreme Court broadened the criteria: a book wasn't obscene unless it was "utterly without redeeming social importance" or unless it went "substantially beyond" the "customary limits of candor."

The High Court put the final bramble in the thicket in 1964 when it decided that these customary limits of candor had to be "national." That is, an Amish village in Pennsylvania had to accept the candor the Supreme Court thought acceptable in New York's Greenwich Village. As a result, so far as diligent research can uncover, the Supreme Court has been unwilling to judge any book obscene. One man's trash is another man's literature, and no man knows how far is "substantially beyond" the limits of candor.

So now we have got to the place where almost anything goes, without distinction as to time, place, or audience. Legally there are hardly any distinctions left between the kind of book that can be sold to an elderly Supreme Court Justice, a sociology scholar, and a ten-year-old who picks up *Fanny Hill* at the drugstore to read while munching his candy bar.

The situation is both outrageous and absurd. Yet apparently the Supreme Court sees no rational way out of the dilemma: by what sort of general legal rule do you preserve the freedom to publish even what many people do not approve of, allowing those who want to read or need to study such writing the right to do so, while at the same time keep the whole country from being buried under an avalanche of pornographic trash?

Perhaps the time has come for a little more irrationality, or at least for a surcease of the sweeping *obiter dicta* that try to make one judicial ruling fit every circumstance. One could readily describe our liquor laws as irrational. In some communities you can buy it anywhere. In others you can't buy it within a specified distance of a church or a school. In some you can't buy it at all. Under the principle of "local option" teenagers can drink in New York State but not in New Jersey. And without any doubt some eighteen-year-olds venture across the border, defeating in part the object of the New Jersey law. Across the nation the whole thing is a bit of a crazy quilt, inconsistent and often illogical.

All the same, it makes some common sense. The very absence of uniformity has social merit. It permits the people of each community to decide for themselves what rules are best suited to their temper and their mores, while requiring of those who think otherwise no more than some inconvenience to be able to get what they want. If the First Amendment requires freedom to publish anything and grants to New Yorkers the right to display any book in their bookstores, as the twenty-first Amendment gives them the right to make their own liquor laws, why does Dubuque, Iowa, have to do it the New York way?

Since communities vary in the wisdom of their other laws, we might well end up with a patchwork of paradoxes. Without doubt some communities might "ban" public sale of some books that would strike a judge as instructive reading. But in so diversified a country why should every man, jack, and toddler have to live at the outer limits of candor that comfortably fit around Mr. Justice Douglas—or his colleagues, for that matter? Some people will envy the judges their long winter's reading, but theirs is no enviable task if they feel called upon to mandamus the mores of every hamlet in the land.

January 4, 1966

PELOPONNESIAN POLITICS

ANYONE who has labored his way line by line through the dactylic hexameters of the *Iliad*—they are now a dwindling band—will recall the endless boredom of Homer's long catalogue of the ships. Here the poet and journalist of the Trojan War gives the detailed battle forces of the Greek invaders—Agamemnon of Mycenae with his hundred ships, Nestor of Pylos with his ninety, Idomeneus of Crete with his eighty, and so on through the long line of this Bronze Age alliance. The list made weary Greek and dull poetry, and for generations of schoolboys the frustration was heightened by the fact that the experts said Homer made it all up. Indeed, for generations experts said the whole story was a myth: no Agamemnon or Nestor, no Mycenae or Pylos, no such war, not even such a place as Troy.

Then the amateurs began to confound the experts. Heinrich Schliemann, a German merchant, uncovered Troy and later Mycenae by the simple device of looking for them where legend said they were. Sir Arthur Evans, who got around to archaeology in his old age, found the great palaces of Crete. Later a professional archaeologist, C. W. Blegen of Cincinnati, uncovered Nestor's Pylos where it should be, on the western slope of the Peloponnesus. Even so, most scholars stubbornly insisted that both Mycenae and Pylos were Cretan in culture, not Greek. Or they did until Michael Ventris, an architect with an interest in ancient languages, broke the secret of the clay tablets found both in Pylos and Crete—the so-called Linear B scripts—and proved them written in early Greek.

All this threw the history of the Bronze Age into disarray. What did happen in the second millennium before Christ? Is Homer's tale all mythology or is it explainable by the working of political forces unchanged in the three millennia to the Atomic Age?

These are intriguing questions to those of political mind, and so once more an amateur has plunged into the Homeric thickets. In *From the Silent Earth* Joseph Alsop, never one to shun speculation about Vietnam or Brazil, has spun some theories on Peloponnesian politics and this earliest of great wars. It's a fascinating book because Mr. Alsop brings to the Bronze Age the interest of the thoughtful amateur and a perceptive journalist's understanding of the political forces that move men and nations, in eras millennia apart. His theories are interesting (the book is a delight just as a whodunit) because Mr. Alsop writes well and because, as a good reporter should, he has done his homework not only with research but with his feet. But his approach— reading the past by the present—is most intriguing because it can tempt others of political mind to speculations of their own, reading the present from the past. History, after all, runs forward as well as backward.

Briefly, Mr. Alsop's thesis is that the then more advanced Crete was subjected to an early Greek invasion from the Peloponnesus around the fifteenth century B.C., and that this conquest produced a new kind of society in Crete. This mixed culture then fed back into the mainland as a Greco-Minoan culture marked by further technical and artistic advances and by the creation of elaborate governmental organizations.

Mr. Alsop's reasoning rests on observations of what often happens, politically, when a less advanced people conquers a more advanced people, a reversal of the more familiar conquest pattern. But his reasoning also fits the recent archaeological discoveries—and the tale as told by that ancient journalist and poet. For example, the date for the fall of Troy set by Eratosthenes of Alexandria, which was 1184 B.C., has been moved back by Blegen and others to around 1260 B.C. Meanwhile, the final destruction of Knossos on Crete is now dated around 1200 B.C., instead of 1400 as thought by Evans. Pylos, it now appears, was overrun about the same time as Crete, and by the same primitive Dorians from what is now Albania.

Ironically, although Mr. Alsop doesn't mention it, this restores the Trojan chronology given by Herodotus. More importantly, and this is Mr. Alsop's point, the "new" chronology restores room in history for Agamemnon of Mycenae, Nestor of Pylos, and Idomeneus of Crete. Furthermore, the Trojan war now makes political sense, as a sort of Gallipoli campaign of the Bronze Age, substituting bronze for oil as the strategic commodity to put the Middle East at the center of a power struggle. Finally, the economic strength and the organizational skill shown by the Linear B tablets lends credence to the power displayed in that long catalogue of the ships that once so wearied schoolboys.

I find that personally a happy thought. What sends a little tremor through the mind is what imagination can now conjure up about what the Trojan War did to those who won it. For a decade the richest and most powerful Grecian nations battered at the gates of Troy, though no more for the sake of Helen than the armies in Flanders for a murdered archduke. The enemy vanquished, the world lay at the feet of the conquerors.

Why not? Sterling Dow, the Harvard historian, gives a graphic description of Mycenaean Greece in the days of its glory: the tremendous authority of the monarch and his bureaucracy. The intricate framework of system with every man's task assigned on a clay tablet. Rich treasuries for ships and swords. Subjects subservient in their duty to the system. Yet the victory won, the alliance fell apart. Odysseus returned to political disorder, Agamemnon to assassination. Within a few years the Dorian barbarians had sacked Pylos, Mycenae, and Crete, the big three of the glorious victory. In Mr. Alsop's words, the collapse was mainly caused by the surge of internal revolution, "most probably resulting from the social, political and economic disruption after the long siege of Troy."

Of course all this happened long ago, so all the reflections offer a relief from the depressing things you read about in the morning newspaper. Or do they?

April 10, 1964

THE MALE MYSTIQUE

THE *Ladies Home Journal,* whose interest for men ought not to be underestimated, devotes a good part of a recent issue to something called the 4–D woman. There's a rather ponderous article by Betty Friedan, inventor of "the feminine mystique," a couple of sparkling ones by Jessica Mitford and Marya Mannes, and a delightful one about how Jean Kerr mixes motherhood and a career by not doing the dishes. To round it off, a husband tells how he overcame a working wife's challenge to his self-esteem, and finally college girls are told where not the men but the jobs are.

The sum of it all is that the ladies, in addition to the usual curvaceous dimensions, also have minds, and with that a problem of how to fill out their fourth dimension. The role of mother, wife, and housekeeper, while possibly necessary for the species, is not enough; it's dull, dreary, mentally imprisoning, and spiritually unsatisfying. For a woman to be truly a woman she must escape this prison built by men. The proffered answer, whatever the variations, comes down to work; that is, work outside in the workaday world. A business job. A diplomat at the UN. A playwright or a concert violinist. A social worker. Anyway, a career of some kind, either as a substitute for or at least a supplement to the demanding business of pleasing a man, changing diapers, or washing dishes.

For a mere man the temptation is great to retort with witticisms, or perhaps some Elbert Hubbard philosophy, or some poet's raptures about the loveliness of the ladies. That would be futile; Mrs. Friedan would but smile at this confirmation of the male mystique. It would also miss the point, just as it is also lost in the Vassar (or Smith or Wellesley or Radcliffe) complex that woman's self-fulfillment lies only somewhere yonder beyond the home.

A part of the point is that the "problem" is mostly imaginary; that is, what psychological evidence is available suggests that women as a group do not in fact feel dissatisfied in their tripartite role of wife, mother, and homemaker. A concurrent issue of *The American Scholar*, for example, reports on a survey by a husband and wife team (no merely masculine article, this) into women's own image of themselves and their aspirations. Ellen and Kenneth Keniston, the one a Harvard psychologist and the other a Yale psychiatrist, conclude that most women "not only accept but largely desire a homebound position." If women are indignant, these researchers found, "it is most often over the social and personal situation that requires them to work. . . . Most women work because they must, and would gladly exchange their 'careers' for a life of a happily married, financially secure wife-and-mother."

The resentment and indignation at the male-structured working world, they say, flares only among a relatively small group of highly educated professional women. "Most women 'fulfill their potential' outside the home reluctantly, if at all. If there is a 'problem' for women in America today, it is that they work only of necessity or by default." So much, then, for the Vassar complex that spills over into the ladies' magazines. Actually the findings will surprise no one who has seen societies, such as the Russian or those of backward countries, where necessity forces women to work in the same way men do. They ought not to surprise any husband with sisters or daughters. What the preachment at Vassar does, quite often, is to create the ambivalences by instilling guilt feelings in those who really don't want to be 4–D women.

277

But this isn't the whole point either. Changing social and economic conditions have altered women's roles; they are better educated, they know they have minds and talents, and their use of them in homemaking has been foreshortened to too few years to fill up a whole life. The real mistake, rather, is equating self-fulfillment with "work."

This is the male mystique. Or, rather, a mystique of the American male society. For thousands of years, and even now elsewhere, "work" was viewed as an elemental necessity of a life, never as an ideal. All men of spirit, from philosophers to poets, disdained it. The ordinary man suffered it, but his one ambition was to achieve a situation where he could forgo it and find his fulfillment elsewhere. The American pioneering society altered that. Work—clear, definable, workaday work—became the only honorable estate of man. Idle rich or idle poor, all were frowned upon. Those fortunate enough not to have to work, whether by virtue of fortune or the relief rolls, may have secretly enjoyed it; "face" required that they pretend otherwise.

The female emancipation movement, culminating in the current Vassar complex, unwittingly took over the mystique. If visible work in the outer world was the caste mark, then by Heaven and come what will the women should be entitled to it.

The whole thing, male and female, is nonsense. Any sensible doctor would like to dispose of 90 per cent of the grubby work he does, so that he can enjoy the intellectual puzzles that come along or muse upon the cause of cancer. Any auto assembly worker above a moron views his work simply as a means of enjoying life elsewhere: the pleasures of his family, his home, or the gathering of kindred spirits at the bowling hall. Self-fulfillment, male or female, is an individual thing. For some there are rewards in what the world calls work, but they can be found too in reading, sewing, fishing, planting petunias, playing bridge, helping the Little League, studying Swahili, or just lazily contemplating life, like Socrates. Only the smug measure all things by themselves.

When you come down to it, it's because work is mostly a means to an end that mankind has spent three thousand years automating labor. Washing dishes may be dullard's work, but not so the enriching of a home with a woman's educated mind. Changing diapers is messy; the rewards for the spirit are in watching a baby grow. Actually, it's probably all an academic argument. That same *Ladies Home Journal* has pages of feminine things, resplendent in color, and not one to be worn to courtroom, laboratory, or office. Never underestimate a woman.

June 24, 1964

THOUGHTS ON A BRIEF VISIT

T HE most interesting thing about the visit, when you think it over, was that it took place at all. It was not so long ago, as time is measured by history, that it would not have occurred to the bishop of Rome to come to the United States of America. If it had, he would have set off an uproar of protest. Yet when Paul VI, pontiff of the Roman Catholic Church, spent a few hours recently in New York not only the city but the whole nation did him honor. The people lined the streets, and television cameras carried his every movement to people across the continent, and the President of the United States journeyed from Washington to receive him.

All this made it a memorable occasion. It was also one to dramatize the great changes that have taken place in this country, in the world, and within the Roman Church itself. Paradoxically, it dramatized as well those things which endure amid the changes of men.

One reason for the change, of course, is a simple statistical one; there are more Catholics in the United States than there used to be. The English colonies from which the country sprang were almost wholly Protestant, which in those days marked a political as well as a religious difference. Although we pride ourselves on the tradition of religious freedom, in most of those colonies Roman Catholicism was legally proscribed. As late as 1800 there were barely 50,000 Catholics in the whole country. Today their number approaches 50 million. But the increase in numbers only partially explains the alteration of the Catholic position in the U. S. By 1928 they had grown numerous; yet the anti-Catholic vote played a great part in Al Smith's defeat in the Presidential campaign. In the Kennedy campaign, thirty years later, it was much talked of but of little effect. And today few suppose that a candidate's religion will ever again be a predominant political issue.

This change, as many have noted, comes from an increase in tolerance of religious differences. Not many people, any longer, can be aroused to fighting anger by the theological arguments which caused so much hostility in the past. But if we are more tolerant, it is because, as a people, we no longer care so much about those ideas. This is as true among the Catholics as among the Protestants, the Jews, or the nonbelievers in anything. Nowadays the arguments are debated without passion on quiet television panels. Or, to put the matter another way, the growth of religious tolerance among the people has been paralleled by an increase in religious apathy.

That this is so is in part due, surely, to changes within the Roman Church itself. It too has altered and is altering more. And if apathy is too strong a word for those who profess its faith, it is certainly true that those who profess it have lost their militancy, their unshaken certainty in the dogmas of two thousand years in whose name, once, men were put to rack and wheel. The saints of the past would find it passing strange to hear assembled bishops debating not the issue but the words to express the acceptance of religious liberty by the one true Church; or hear priests raising voices to debate birth control and other long-settled dogmas. There is no doubt that the winds of change blow through Rome.

So it must be put down that the visit of the bishop of Rome passed as an unruffled triumph in part because religion itself has lost its one-time grip upon the minds of men. As faith languishes, schisms diminish. Yet if this be true, there remains a paradox

281

unexplained. For while the welcoming crowds along the pontiff's path were predominantly Catholic communicants, they were by no means exclusively so. Protestants, Jews, and confessors to nothing joined the throng or watched on TV. And all the world waited to hear what this man would say to the ministers of nations.

Perhaps some of these were drawn by pageantry, as to coronations or to funerals of the great. Or perhaps for some it was merely idle curiosity. But you did not have to mingle with those who stood along the chilly streets to be aware that there was something more than this. What that something is can only be surmised, and that only by asking yourself a question. If this is such a secular age, why should men anxiously await the outcome of a Consistory of an institution they think outmoded, as men have awaited the recent Roman councils; why should they weigh the words of a man of God if they profess no God at all?

There is one simple explanation for the paradox. When men have lost old faiths they can still hunger for something to have faith in. You do not have to be a Catholic, or even a Christian, to long for something that will restore to man his spirit, his kinship with something outside himself, a spirit stripped from him by the rationalizations of science and the materialism of ideologies. Put briefly, the surmise is that great numbers of people watched this bishop believing not in anything but wanting to believe in something, hoping for some mystery that would give them back again their faith.

This is the strength of the Roman Church. If you read its history as a rational man, you cannot escape its brutality, its terrors, even its evils in times past. Though raised up in the name of God, it was an institution created by men no less frail and fallible than their brothers and therefore not immune to the failings of mankind. Yet as an institution it has outlasted all other institutions of men; states, and even empires, have come and gone while it remains. In some mysterious way, the idea of the Church transcends the man-made institution. This gives its bishop pre-eminence among all others. There is no priest of any Protestant church, no rabbi, no mullah, no Buddhist monk who can speak with such authority to so many. None, then, with so much power to rally men if he can find, for a modern age, the touchstone of the spirit.

No man knows whether this bishop, or any other, can find the way. Not all would follow anyway. But all men can wish that some man could find the way, because we all long for what is lost. And so perhaps this brief visit served, if nothing else, to remind us of the paradox of our age.

October 7, 1965

COMMENCEMENT—OF WHAT?

LET us consider now the season of Commencement speeches, one of those pleasant ceremonials of life that everybody wants to get done with as soon as possible. Both the pleasure and the impatience are shared by parents and offspring. There are generally two kinds of Commencement speeches. One, usually given by political figures, deals with some major current issue, like Vietnam or civil rights. Even when they contain a useful thought, hardly anybody's listening. In the other kind of Commencement talk the speaker avoids the pitfall of irrelevancy only to get bogged down in platitudes. This is not the speaker's fault. The ceremonial occasions of life have been so endlessly repeated that the wiser the observations they invoke the more time-worn they are.

It was ever thus. Can you recall a single word uttered by your Commencement speaker on that auspicious occasion, lo those many years ago? The reason, one may suspect, is that hardly ever does such a speaker put to words the thoughts that are really in the minds of all those gathered on the greensward; quite conscious thoughts on the part of the elders, no less burning to the young for all that they are covered over as much as can be. These thoughts have nothing whatever to do with advice. If we elders prattle it, it's mostly out of nervousness and not knowing what else to say. In our saner moments we realize it's not only futile but probably ill advised because none of us can really tell another what to do.

Our real thoughts have to do with questions, not answers. What we'd like to ask, as we sit there counting up the years and the bills, is—okay, now what? But of course the young have always fled that question when they could. There was no Peace Corps in grandfather's day to offer youth a chance to escape to Nepal, where for another year or two he can avoid the question of what the devil he's going to do with his life. But the spirit wasn't much different for those who ran off with Clive to India, or dropped out of college to spend two years before the mast.

As for the female of the species, there are a great many great-grandmothers who went stagecoaching west to be pioneering schoolmarms rather than settle down with the boy next door. And quite a few grandmothers who thought it more exciting to march with the suffragettes than to sew a fine seam. If things seem different today it's largely because we, the elders, have given our young more opportunities to postpone the putting away of childish things. And have contrived to make them think that the grubby workaday world is dull and unrewarding.

The first part of this, as many have noted, is a by-product of the affluent society. Working your way through college is not only rare but square. Commencing to work on Commencement Day is hardly ever necessary. Except for the dullest of dullards there's a scholarship for graduate study, and for the dullest there's the beneficence of the welfare state. That is, society has postponed the necessity for adulthood. The Bar Mitzvah is ceremonial only; one and twenty is a legal fiction; even marriage no longer separates the boy from the man. How, then, can there be a "graduation" day to mark an end and a beginning?

But somehow affluence doesn't explain it all. Perhaps unwittingly, we elders have also created a new folklore which has been more influential than our formal precepts. To be a wife and mother, in this folklore, is to be a woman unfulfilled; or, worse, to be less than a man. National magazines emblazon their covers

285

with the query: "What Role for the Educated Woman?" The avid readers will offer divergent answers, but both questions and answers all assume that to be "educated" must demand some other role.

The young men are reared in just as strange a folklore. Among the intelligentsia it's tolerable to be a lawyer, doctor, or scientist. Although even here it's better not to work at the main function of any of these. The doctor who studies nine to five in a foundation laboratory is much more "fulfilled" than one who takes pay for taking out your appendix in the middle of the night.

For the rest, so the bright young ask, what is the point in studying Shakespeare or Kierkegaard and then "throwing away your life" as a stockbroker, a manufacturer of auto gears, a merchant of soap, or a banker in a countinghouse? In the folklore, indeed, anything connected with the real work of the world is not only grubby but unrewarding to the soul of the "educated" man. All this is the legend, from the dust of Main Street to the dying salesman on television. The workaday world is routine and unexciting; where's the poetry in working out a sales contract or changing diapers?

To top it off, we've fostered the idea that work is unnecessary; possibly even degrading. Society—i.e., the government—will pay for your school, your rent, your food, your medical care, and guarantee you an annual wage, labor or no. Of course it's true that all this is nonsense. But who should blame the young when they yawn at the Commencement orator's precepts—whether he's preaching valor for one's country, the rewards of virtue, or the dignity of labor? These things the young must learn for themselves. And curiously enough, they will; or at any rate, most of them will. In due time they'll build roads, raise bridges, dig oil wells, finance industries, sell shoes, fly to the moon, change diapers, manage great enterprises, cure the sick, lay sewers, do the work of the world. One of them, astonishing as it may seem, will be President of the United States.

286

Then they will make a discovery we have hidden from them. Not only does the world belong to the squares, but that's where the excitement is. The real poetry is in the rhythm of life; the real adventure is in delivering babies, clothing the masses, moving the earth, keeping the ledgers that will determine the future. The wildest soap opera on television pales by comparison. But when the elders act as if it were otherwise, it's a bit hard to sell that wisdom in a ceremonial oration. And to tell the truth, did you know what you were commencing that distant summer's afternoon?

June 13, 1966

X

BULLS AND BEARS

TRACKS IN A WILDERNESS

WALL Street starts at Broadway and runs a scant seven blocks (eight if you count the Hanover crossing) to a dead-end at the East River. Yet more people have gotten lost in its thickets than in the forest primeval. If you think it's only the country boys who are bewildered by this strange market place, turn to the newspaper's back pages where the stock tables are. There you will find published some little snippets of wisdom from the expert guides. On almost any given day you will find one expert announcing that the underlying forces of the market are strong, there are wonderful buys about, and that you should gather them in. And another, with equally impeccable credentials, suggesting that the best thing to do is to run for the storm shelter. So we walk warily into these tall trees.

I well remember the first time I decided to risk a few bob on the future of America. It was in the depths of the depression, my journalistic talents were grossly underpaid, and all the learned economists were announcing that ours was a mature economy with no hopes of future growth. Anyway, I bought five shares and felt like J. P. Morgan. Then with studied casualness I dropped the news to Oliver Gingold, for whom I occasionally fetched a cup of coffee. Mr. Gingold, even then, was the doyen of all financial journalists, the last *Wall Street Journal* writer who worked for Charles Dow, founder and first editor of that worthy enterprise. Mr. Gingold received the news quietly and equally quietly remarked, "Maybe the fellow who sold the stock was smarter than you."

It was a sobering thought. Since then I've never forgotten the simple truism of the stock market, of any market place, that for every buyer there is a seller, and *vice versa*. In the biggest bull market there's as much selling as buying; in the biggest crash somebody buys every share that's sold. What this means is that whatever your opinion there's somebody willing to put up money that you're wrong.

This explains why there are no real experts on the stock market. You can analyze a particular company, or an industry, or the whole economy, with great acumen and yet miss on the stock market because you don't know what people will do. Sometimes a company's earnings go up and the stock goes down. Sometimes the other way around.

In any auction market prices are not set by some abstract values; they go up or down depending on who has the most enthusiasm, buyers or sellers. This is, in fact, the great democratic virtue of any free market place. Prices aren't determined by any authority's notion of what they "ought" to be but by mutual agreement among all would-be buyers and would-be sellers. This, of course, makes nonsense of proclamations from Councils of Economic Advisers in Washington that the market is "too high" or "too low." They haven't the foggiest idea what it ought to be. But it also fogs up the predictions of those who pretend to tell you what stock prices will be tomorrow.

Still, the stock market isn't a trackless wilderness. There are certain patterns which, if not immutable, have been so often repeated that they are useful guides. One is that in the long run the buyers in the market will pay only for earnings, future as well as present, and that what they will pay for earnings bears a relationship to what they could otherwise get if they simply lent their money for interest, where the return is fixed but less hazardous.

The question that bedevils the market experts is whether this traditional relationship between stock yield and interest rates has been permanently changed in the public's mind. For example, just before the crash in 1929 stocks were yielding about 3 per cent, well below the return on interest-bearing bonds. Nonetheless, people kept on buying stocks because they were convinced that earnings and dividends would rise further and thus rising yields would restore the traditional relationship with interest rates. Much the same situation, and the same mood, prevails today.

Of course a number of things have changed. The American economy is bigger and richer; American business more experienced and, on the whole, more stable in its operations. Things are booming along; earnings and consequently dividends are indeed rising. The price-earnings ratio on the stocks in the Dow-Jones industrial average hovers around 20 at this moment in history, which is about what it was in 1958 when the average was 200 points lower. The ratio is several points lower than it was in late 1961.

Another major difference from the past is the inflation factor. Today the debasement of the currency is a deliberate policy of the government and is expected to continue. This makes fixed-yield investments, like bonds, less attractive because it means that the future interest payments will come in cheaper dollars. It also holds out the promise of higher stock prices just because the future prices will be measured in those cheaper dollars. But among stock market patterns there is another noted long ago by Charles Dow, who was an acute observer and in no way responsible for what others have done to elevate his common sense to prophetic dogma. This is the tendency of people to project present trends into an indefinite future. In recessions they get overgloomy, in booms overoptimistic.

Technicians will argue the length of the present bull market; it depends on what dip you think makes a bear. But an ordinary man looking at the wiggly track of a Dow-Jones chart might conclude that since 1949 the movement has been pretty steadily upward, making it the longest sustained movement in history. In the past eighteen months there's hardly been even a pause. And because of this, the market is bound to look bullish right up to the moment when it suddenly ain't. If I knew that moment I could stop scribbling and retire to the Riviera; so could the writers of those market letters. Which leaves a country boy nothing to fall back on but his common sense.

His common sense might tell him to be always optimistic about the long future of the American economy. But also remind him that in Wall Street, as in any other arboretum, no tree grows to the sky.

February 10, 1964

HEMLINES AND BUSTLINES

ONE of the peripheral pleasures of an editorial sanctum is reading the mail. Of course I get a lot of thoughtful letters on such drab subjects as socialism in Washington, chaos in the Congo, and crisis in the balance of payments. But however enlightening, these aren't as delightful as some of the theories proffered about prosperity and the stock market. The configuration of the planets is quite commonly advanced as either a cause or a measure of economic tides. One correspondent used to write us elaborate formulae for predicting the Dow-Jones averages in terms of Einstein's time-space continuum; I always referred him to the Dow theorists. And of late, naturally, I've been getting letters about the relationship between the Gross National Product and strontium fall-out.

From time to time all this has inspired some Pickwickian thoughts of my own, and they were crystallized the other day by the research of *The Wall Street Journal*'s news department on the hemline situation. The substance of the findings as published on page one was that business office managers by and large get short-tempered about short skirts. This strikes me as a rather short-sighted attitude. In fact, the reporters may have taken a too narrow view of their subject in limiting themselves to hemlines. For it is demonstrable from the historical evidence that the horizontal elevation of ladies' dresses, at the top as well as the hem, is a far better economic indicator than planetary relationships with the points of the zodiac.

The demonstration was first made to me many years ago in Professor J. P. Harland's course in Mediterranean archaeology. His lectures may not have left many lasting impressions, but they did leave me with a vast admiration for the sewage system of ancient Crete and they did acquaint me with the charms of the lovely Cretan maiden whose statuette is a perennial adornment of Christmas art books. Professor Harland noted at the time, if memory doesn't play tricks, that this statuette was from the period of Crete's greatest prosperity and glory. And even the most obtuse student could hardly help noting that the bustline of the lady's dress had fallen to the lowest possible level. Soon thereafter Crete fell upon hard times.

The line of reasoning this opens up can be stimulated by a tour of Europe's great art museums. The Renaissance, for example, marked not only the emergence of Leonardo and Cellini but also the re-emergence of the female form, at least at the top. After the usual cyclical variations, the lowering of bustlines and hemlines reached their peak (or nadir) in the luxury of the French court just before the Revolution.

But it isn't necessary to rely on ancient history. In 1910, when as you'll remember the economy was on a plateau, bustlines were at the neck and hemlines at the floor. By the booming era of the Charleston, hemlines were approaching their present elevation and bustlines were forming what the chartists call an inverted bottom. After 1929 the skidding stock market had the hems sagging again. As befitted a period of uncertainty, bustlines were confused and showed diurnal fluctuations during the thirties, up in the morning and down at night. This suggests a tentative conclusion that the less the ladies have to spend on clothes, the more clothed they are.

The present upward hemline movement coincides almost exactly with the great bull market. It began, rather timidly, in the middle of the war with a rise to about the halfway marker,

296

then drifted slightly downward until, like the Dow-Jones industrial average, it rose sharply with the soaring sixties. Bustlines have tended more to follow bond prices; that is, to move contrariwise to interest rates. Not until the unpegging of the government-bond market in the fifties was there a marked downward décolletage. But with the sharp rise in the prime rate, both here and in Europe, bustlines have plunged until they are almost nonexistent. It's plain enough, then, why businessmen and economists ought to pay close attention to the rhythmic hemline and the undulating bustline. Royster's Rule, which I intend to expound at the next meeting of the Pickwick Club, is that hemlines vary directly with the rise and fall of the GNP while bustlines rise and fall in inverse proportion.

What needs some further research, however, is whether these are to be classed as leading or lagging indicators. The most you can say right now is that hemlines seem to tell us where we are but that bustlines—as evidenced by what happened to Crete and Louis XVI—are rather ominous when they make new lows.

While awaiting the computer, I'll go back to reading the mail. That'll get me in the right frame of mind for pondering all those New Year's economic forecasts soon to come flooding in.

December 15, 1964

PAINFUL REMINDERS

THE stock market has lately been giving some nip-ups to those with weak hearts. And some painful reminders to those of us with weak memories. The reminder is simply that whatever you read in your brokerage letters, or whatever the preachments of the new economics in Washington, the copybook maxims aren't wholly outmoded. One of these was succinctly stated years ago by J. P. Morgan, who when asked for his expert opinion on the stock market, replied: "It'll fluctuate." It was a remark of such simplicity as to cause a great deal of hilarity.

But right now nobody's laughing. Not so very long ago the Dow-Jones industrial average was flirting with the magic thousand, that talisman of the superstitious, and in brokerage offices from Seattle to Syracuse euphoria hung high. Since then practically everything's been a downhill zigzag. Some weeks it's been downhill all the way, with the averages sliding eight, nine, and ten points a day. One day the averages dropped more than fourteen points, for the worst one-day slide since President Kennedy's assassination and without that dramatic provocation. There've been a few upward zags, but even so the averages have not scaled the heights.

So the euphoria has been replaced with what the psychologists call "free-floating anxiety." The phrase describes that vague feeling of uneasiness which overcomes all of us from time to time and yet finds us unable quite to pinpoint the reasons for our premonitions. Not that you can't find causes for alarm. There's the war in Vietnam. There's bigger government spending. There's clear evidence of inflation. There's the manpower squeeze and shortages of some commodities. There's costlier money. And there's the threat of much more government economic management.

Yet all these things—remember?—are exactly the same things that were once cited to explain why the stock market tree was going to grow to the sky. The war spending would make factories hum. Bigger government spending would give people more money to spend on consumption. The manpower squeeze would add to this with higher wages. Higher yields on bonds were just proof that smart money wasn't going to risk being wiped out by inflation. As for that inflation, what better hedge than common stocks, yields or no yields, for which somebody would pay more tomorrow than you paid today, even if in cheaper dollar bills? Inflation meant that the "new valuation" of the stock market would be permanent, and you could forget all the old rules about price-earnings ratios or the relations between dividend yields and bond yields.

Finally, there was the "new economics" discovered in Washington. There couldn't really be a down-turn because of all those built-in stabilizers. Anyway, if any little trouble should develop the government managers would manage us right out of it.

Ah, well. It isn't the first time that the same arguments have been turned inside out, as the mood fancies, to justify both euphoria and the jitters. And often with not much real sense, either way. It's probably unkind to mention 1928–9, because the minute you do everybody gets the shudders and thinks you're predicting a similar debacle. All the same, as the late Oliver Gingold was wont to remark, sensible people do keep making the same silly statements. There was Professor Irving Fisher, the Samuelson of his day, who thought stocks had reached a "permanent high plateau," and two other then famed but now forgotten experts who said the road to plenty was to spend more and more freely. And there was the Harvard Economics Society, from a locale then as now providing soothsayers, who explained that "if recession threatens . . . there is little doubt that the Reserve System would take steps to ease the money market and so check the movement."

As for the dreadful aftermath, there are a lot of people who can remember when we were all later being told—and many believing it—that we had a mature economy that wouldn't grow any more and that the stock market had found its permanent plateau in the 100 to 200 range for the Dow-Jones average.

Each successive wave of "new economics"—and new brokerage customers—forgets that the more things change the more they remain the same. Undoubtedly there's a new valuation in the stock market, for the simple reason that the country is bigger, more populous, more productive, and because the dollars that measure value have changed. Doubtless this change will continue. One of these days, like as not, the Dow-Jones industrial average will hit 2,000. Count us not among the bears. Still, there are a few things unchanged. The new government managers are more powerful; the gods have given them no extra genius. Inflation, though it charms with a new décolletage, demands the same wages for favors. War is not to be numbered among a people's economic blessings.

As for the stock market, those who recklessly pay tomorrow's prices today will surely be undone. The investment market is a shopping center with a vast array of choices—stocks, bonds, land, and chattel. Except in brief moments of aberration, investors with savings for hire will in time find their way to those types of investments which reward them most.

What we've witnessed lately isn't a debacle or even necessarily the beginnings of one. The relationship between bond yields and stock yields has simply been reasserting itself. And in making that reassessment, the thought has dawned on a lot of people that inflation doesn't automatically make a stock certificate worth more if for one reason or another (taxes, controls, rising costs) it can't be matched with rising yields.

Ask not the when and where of the new relationship. If a man knew, he wouldn't be writing your market letter. Just take to heart this painful reminder that there are some things the Council of Economic Advisers can't repeal. And reflect that perhaps, after all, old J.P. was as profound a philosopher as Heraclitus.

March 11, 1966

HIGH ALTITUDES

M OUNTAIN climbers, balloonists, and jet pilots like to tell
about the exhilaration of high altitudes. But they are
also wont to warn that there are perils amid the pleasures. For
the same rare air that brings cheerfulness can also addle judgment
and make the heights look safer than they are. That effect is not
unknown in everyday affairs. There's always a tremendous exhilaration when business is booming and the stock market is
soaring, especially when a few months earlier everyone's mood
was deep in a recession trough. Then it becomes very easy to
forget that enthusiasm, as well as discouragement, can sometimes
overreach itself.

I am not suggesting that there aren't some good reasons for
continuing business optimism. The American economy has again
proven its tremendous resilience. To look back a bit, the 1957–8
recession was sharp, and in some places deep, and yet the worst
forebodings were never realized. There's no question that business
is once more pointed upward. Nor would it be wise to suggest
that the stock market, high as it is, is necessarily "too high" in
relation to the business outlook. We must keep in mind that such
traditional measurements as the ratio of stock prices to stock
earnings, now so high as to puzzle many people, can be brought
down either by a decline in stock prices or by an increase in
earnings. A continued increase in earnings is certainly a possibility. And I would be the last to suggest that the prospect of inflation, which can knock all traditional measurements cockeyed,

302

is not a very real one. When you read the wild spending plans of the dominant wing of the now dominant Democrats, you realize that the man who buys "things" to beat inflation is not acting without some reason.

Nevertheless, it is when the heights look most lovely and the path most sure that it's time to watch for that risky overoptimism that overcomes a mountain climber just before his foot slips. It's always impossible to name the moment when that will happen. But when you see the stock market soaring day after day without interruption, when prices discount not only next quarter's earnings but the most glowing prophecies of future prospects, when the market jumps nervously at the most insubstantial of rumors, when every Tom, Dick, and Harry decides to pile his savings on this bandwagon—well, you begin to wonder.

It's one thing to have confidence that the American economy will climb higher; or to recognize a long-term inflation trend that may make dollars worth less and prices higher. It's another thing to think this new inflation is going to be here the day after tomorrow or that next quarter it's going to be transferred into double profits for business. The danger doesn't lie so much in what has happened as in what can happen. Although nobody can say when the market is too high, anybody can be sure that it will soar too high when the public gets caught by the idea that the thing to do is to buy stocks no matter what, to pay any kind of prices today because tomorrow inflation or prosperity or whatever is going to make bad purchases good.

November 12, 1958

WHO'S INSIDE?

I T was a couple of months ago and the man next to me at the luncheon table was making polite conversation, in the time-honored way of the neighbor who asks how's the missus and the kids. Only this time the appropriate question was: How's business? In the time-honored way the reply was that vague sort which politeness decrees should be used with casual but friendly acquaintances—after all, most people aren't really interested in hearing the details of your wife's arthritis, your problems with the mortgage, or junior's lamentable failures as a scholar.

Business down at the shop, I said, was pretty good. Might even do a bit better than last year, what with circulation up and the advertisers being in a generous mood. As it turned out, I was a rather cautious prophet. The first quarter earnings of the estimable enterprise I work for, duly presented to the public and published in the financial columns, were up sharply. In the over-the-counter market the company's stock rose nearly five points between that luncheon and this morning's breakfast.

Nonetheless, it was the kind of conversation that ordinarily passes without a second thought. Ordinarily, but not now. Any moment I expect a visit from the SEC Commissioner. For the Securities and Exchange Commission, as you may have heard, is taking a more jaundiced look at the way "insiders" use (or misuse) the information they have about their companies. The trigger for this interest was the tangled affair of the Texas Gulf Sulphur Co. The SEC alleges that certain company officials knew in November 1963 that a rich ore discovery had been made in Canada, but didn't inform the general public until April 1964.

Of course, Texas Gulf isn't the only cause for the present discussion about insiders. Since the days of Jay Gould and the famed Commodore, stock market habitués have been as much devotees of the inside tip as characters in *Guys and Dolls*. Sometimes, like a three-way parlay, a tip even pays off. More often, it's an expensive reminder of the virtues of right conduct. Anyway, it's true enough that insiders are no more resistant to temptation than outsiders. So it's true enough that the SEC, along with stock exchange officials and others, ought to give some thought as to what to do about it.

But that's where the rub begins. There are already a peck of rules and federal laws on the subject. For example, officers, directors, and large stockholders must report to the SEC every time they buy or sell the company's stock. In some cases if they make money they have to give it back. However, these rules don't, and can't, cover the assistant bookkeeper or the office boy, from whom a company can keep few secrets. And they perforce leave unanswered a lot of troublesome questions, such as, what is "inside information," and what is the right time to make it public? These aren't simple questions even when a company lands a big new contract or strikes oil. The contract may be so loaded with ifs and whereases that nobody knows whether it will be profitable. It can take months to be really sure about what's in that hole in the ground. So a company can—and sometimes does— mislead the public by making wonderful-sounding announcements, even when done with the best of intentions.

There are other immeasurable factors. Those who spend a lifetime in any business acquire feelings about the way things are going, often with only vague facts to pin to.

Question: Which is more moral, for them to hide their feelings from present or prospective stockholders, or to express them

305

when of course they might turn out to be mistaken? A few years ago the president of a large corporation caused a three-day sensation because, when asked, he forecast publicly that earnings would show "an improvement over last year." The stock promptly plummeted because the "tone" of the statement seemed less optimistic than the public's expectation. Indeed, the statement was conservatively cautious, as the event showed. Still, it seems odd to pillory a man for careful words. What if he'd touted his stock —and been wrong?

Finally, where's the virtue in saying-nothing-until-it's-official, a policy behind which some businessmen take refuge and some lawmakers would make a rule? This too can do injury by misleading people. The questions here posed are deliberately metaphysical, not to treat them as unanswerable questions in ethics but to express some wonder whether they permit laws to be drawn to fit all occasions. In this area men are dealing with the imponderable questions of judgment, judgment to be exercised both by those who speak and those who listen. And anybody who has spent more than a quarter century around Wall Street knows that that world is muchly improved on both counts.

Facts that can be determined—quarterly earnings, dividends, and the like—are universally announced as soon as they can be ascertained. The practice of company presidents talking "off the record" to privileged inner groups has all but disappeared. There's a growing practice of making interim assessments to the leading press media, where all who are interested may read and be informed. If there is still hanky-panky, and there is, the mark of its rareness is the furor even a suspicion of it creates. If the "rules" can be further improved, and doubtless they can, they need only follow further along their present course toward full and quick disclosure of the "hard facts."

Yet after all this is said—and done—there remains that area which must be left to the good sense of those on both sides of the dialogue. Rules that try to answer every question and protect every fool always cause more trouble than they cure. There's no need to read dire plots into every luncheon conversation. All the same, the next fellow who asks me over the soup how's business will see a pudgy face staring in frozen imitation of Buster Keaton.

May 4, 1965

A LESSON IN VIGILANCE

IT's been many a year now since the Richard Whitney case, which ended with his expulsion from the New York Stock Exchange and later imprisonment for mishandling other people's money. That case was a national scandal. Recently another stock exchange member was expelled and one of the firm's partners has been charged with "fraudulent acts." This time there has been no public outcry against the whole of Wall Street. That alone, I think, suggests how much the intervening years have changed not only the complexion of the financial community and the stock exchange itself, but also the attitude of the public toward Wall Street. But there is more to this particular story, and it is worth telling how it all came about and what the reaction to it has been among those most immediately concerned.

The story began when the New York Stock Exchange, as it has been doing for many years now, called for a routine surprise audit of member firms' accounts. One purpose of this audit is to make sure that every member firm maintains at all times a fixed, and safe, ratio between its liabilities and its capital. In measuring a firm's capital the rules are exceedingly strict; the value of its stock exchange membership, for example, cannot be included and even the bluest of blue-chip stocks are valued at only a part of their current market value.

As a result of this routine audit, it was found that Du Pont, Homsey and Company of Boston, a relatively small firm, was in technical violation of this capital ratio rule. By itself this is not unprecedented; perhaps five or six times a year some firm may, very briefly, fall short on its capital requirements; in every case it is immediately required to bring its capital up to the mark. In this instance, however, there was a prior violation on record and the exchange officials decided to bring charges against the firm before the Board of Governors and to discipline it. Thereupon a special auditor from the exchange was sent to go over the books more thoroughly.

This auditor did not like what he saw. He was promptly reinforced by the exchange's chief auditor and for several weeks the accounts of this firm were thoroughly scrutinized. The result was that the Securities and Exchange Commission and the district attorney's office were notified.

It seems to me that the significant thing here is not that a bad apple cropped up among the stock exchange members, but rather that the bad apple was found in the process of a routine check to make sure of compliance with definite and strict requirements. Furthermore, both the requirements and the check on them were instituted by the stock exchange itself. Neither the SEC nor the district attorney had anything to do with uncovering the situation.

And there is more. In an unprecedented statement, its president said that the exchange "feels that its moral responsibilities [in protecting the firm's customers] are not ended with the act of expulsion" against the Boston firm. If, after the firm's accounts are straightened out, there are losses to some customers, then the exchange itself hopes to make restitution.

Here, then, is a clear lesson in the rewards of self-vigilance. Sound rules and a system for spotting transgressors quickly; prompt and forceful action at the first faint signs that all is not as it should be—these are the essential ingredients for avoiding more federal intervention and, more importantly, for protecting the financial community's good name and the money of those who come to it. If this case suggests anything, it is the need for even more vigilance and a full appreciation by all exchange members that sound exchange rules are the best safeguards.

For it is in this way that the New York Stock Exchange, as an institution, fulfils its true function. It is not the function of the stock exchange to sell stocks or drum up business for its members. In addition to providing a market place, its job, which it has performed so well in this case, is to be sure that all who do take their business there can do so in confidence that their affairs are honestly conducted under the watchful eye of a vigilant guardian.

October 10, 1960

GAMES PEOPLE PLAY

MARK Twain, who achieved some fame as a Mississippi riverboat pilot, has not been honored as much as he ought to be for his pioneering work in statistical analysis. You'll recall that Mr. Twain, who among other learned degrees held a doctorate from Oxford, did a depth analysis of the mortality statistics and by adjusting the correlation coefficients to the extrapolation of the skew pattern concluded that nobody could live to be eleven years old but that those who did were immortal.

The famed philosopher, who in his portraits somewhat resembles Hal Holbrook, also turned his attention to the stock market. His conclusion has never been refuted; namely, that May is a dangerous month to speculate. Other dangerous months shown by his analysis: October, June, January, March, November, August, February, April, December, September, and July.

From this pioneering conjunction of the stock market and mathematical analysis there has, subsequently, never been a respite. Every prophetic principle, from astrology to Zoroastrian metaphysics, has been used to solve the esoteric mysteries of the stock market. The forecast systems flourish especially in boom times. Also at times when the market can't seem to make up its mind what it's doing. Also when it looks like it's made up its mind to go down.

The excuse for these remarks, including the recollections of Dr. Twain's seminal work, is a fresh reprint of an old stock market study by the Graduate School of Business of the University of

Chicago. That plus the fact that just the other day the elevator operator asked whether he should stay in or get out of the market. So maybe there's some passing interest in the subject.

The Chicago study, you'll remember, took an outrageous approach to the whole problem. It didn't seek a better system of market judging. It simply measured with a computer the results of various investment methods against the actual performance of the stock market. The results shook up Wall Street. They were, in fact, enough to destroy a man's simple faith that somehow there's a way to know where the little red ball will drop or what General Motors will sell for tomorrow. The Chicago analysts recorded closing prices for 1,700 New York Stock Exchange stocks over a thirty-five-year span, adjusting for stock-splits, dividends, rights offerings, mergers, spin-offs, and, for some companies, the distribution of warehouse receipts for whiskey.

With this tipsy conglomeration of data the researchers spent four years searching for Newtonian Great Principles. What they found more nearly resembled the Heisenberg Uncertainty Principle. Not that everything was confusing. The data proved that it pays to be tax exempt. Likewise the study found that over the long run you're better off if your assets earn 9 per cent rather than 3 per cent. And discovered that the return on investments made at the height of a bull market, as in 1929, is less than if you buy at other times. Number these among the rewards of research.

All the same, there were some shockers. For one, the study calculated frequencies for the purchase and sale of stocks during the sixteen business expansions and the sixteen contractions over the period; one stock over 420 months can be bought and sold at approximately 88,000 combinations of dates. It turns out that, for the most part, you're wasting your time trying to decide whether to put that order in today or tomorrow. Or, in the words of the report, "Generally it doesn't pay to try to be clever in timing."

But the conclusion most disconcerting to clever people was that even when they are professional experts they don't do any better than ordinary folks. This was tested by selecting some stock portfolios purely at random. This whimsical investment program was then compared with the performance of the mutual funds, taken as a group. "On the average," reported Professor James Lorie, "returns to investors in such funds were slightly less than from investment in the randomly selected portfolios." Much the same result came when the random portfolios were compared with the performance of other professional managers, such as the managers of trusts, pension funds, and the like.

Two comments. This is not an argument against mutual funds or other professional managers, as some people took it; their services are useful to investors on many counts. The second comment is that the somewhat startling conclusion about the pros versus the dart players isn't as irrational as it seems. The explanation is that when you get competent people competing with competent people in selecting stocks they will all seek out the same information and generally make the same judgments.

Furthermore, because they deal, collectively, in such huge sums the judgments they make about what will happen can have an appreciable effect on what does happen. If they all, for the same good reasons, expect the XYZ stock to rise (or fall), their combined actions will tend to make it do just that. The effect is intensified if the sheep, hearing what the goats are doing, decide to follow.

There's no profound philosophy to be drawn from all this. But there may be a salutary reminder or two. One of them, doubtless superfluous right at the moment, is to be skeptical of those who in nice boom markets assure you it "can't" go down because of all the built-in checks and balances, the sophistication of analysts' techniques, or what-have-you. The converse is an equal skepticism at expert unanimity in gloom.

You might even spare some leftover skepticism for those

experts in Washington with the prescience to have the future all buttoned down, knowing just how to beat the averages and assure us unbroken prosperity forever. But maybe the best reminder is the simplest. If you want some advice on what the stock market is going to do, don't ask me, ask the elevator operator.

May 10, 1966

INFLATION AND BUSINESS

FOR almost a generation now the thinking of the country has been pretty much dominated by the idea that inflation is a sure warranty of prosperity. True, inflation has been complained of on many grounds, such as its unfairness to widows and pensioners and its propensity for turning economic life into a rat race. But while these ill effects have been deplored, it has still been accepted as gospel that inflation will nonetheless keep business swirling and provide a bulwark against depression.

As preached in Washington, this gospel says that while inflation cuts the purchasing power of each dollar this effect is more than offset by the increased number of dollars which increase purchasing power and raise the Gross National Product. It's even been argued that by this simple device a multi-billion-dollar government deficit will create a surplus because the government will get back so many more of the cheaper dollars in taxes. The government is now budgeting on this theory.

Along Wall Street and Main Street this has been interpreted to mean that you can protect yourself against the disadvantages of inflation and reap its rewards simply by buying real estate or common stocks. After all, if inflation has become a "way of life," how can the stock market go any way but up? These articles of faith rest upon two assumptions. The first is that the inflationary process can be endlessly repeated with the same stimulating effect. The second is that the effect will be more jobs for labor and more profits for business.

This, of course, was the effect in the first years of the postwar inflation. The war years not only brought huge increases in the supply of credit dollars but they also left the country with an enormous pent-up demand for just about everything. So from 1946 to 1950 inflation and rising profits for business did go hand in hand. For one illustration, in 1946 the earnings per share of the stocks in the Dow-Jones industrial average amounted to $13.62. A bare four years later, in 1950, they had doubled, to $30.70. Here, or so it seemed, was proof positive of the doctrine. And so the country continued in the decade after—through Democratic and Republican Administrations—a policy of inflationary deficits. The public not only accepted this from the politicians; it encouraged them.

But later the effects were quite different. Although the monetary inflation continued, with both wages and prices rising, the number of unemployed steadily increased and the profits of business increased hardly at all. Look at the earnings per share of those same companies that make up the industrial average: in 1950, $30.70 a share; in 1960, $32.21 a share. Or consider the case of one of our biggest industrial companies, which has lately been in the news, U.S. Steel. The first postwar inflation shot its earnings from $1.22 a share to $3.65 a share. But in 1960, after ten more years of inflation, it could raise its earnings to only $5.17 a share. And the following year its earnings dropped below what they had been a decade earlier.

This being the case, why did the stock market take off on the biggest boom in history? For it did. During the same decade, the Dow-Jones industrial average shot up from the 200 level to the 700 level. The market price of U.S. Steel itself rose from $20 (adjusted for changes in the number of shares) to $100.

The explanation can be found in another statistic. In 1950, for the shares represented in the industrial average, the market price was about seven times the per-share earnings. In 1960 this price-earnings ratio was more than 21. On U.S. Steel stock, to choose a particular example, the price-earnings ratio skyrocketed from less than 9 to more than 27. In short, for stocks having roughly the same earnings capacity a decade apart, people at the end of the decade were paying many times the price for those same dollar earnings as at the beginning of the decade. They did this largely under the spell of the gospel that continued inflation was a guaranty of more economic growth in everything, including profits for business.

This gospel never made much sense; at the very most it expressed only a half-truth. Conceivably if the inflation of the monetary supply could spread its effects evenly at all times throughout the economy, profits measured in dollars might have increased. Of course this would still give only an illusion of greater prosperity because the dollars would be worth less. But in practice even this did not happen. The costs of doing business—particularly labor costs but also taxes—rose far more rapidly than prices for the end product. At the moment wage costs are still rising; prices are not.

Thus the cost squeeze, dramatized most recently by the steel industry. Its wage costs went up another 10 cents an hour. It could not raise its prices. But it's not only in the stock market that the boons of inflation have proved a delusion. By almost any standard you choose for measurement—unemployment, our economic position in world trade, the strength of the dollar, as well as business profits—a decade of almost continuous monetary inflation has simply not produced the wonders that the economic managers promised in their prospectus.

I don't know, really, why anybody ever thought it would.

May 7, 1962

317

XI

A WHIG
ON WALL STREET

HOW TO PICK A POCKET
OR TWO

To a small-town fellow come to the big city it was bound to happen sooner or later, and finally it did. On the way to Wall Street, that den of iniquity, my pocket was picked in the subway, that haunt of the huddled masses. Along with a couple of credit cards, an unfilled prescription for the drugstore, and a shopping list from the lady of the house, this skillful disciple of Fagin made off with $100, which for years I've kept secreted in the back of my wallet against such grave emergencies as running out of expense-account money in San Antonio or St. Paul.

Now being imbued with a Puritan ethic, I do not approve of pickpockets, especially those who pick my own. But in all honesty I must confess that purely from the standpoint of the nation's economic balance sheet there was no net loss to the country. Indeed, if some of the economic theories bruited about today are correct, it could be argued that the nation's economy had been helped thereby.

For my loss of $100 was somebody else's gain of $100, the one canceling out the other insofar as economic statistics are concerned. Furthermore, since there was a transfer of funds from one party to another there was a gain in the Gross National Product as well as the national income. The fact that I paid an exorbitant price for the service received—namely, a lesson in personal finance management—is no concern in abstract economics.

Finally, I suspect the unknown artist of the subway is less well endowed with worldly goods than I am, less likely to keep the money out of circulation as idle savings for a rainy day. So this transfer of my funds to his pocket probably resulted in an increase in the nation's consumer spending.

Whatever my personal feelings, then, the result represents a consummation devoutly to be wished by the influential thinkers of the day. The whole object of current economic policy is to increase the transfer of funds, raising the statistics of national income and the GNP, and especially such transfers of funds as may increase consumer spending. The sociological objective is called the "redistribution of income." Hence the great emphasis on government spending, which has gotten to be a large part of the GNP. There's no surer and more efficient way to transfer huge sums than to take taxes from citizens of, say, New York and spend them in New Mexico or Mississippi. According to this thinking, it's a further help if the dollars can be transferred from corporations and rich folk, who might have a proclivity toward savings, to the hands of those who will inject it more quickly into the spending stream.

We are told that the good effects of all this are enhanced if the government, unlike my friend on the subway, can spend more than it takes or at least seem to. Big deficits, especially those arising from tax cuts, allow more dollars to be put in some people's pockets. True, this is illusory; what the government spends it must take away from somebody in some form. Nonetheless there's no denying it's less painful to steal a bit from everybody's dollars by inflation than to take the money away from them in immediate taxes.

On the subway I had a blissful ignorance of being plucked until, much later in the day, I found myself less well off than I thought. And even now I think there must be many a helpful pickpocket who wishes that policemen understood the ethics of the new economics.

March 13, 1963

POSTSCRIPT: the above comments somehow reached the Russian magazine *Soviet Press,* house organ of the USSR Union of Journalists. The following is the reaction of a Mr. I. Davidow, appearing in the *Soviet Press:*

> It is possible that the above figures (in the preceding item, concerning the cost of the New York newspaper strike to those involved and to the government) acquired special interest in the reasoning of Mister Royster, the editor of the newspaper *Journal* (town of Vermont, state of Connecticut).
>
> "Whose Pocket Is Being Picked?"—Such was the disturbing theme of the leading article by Royster in a recent number of the aforementioned newspaper. The event which suggested this theme to Royster was an adventure in the New York subway.
>
> However, as the author himself writes, when one commutes from a small town to a big one, sooner or later such an adventure is bound to happen, and indeed it did.
>
> "On the way to Wall Street, this nest of vices [As we see, Royster is not lacking in powers of observation.—I. D.], my pocket was ravished in the noisy and bustling throngs of the subway," the editor of the *Journal* stated.
>
> Royster, from whose pocket the thief extracted documents, druggists' prescriptions and $100, properly admitted that he used what had happened to him as the theme for his statement. True, it was in rather unexpected form: he came to the conclusion that "according to economic theory, if somehow an adroit pocket-picking operation could immedi-

ately be put to use, it could be of great aid to the economy of the U.S.A."

In what manner?

"We do not excuse the habit of picking someone else's pocket, particularly if this pocket belongs to us," writes Royster, "but in line with contemporary thought it is necessary to halt before these facts and do some thinking."

And Royster pursues these reflections further. At that moment, as $100 moved from our pocket to another, we read in his article, the Gross National Product, as well as the national income of the United States, showed a definite gain, in that money migrated "from a corporation of rich people, with a tendency toward accumulation, to the hands of those who quickly will put it in circulation."

In a word, pickpockets perform a socially useful function.

Later on, this economist from Vermont draws the courageous and, it would seem, justifiable conclusion that the American ruling circles, as a matter of fact, practice this very same "economic policy" of the pickpocket in the New York subway, whether by means of inflation or by taxes, etc.

We will not intrude with an analysis of the scientific value of the *Journal* editor's reasoning. We only pay just due to his journalistic skill in interpreting certain phenomena in American life as they really are.

BACK TO BRYAN

I ONLY remember William Jennings Bryan as an old man wrestling with the devil and Clarence Darrow. I wish I could have known him in the days of his glory, when as editor of the Omaha *World Herald* he was wrestling with the crown of golden thorns, the horns of William McKinley, and the shades of Adam Smith. For it always struck me that Bryan had the simplest, most straightforward, and logically irrefutable diagnosis of poverty I ever heard of. Poverty, Bryan argued, is when people don't have enough money—an observation that surely ranks in acuteness with Cal Coolidge's remark that unemployment arises when people don't have jobs.

Moreover, Bryan had a straightforward program to cure poverty that was simplicity itself. Since poverty is not having enough money, and since one of the sovereign powers of government is the authority to create money, Bryan reasoned that if the government would just stop being so miserly and would coin enough money then poverty would be easily abolished. Bryan's trouble was that he was a man ahead of his time. Today he would find himself right at home on the Council of Economic Advisers and his ideas echoed in the Johnson Administration's current "poverty program."

Not all the Johnson poverty program, to be sure, is a throwback to the nineteenth century. Some of it, like the proposed revival of Roosevelt's Civilian Conservation Corps, is only about thirty years old. Other parts are just current projects wrapped in a new package: federal money for urban and area development; federal aid to handy and worthy causes like schools, libraries, and hospitals; the medicare plan; expanded minimum wage coverage and unemployment insurance.

But the real aim of the "poverty program" is not to urge these things on their individual merits, of which perhaps there are some, but rather to use them as an excuse for creating more government-made money and as devices for spreading that money around. A library is a good thing in itself, and can be a comfort to the poor equally with the rich, but nobody pretends that reading a good book cures hunger pangs.

The essential point in the new economics is that the government must spend more in total than it takes in from taxes. Even the proposed tax cut, which certainly has merits on its own, is part of the plan for making the government's deficit larger than it would otherwise be. And if President Johnson doesn't promise a deficit quite as large as President Kennedy might have offered, it's still not small.

With all these spending programs, plus the tax cut, Mr. Johnson plans to spend a minimum of $5 billion more than the expenditures in the last fiscal year. For fiscal 1964 and 1965 combined the deficit will be not less than $15 billion. A small part of this may be borrowed from the real savings of people, as in the Savings Bond Program, but most of it—and this is the actual idea—will be simply created by the government.

True, there have been some technical advances since Bryan's day. The Great Commoner was still imprisoned by the idea that money needed to be backed up by something so that it would represent at least something of value. Thus while he was impatient with the restrictiveness of the gold standard, he could think of nothing better than to base the money on both gold and silver. This bimetallism would have increased the money stock considerably. Yet it would have had its limitations. In time the rising prices from the cheapening of the money would have meant that again there would not be enough money to meet the demand, and the poor—though having more dollars—would be poor again. The Bryan plan was up against the fact that the quantity of silver, while more plentiful than gold, is still finite.

The new economics suffers no such deficiency. Walter Heller wouldn't dream of advocating bimetallism. The current doctrine is nonmetallism. A dollar now is just a piece of paper; even the Treasury's silver certificates are being withdrawn. The beauty of this is that the supply of paper is practically infinite. You can print up all the dollars you wish, and with a little ingenuity you can put them in the hands of the poor by the bale. It's not very fashionable to point out that this won't cure poverty any more than incantations will cure cancer. Senator Goldwater, poor fellow, tried to point it out and all he got for his pains was a public pillorying as a heartless fellow "soft on poverty." And to-day any economist who challenges the fashionable view risks be-ing read out of the fraternity, or at best being kindly tolerated as a museum piece.

Yet some people, I suspect, have a few nagging doubts. The war on poverty has been the long occupation of mankind and the worthy aim of every economic thinker from Adam Smith to Karl Marx. But there is no instance on record of poverty being abolished by kings clipping coins or parliaments printing up money. It has come closest to being abolished in those lands, like the United States, where people have the most economic freedom to lift themselves from poverty and where the government has done the least damage to the money for which the poor labor in order to escape poverty.

Those doubts, just possibly, explain why Bryan was twice defeated for the Presidency by William McKinley. The common sense of the people may have suggested to them that if it were all so simply done just by minting coins and handing them to the poor, then the heartbreaking battle would have been won long ago.

That double defeat, which blocked that wonderful poverty program, may also explain why McKinley has got such a bad name. What it doesn't explain is why it's reactionary to want to turn the clock back to McKinley but forward-looking to turn it back to Bryan.

February 4, 1964

VERILY, A PROPHET

C OME now, and let us reason together, saith the Lord. And so also, at every opportunity, saith Lyndon Johnson. This advice from the prophet Isaiah has certainly served Mr. Johnson well. By appealing to men's vanity that they are reasonable the President has gotten a number of things done that might otherwise have been difficult. Congressmen, for example, have rushed through a number of hasty laws rather than risk the charge of being unreasonable with questions. Labor and management, bombarded with the biblical text in long night sessions, have agreed to wage contracts that satisfied neither rather than lose the accolade of reason.

The steel industry has been dissuaded from raising prices to meet the cost of the raised wages. So has the aluminum industry. Banks have been persuaded to frown upon higher interest rates. All manner of enterprises have agreed to reduce foreign investment programs, voluntarily. Copper producers too are voluntarily cooperating in an "orderly" disposal of copper surpluses in the government stockpile. And so on. Throughout it all the words of Isaiah have marked the President as a most reasonable man, particularly within the business community. At the White House businessmen have found a welcome, a courteous hearing, and an interest in business prosperity. To most businessmen it's seemed a lovely honeymoon.

Or did until lately. What with a few things like the dumping of the government's aluminum and copper to break the market, the mood has changed. Now you hear grumbling that Mr. Johnson is a very unreasonable man. This is not really fair to the President. For if you look at the problems from his point of view, his methods of suasion are quite reasonable. Consider: It is a fact that the total outflow of dollars from the U. S. exceeds the inflow of other currencies and this has created a serious balance-of-payments problem which, if unresolved, threatens the stability of the dollar itself.

This excessive outflow is composed of two parts, one the dollars paid out by the government and the other the dollars paid out by the public, the largest being private investment abroad. But the government does not want to reduce its own spending abroad because this would interfere with the things the political leaders want to do with this foreign spending. It follows, then, that the people must be stopped from spending their money abroad, whether to buy lace in Belgium or to build factories in South Africa. If you agree that the government's desires are paramount to any other interests, then it follows that if people cannot be persuaded to check their spending "voluntarily" they must be made to.

Or again: It is a fact that if the price of steel or aluminum or other commodities increases, the effect will be to decrease the purchasing value of the dollar. That is, we shall have price inflation. This will have consequences for everybody, including the government itself, seeking to buy things with dollars.

There are two ways to deal with inflation. One way is to stop creating the new money and credit which causes the inflation. This would halt the process entirely, but of course it would mean that political leaders would have to postpone many things they want to do which cost money. For the political leaders this is patently an unreasonable suggestion. There is left, then, only the recourse of trying to hide the inflation. Price rises must be stopped at any cost, because if they take place they undo the sought-for benefits of the inflation itself. It follows then that people must be stopped from raising prices no matter what happens to their costs— voluntarily, if they are "reasonable," involuntarily if they aren't.

There is nothing particularly new in any of this. It is simply the current outcropping of a fundamental clash of interest between the political part of society—i.e., the government—and the economic arm of society—i.e., business. This divergence of interest is timeless, immutable, and unavoidable, regardless of the form of government or the manner in which "business" is organized.

It is just as true in Soviet Russia, for example, as it is here, even though everything in Russia is ostensibly under the government. That is to say, the political leaders in the Kremlin and the managers of Communist farms and industrial enterprises want to put the economic resources of the country to different uses. The reason is simple. The function of the economic organizations is to create wealth for the community. The function of the political organization is to spend the community's resources.

This isn't an invidious comparison. We need government to spend our resources for community purposes, on such obvious things as defense or highways, or on such other things as education, welfare programs, or whatever the people consent to. The point is simply to note that the rivalry is inevitable. Never at any point in history has the economic part of the community been able to create enough wealth to satisfy all the desires of the political part for wealth to spend. Nor will it.

In the inevitable tug of war between "business" and "government" there have been times when one or the other has been in unquestioned control, and always to the injury of society. The remarkable achievement of this country, up to now, is the relative power balance between the two. Business has never controlled the government; we have never had a totalitarian political control over the economy.

But we bemuse ourselves if we are misled by brief honeymoons. Wage and price controls are no more unreasonable than dumping copper to make men do one's bidding. Let us reason together, says the President, halting before the prophecy in the next verse: "If ye be willing and obedient, ye shall eat the good of the land. But if ye refuse and rebel, ye shall be devoured with the sword."

November 24, 1965

332

FACTS OF LIFE

T HE rubric which heads this essay is also the title of one of those delightful stories in which Somerset Maugham so often pinned life to its sardonic facts. It's a ribald sort of tale to turn the copybook maxims topsy-turvy.

The story, as you'll recall, deals with the adventures of a young man sent on his first solo trip abroad laden with sage fatherly advice. Don't gamble. Beware of lending money to smooth-talking strangers. And shun the company of smooth-talking ladies of the evening. Even if you've forgotten the story, you can guess what happens. The adventuring young man gambles on a charming stranger and on the wheels at Monte Carlo, both of which increase his fortunes, and he winds up with a wild evening's gambol in gay Paree which returns him both pleasure and profit.

Thus is sage advice confounded. The tale ends with the young man convinced of the stuffiness of fathers, and poor father himself reduced to helpless frustration. Recounting the story at his club, the father gets not sympathy but gales of laughter.

Perhaps you'll find the story a little less amusing now than when you were young, but the frustration will certainly be familiar. You can say, as you doubtless do, drive carefully, or deliver other wise little homilies. But the facts of life are that not every wild drive on a holiday highway ends in a smash, nor every teenage drinking party in a Darien disaster.

The difficulty with copybook maxims is that perforce they

rest mainly on probabilities—drive like a madman long enough and you're almost sure to park in the cemetery. But not absolutely and positively. And meanwhile, why spoil the fun? That's a point of view, let's confess it, we all sometimes partake when the probabilities deal with facts not experienced in our own lives. History repeats itself for the same reason that the tables at Las Vegas are crowded afresh each season.

The annals of business, for instance, are thick with examples of enterprises built high by pyramiding credit in easy times only to come crashing down in ruin, even as frantic creditors rush in to pour good money after bad. But with the history books full of Samuel Insulls, there are supposedly hard-headed businessmen right today walking the same precipice. The newspapers are filled with their tales.

Even whole nations aren't immune. Almost every economic absurdity you can think of has a glorious history of repeat performances. At one time or another ancient Pharaohs and Roman emperors tried all the tricks of clipping coins and then all the devices of controlling the resultant inflation, including the beheading of those wicked, wicked speculators who got blamed for it all. And not all of it is ancient history either. Any economic textbook, including those of Professor Samuelson, will cite you examples of nations come to grief defying the stuffy copybook maxims of fiscal policy. And the last great collapse of the world's monetary system built on just such a defiant pyramid is within the memory of many living men.

No matter. With a little bit of luck Sam Insull might have made it, or so anyway runs the comforting thought for those now engaged in our more renowned current juggling acts. After all, the world is different from Insull's day—isn't it?—and governments just aren't going to let things happen the way they happened before. Today's government managers are too smart, aren't they?

Look at the British. For years they've been following the

classical road to trouble—repeated internal deficits with rising wages, costs, and prices; taxes that discourage investment in new facilities; jogging along with a mounting balance-of-payments deficit. Then the Labor government suddenly upped taxes, upped welfare spending, upped tariffs, threatened renationalization of the steel industry, and generally comported itself in happy socialistic fashion. So much so that not long ago it seemed that the collapse of the British pound was at hand. But no. Like Mr. Maugham's youngster, Britain found that something turned up. In this case, $3 billion from kindly Uncle Sam and assorted friends. So why, really, should anyone expect them to reform their ways and spoil the fun?

Meanwhile, back at the ranch, President Johnson was informed that the United States just lost another $37 million of its gold supply because it too has been spending more abroad than it takes in. But in Washington this was considered good news because the rate of loss was smaller than heretofore, which means it will be longer before we run out entirely or the dollar gets into trouble. Anyway, don't worry. The rest of the world can't let the dollar topple, can it?

As for our fun with inflation, who wants to stop it? After all, the statistics show quite clearly that the dollar isn't rotting nearly as fast as it did a few years ago. Its current rate of depreciation is only about 1.3 per cent a year, whereas between 1945 and now the dollar lost about 70 per cent of its value. At the new, slower rate it'll still be a long time before it takes a dollar to buy a loaf of bread. Even that, so we're told, won't matter too much, a disappearing dollar being a small price to pay for the pleasure and profit of an economy with no more poor and never any more depressions.

Well, it's always possible the yeasayers may be right. Stuffy naysayers can only note what's happened in the past to others. No one can say absolutely and positively that a government can't go on forever spending more than it takes in, just because the probabilities are against it. It's always possible that somebody will find a system to beat the bank at Monte Carlo.

And of course there's always luck to return sardonic laughter to sage advice. For one of the facts of life, though it confounds philosophers and fathers, is that the wages of sin sometimes aren't collected until we are too old to care. Still, Mr. Maugham was clever not to write the sequel. When you're just spinning a yarn it's best to quit with the joke and pretend everybody lived happily ever after.

December 3, 1964

DOWN THE UP STAIRCASE

I N case you hadn't noticed lately, the cost of living is inching up. Slowly but relentlessly month by month the Consumer Price Index tacks on another half a point, which is no surprise to the lady in your house who pushes the grocery cart. And in case you're wondering what's going to happen next, the portents are for more of the same. Even the official seers in the Council of Economic Advisers dispute no more the fact of inflation. The debaters differ only on the question, How much?

In case you're puzzled as to how you got into the situation where the dollar you earn today will daily buy less and less, the explanation is quite simple. It was planned that way. Indeed, until the inflation got a bit more than planned for, the gentlemen of the CEA, the members of the Cabinet, and the political leaders of the controlling party boasted of the accomplishment. They had, so they said, unlocked the secret of inflation without pain.

And in case you're interested in what they are planning to do now to mitigate the unplanned effects of the planned inflation, that too has become clear enough. Your governors are going to protect you against the rising cost of living by raising your cost of living. Or to express it in terms deemed more suitable for grave talk around the economic council table, the government is going to increase your taxes.

Marvelous, is it not?

Of course to savor the full flavor of this marvelous idea, you have to go backward a bit in time to the moment when it was

337

decided to send the economy charging up the staircase. This was several years ago when, as you'll recall, we had to "get the country moving again" out of all that sluggish Eisenhower prosperity. The means adopted were several-fold, ranging from tax cuts to enlarged spending for both old and new programs, spiced with dashes of easy credit. But the purpose of all was the same, to open the economic throttle as wide as possible, in the conceit that such obstacles as domestic inflation or a foreign balance-of-payments problem could be safely skirted with deft management.

To be fair, nobody then anticipated the Vietnam war with all its imponderable economic effects. Had they been so prescient, perhaps they would have done otherwise. Also, it's only fair to concede that it is this unanticipated Vietnam war—with its extraordinary pressures on the budget, on materials, and on manpower —which now threatens to play such hob with all the nice plans. An explanation, however, is not the same thing as an excuse. It's certainly equally fair for those critical of the economic policies of the past five years to point out that men who deliberately plan to stretch resources to the limit, with no allowance for the unexpected, hardly deserve the name of prudent.

Moreover, neither explanation nor excuse alters the fact. The economic impact of the Vietnam war threatens serious economic problems only because it catches us with everything already taut as a drum. This tautness is felt in many places. Many defense commodities already under booming demand are getting in desperately short supply. Manpower shortages are busting every wage guideline. The balance-of-payments deficit is worsened by overseas war expenses.

But most of us most feel the pinch at the shopping center. What the economist calls "disposable personal income" disappears more quickly and buys less food, clothing, housing, or housewares. What we have, in the economist's phrase, is demand-pull inflation. What you have, in the phrase of the lady of the house,

338

is not as much useful money as you thought you had. This is the inflation pain the wise men of Washington are going to ease by raising your taxes.

The theory here, in case it's escaped you, is that higher taxes will soak up some of the "excess money" and so reduce the demand-pull. This excess in the money supply came from the government in the first place, since the government supplies the money. So what is more logical, if this excess money supplied by the government is causing you trouble, than for the government to take back what it put out to cause the trouble?

It might be quite logical if the government, taking the money from you in taxes, would then withdraw it from the money supply, thus decreasing the demand-pull. But this isn't part of the plan. The money the government takes from you in extra taxes will be spent elsewhere, merely shifting the demand-pull from your local shopping center to some other place. Indubitably, raising the price of government will leave you with less money to spend. The same thing would happen, to be sure, if the price of cigarettes went up. But if the price of cigarettes goes up, that's inflationary; the President said so himself. Anybody who raises the price of steel is a robber baron and gets investigated by the FBI.

Mind you, nobody wants to raise the price of government either. But everybody agrees that if necessary it's just the trick to halt inflation. The price of government is different. For one thing, the price of government, being called a tax, isn't figured into commodity price indices. You can explain to your wife, therefore, that a bigger tax bill hasn't officially raised your cost of living at all. Just eat less.

For another thing, if the price of cigarettes goes up you can defeat its effects as a net reducer of disposable income for other things by cutting down on smoking. You could even postpone buying a steel T-bar. But when the government raises taxes, you've had it. You just plain don't have that money to buy any-

339

thing, regardless of the price. This should make it clear why raising taxes is such a marvelous idea. It helps the government keep its spending up but saves you from paying higher prices by keeping your spending down.

April 1, 1966

TOMORROW ALWAYS COMES

I T was Scarlett O'Hara, that scatterbrained minx, who compressed in a phrase an enduring bit of philosophy. As Rhett Butler walked off into the sunset, the little lady gently wiped away a tear and remarked to no one in particular, "I'll think about that tomorrow." Over the years that cheerful thought has done yeoman service for all those to whom the realities of the world are sometimes too harsh for contemplation, which includes all of us at one time or another. But it is the especial motto of adolescents and politicians.

The young, of course, adopt it out of ignorance. It's not easy for them to imagine that what they do today, having fun kicking over the traces or knocking down icons, will have its consequences tomorrow; or that someday they too must wrestle with the same prosaic problems that make their parents careworn. Anyway, when you are young, tomorrows seem very plentiful and a long way off.

With politicians the motto is often a matter of policy. A Winston Churchill may foresee in the Nazi clouds over Europe a gathering storm for the world. Those in office usually see no need to borrow trouble from the future. They have enough problems keeping people happy in their own times, failing which they may not be long in office. Politics is in part the art of postponing trouble until somebody else will have to deal with it. This isn't always as wicked as moralists may suppose. It's true enough that not every distant cloud turns into a storm. Generations that were

XI · A Whig on Wall Street

the despair of their elders turn out quite well, and despair of their young in turn. Many of yesterday's great political crises disappeared no man knows whither, and sometimes passed more quietly for lack of ill-considered remedies.

Yet it is also true, just as the copybook maxims have it, that today is the consequence of yesterday, in great affairs as in small, and to ignore it truly compounds trouble. Take a look at the problems which press down on President Johnson and hence on all of us. The most dramatic of them is Vietnam. That the present situation is a consequence of many past mistakes is self-evident. One mistake, and quite possibly the one fatally irreversible, was the manner in which the Diem government was overthrown, with the approval if not the instigation of the U.S. government. Its consequence was the chaos in the Vietnamese government which continues to this day and which makes every difficulty more difficult.

But the depressing thing is not alone the fact of mistakes. Political leaders are not relieved of human fallibility by election to office, and those of historical mind can trace a chain of errors backward through many political Administrations. What has compounded all has been the propensity to shove one day's problems to the morrow.

Since the Vietnam drama began, every Administration has tried to postpone true reckoning. The war has been patched, shored, and wrapped around with baling wire. At no point has our government been willing to take its harsh measure, to face and weigh the cruel choices, to act resolutely for one choice or another. The only policy has been to temporize. One result, planned or otherwise, has been to deceive the public. At every flare-up emissaries have jetted off to Saigon with the frequency of the Times Square shuttle, and returned to offer us reassurance that all goes well—right up to the point where it clearly doesn't. Vietnam is not the only example, either, of this temporizing. The problems of the world's monetary system may not be so dramatic for the man in the street; they are not the less important to him and they may be equally dramatic in their results.

It was the collapse of the world's monetary system in the twenties that ushered in the great depression, which surely ranks next to World War II as a holocaust in our time. Again we risk a like collapse, and from like causes. This possibility has long been known to all concerned. But to those in authority it has also appeared, at least until very recently, as a possibility of the remote future. The danger, then, was distant, whereas the necessary measures to avoid it—the halting of inflation, domestically and in international credit—meant the sacrifice of present political desires. A simple example: one part of the danger has been the ceaseless increase of U.S. dollar credits abroad, all of which are claims on our gold supply. But to halt the increase would mean not only curtailing foreign aid but also halting the budget deficits which create the dollar credits and, incidentally, enabling us for the time being to pay our debts in "printed" dollars. Few politicians want to do that.

So the balance-of-payments deficit—a symptom of the illness —continues unabated. So does the drain of our gold supply, as more foreign creditors grow wary of our "printed" dollars and demand payment in hard gold. So too, unabated, does the temporizing. Our government has cut the customs allowance for tourists. It has tried a special tax on purchases of foreign securities. It proposes to reduce the gold cover requirements for the American dollar. It scratches its head thinking of other patchwork measures. And of course it gets out the baling wire whenever, as repeatedly with the case of the pound sterling, some part of the system threatens to give way. The pound is shored up while the pressures continue on the whole dike.

It also gets out the reassurances. The temporary rescue of the pound is hailed as a master stroke. A drop in the size of the balance-of-payments deficit, or a quarter's reduction in the rate of our gold loss, is seen as a comforting sign. And any lone voice that suggests otherwise is dismissed as a contemporary Cassandra.

That may be the saddest part of it all. No one supposes great problems admit of easy solutions or expects unfailing wisdom of those appointed to lead. But surely what we ought to expect is that, unlike young ladies in crinoline, they not brush away the problems of the day to make them harsher tomorrow.

February 11, 1965

SOME THOUGHTS ON
AMERICAN BUSINESS

UNLIKE some of my friends in Washington these days, I am old enough to recall the great depression not as a studied lesson in a history book but as a remembered personal experience. No one needs to tell me that it was a time of troubles. Yet curiously it is hard to convince my younger friends that in those days not everyone was sunk in despair or believed the gloomy myth of the day that America was a "mature economy," with all its growth and greatness behind it.

Most of all, my young friends find it hard to believe that such depressed times could also have been times of economic growth. The myth today is that growth and prosperity are one and the same thing, so lack of growth and depression must also be equated. And because the U. S. does not seem to be growing as rapidly as it has at some other times, the fashion is once again to be gloomy about the future of the mature American economy. Well, it wasn't quite like that; and I doubt if it's going to be. There's no reason to believe that the pessimists about this country's economic future will be less wrong than they have been in the past. In any event, count me not among them.

This doesn't mean that I am cheerful about all that's being done to the American economy right now, or think it can be abused without a price. Rather, it's just that the record suggests the American economy can take an awful lot of abuse, and that it is sensible to be skeptical about the durability of high fashion in economic ideas. The delusions of one era pass as surely as those of another.

Take the fashionable ideas about growth. The thirties were, right enough, depression years. They were also years of growth by the yardsticks it's now the fashion to use. Between 1933 and 1940 the Gross National Product practically doubled and the national income more than doubled. This coinciding of growth and depression hardly suggests growth is a bad thing—between 1950 and 1960 there was the same doubling of the figures, and by anybody's standards the fifties were years of prosperity. It's simply a reminder that "growth" and "prosperity" are not synonymous. You can have one without the other, and in our history we frequently have.

Indeed, the history of the United States is strewn with passing economic troubles, recessions, depressions, and downright panics, but over the whole span of that history the bright years far outnumber the dark ones and the total record of economic growth and rising material well-being for its citizens is unsurpassed by any country in the world.

One moral from this is to beware of anybody who takes the statistics of a few brief years, gloomily projects them into the future, and then says the country is going to hell in a hack if it doesn't forthwith adopt some particular nostrum. There's another moral, too, when you look back at what brought on the times of troubles.

Almost without exception they were preceded by plain foolishness, the belief by people or politicians (or both) that the elementary principles of economic health no longer applied, or could be ignored. Land speculation, currency tinkering, wild credit expansion, overinvestment, unchecked government deficits, mounting state debts, attempts to prop prices, and a cavalier attitude toward "foreign" balance of payments—all these things have played their roles in the recessions of the past. Each was brought on by the excesses that went before. The trouble, of course, was that the excesses did not seem like excesses, nor the nostrums like quackery, until it was too late. It would take a bold man, looking at the nostrums now being offered, to say we have outgrown that human frailty.

Yet the real moral is that American business does not succumb easily to abuses. Even in the long and deep depression of 1873–8, as in the depression after 1929, there were many segments of the economy that retained much vigor, and some that even expanded. More to the point, the nation's recuperative powers have been immense. In the collapse of 1893—brought on by uncertainty over the dollar and a flight of capital to Europe— nearly five hundred banks failed and business bankruptcies were numbered in the thousands. Once confidence was restored in the dollar and the gold drain halted, recovery was rapid. Finally, none of the foolishness, or the troubles it caused, stopped the upward march of the American economy.

The reason, surely, lies in the enormous resiliency of private capitalism and a free enterprise society. Repeatedly, as in the 1930's, direct government efforts failed to recapture prosperity; just as repeatedly, once given a chance the country got itself moving again. Right after World War II, for example, it made liars out of some supposedly learned economists who again wailed that our growth was at an end, as well as our prosperity.

This resilience is not easy to define in a textbook. For essentially it involves the accumulating effects of thousands of minor decisions of individual businessmen, of their wit or their luck in finding ways under, around, or over whatever is the immediate economic problem. If the problem is depressed business, some people will find a way to sell things even so. If the problem is high taxes, somebody will find a way to accumulate capital and put it to use in spite of the tax collector. If the problem is foreign

347

competition, some businessman will find a way to meet that competition in spite of high costs. If the problem is inflation brought on by government tinkering with the money, some people will somehow find a way to protect their savings and capital to a marked degree.

Beyond that, the country has always come to recognize bad policies at last and halt them before the damage was irreparable. Nobody argues any more for 16-to-1 silver, any more than they do for prohibition. We still have the farm program, perennial deficit spending, lopsided labor laws, punitive taxes, and those who preach inflation as salvation. Yet already all of these things are in doubt if not yet disrepute. Even some politicians are beginning to wonder if you can fool the people forever.

Of course, even if you could plot these favorable factors on a piece of graph paper they still would not tell you whether business will be up or down in the next few months. But what this economic discussion is all about, or ought to be, is the reach of America's economic horizon in the years ahead, not just how business will be nursed along between now and the next election. If that be true, the real pessimists are those who tell us all will be lost if we don't swallow a huge dose of the latest patent medicine brewed by fearful men in Washington. These desperate economic remedies are prescribed only by those who no longer believe in the free economic system.

I still do. Nothing can guarantee this country against some painful consequences from bad economic policies. Yet when you take the enormous resources of this country, add to them the ingenuity and industry of its people, measure these things against its record for recuperation from punishment, and finally project it all against the horizon of opportunity that lies before it—then you cannot really be a pessimist about America's economic future.

March 5, 1963

XII

L'ENVOI

THE EPERMANIS STORY

EARLY the other morning a Navy transport slipped past the Ambrose Channel lightship, past the Narrows and Bedloe's Island, past the Battery and the towers on the tip of Manhattan. As it nudged its way into a slip, a corps of waiting dignitaries stood bareheaded at attention while a brass band struck up "The Star-Spangled Banner." The dignitaries and the band were there to meet a twelve-year-old girl from Latvia, Dace Epermanis by name, whom fortune picked as the 150,000th of the new refugees and the uncounted millionth of all the exiles that have fled from the ancient lands in the hope of haven.

The little girl in pigtails seemed bewildered by the pomp of the official welcome, which was to include a trip to Washington to meet the President of the United States. But there had been an earlier welcome that was simpler and less bewildering. And one that meant more than pomp to the twelve hundred other homeless who rode with her on the long sea voyage. The earlier welcome was a glimpse of the Mother of Exiles, the tall, bronzed lady who keeps vigil on an island home, the lady whose towering torch of imprisoned lightning was the harbor beacon for most of those hopes. Her greeting to the passing ship was little more than an upraised gesture and a few words on a graven tablet. Yet the compassionate lady who lifts her lamp by the doorway knows better than the dignitaries how to welcome the dispossessed. For she too was an immigrant. And she remembers what it is they flee from—and what it is they come here seeking.

Dace Epermanis, who by happenstance became a symbol, was born in Latvia, the second child and only daughter of Bernhards and Walda Epermanis, a middle-class farming family who tilled their own land. She was born in the last year of peace for Europe. Dace—she calls it "dah-chee"—does not remember the family farm as it used to be because when she was two years old the Russians destroyed the Republic and overran the country. Their farm was confiscated by the state and father Bernhards fled with his family to Riga.

A year later it was the Nazis' turn to invade the country. For a brief time the Epermanises went back to the farm, but it was very brief indeed because Bernhards quickly clashed with the new masters and was again driven out of his fields. Then the war tide turned and the Russians came a second time. This time the retreating Germans seized the whole family for forced labor, and for the next several years Dace wandered in an Odyssey of Europe as her parents were dragged from one labor battalion to another.

Yet perhaps all this was a blessing in disguise. When the liberation came in 1945 it found them not in Latvia with the Russians but in Bavaria, where they were able to get into a refugee resettlement camp. There was suffering behind, but there was hope ahead. Soon there was an opening for father Bernhards on new fields in New York. They patiently sat out the long waiting period and so arrived on a Sunday morning in the new land. Twelve years had brought wisdom to Dace. With simplicity she told the dignitaries her desire: "May God help me to find my place among other children."

The Epermanis story is personal and unique. Yet the Epermanis story is also the story of all the homeless and the tempest-tossed. They all come seeking a place for themselves among men. They are fleeing wars and man-made devastations; they come for peace. They have heard that the Mother of the Exiles does not stand like the ancient colossus with conquering limbs astride, and they are grateful. They have had enough of conquerors and conquering.

They are fleeing oppression and the man-made burdens that crush even hope in a poverty that knows no ending. They come risking new and unknown hardships in an alien land because they have heard that on the shores beyond the statue there is hope for a man and a future in the world for children. They do not flee because in their native lands they suffer from too little government. They do not come seeking a more attentive state to make them its wards and nurse them till the grave. If they were lured by the vision of the Great Provider they know many other nations where they might journey.

Dace Epermanis and the millions have come trusting in a chance to build destiny with their own hands and the help of God. There is no promise of security written on the pedestal of the Statue of Liberty. Her lamp lights only one hope, but it alone is bright enough to glow world-wide. It is only those too close to it who are blinded and go groping backward in the dark and wasteland.

The Mother of Exiles has watched ships pass with legions of the nameless and she knows what words to speak with her silent lips to bid them welcome. "Give me your tired, your poor," she whispers, "your huddled masses yearning to breathe free." This, and this alone, is the yearning and the promise.

May 18, 1950

A MOMENT IN TIME

ONE of the sad little things about life is that the moments that touch us most deeply are touched with triteness, that when the mind asks the most profound questions it grounds upon the most superficial shallows. The playwright who clothes his hero in inky black, or leads his lovers to a star-crossed end, deals in the stuff of literature, however feebly he draws. He deals then in passions that can be put to words. Let him set upon the stage a happy life, or have love both requited and fulfilled, and he's left with a fairy tale for children or a morning's soap opera, for what lies beneath happiness is inexpressible.

The scientist who in his laboratory puzzles over a cure for cancer asks something the mind can grasp. He knows that if not he then some other will one day have an answer. Let him ask what is life itself, or the meaning of man, and like every philosopher before he flounders at last in futility.

So it is when you sit by a bedside and watch an old man die. Or see a boy and girl hold hands in a park. Or peer through a glass at a first grandchild. If you think about it, standing before the glass, you know that yours are shopworn feelings, repeated endlessly in the milliards of time. What you see is a shriveled bit of flesh, wrinkled, misshapen, a primordial animal struggling desperately to survive in a suddenly strange environment. Yet what you see also is a thing of beauty which men have found a joy forever. And if you are bemused to wonder what life will be for a granddaughter, what sort of world she will live in—or more, to dream of what you hope it will be—you know you are lost in vain preoccupation. Like a wisp of heather on a wild moor she can be driven no man knows where by what unknown winds.

Yet men persist in just such dreaming, or always have in times past. Were it not so, we would not enjoy this world we never made. And enjoy is the word, though some would have us despair it. For if it be still a world full of troubles, it is still a world less full of pestilence, famine, and of darkness than other men have known.

Most especially, were it not so, we here would not enjoy this wide country that other men conquered, the bounty other men created from a desolate wilderness, the freedom others left us as our heritage. If there be one mark common to all those who played their parts in our beginnings it was that, whatever their differences, all were dreaming of a world for their children's children. Not for themselves alone, they wrote it down, but for their posterity. It's a dream that recurs, peering through a window. It is not the cheap wish that your child's child will be spared all sorrow and trouble, although the heart hopes they will not be too cruel. These things are the stuff of life, as of the things men write about life, and deep within lies the knowledge that it is by these things that men grow in wisdom and in stature and in favor with God and man.

Certainly some of the thoughts, as in all moments of emotion, are quite mundane. Let us say you may prefer that some other man had been chosen to lead your country; suddenly the wish is that whoever wears the crown be favored with wisdom and good fortune. You may think that this or that affair of the world were better organized otherwise; for once the hope is that you are wrong, that it is better thus and all foreboding foolish.

But the thought is something more than that we escape mistakes. Our times will not do so, any more than others. Rather it is a fervent prayer that, in choosing what we do, our thoughts

355

not turn upon ourselves to the forgetfulness of those who come hereafter.

When we act in a perilous world not for the morrow but for the moment's respite, we betray both forebears and posterity. So do we when we spend our substance for selfish increase. Or yield that heritage of liberty for present ease. Or when we tear away old mores because we find them bonds to chafe our pleasure. Most of all, we so betray ourselves. For then, and only then, is it true that in the long run we are all dead, and so embarked on a pointless journey.

It's all very trite. If the dream persists, it's because men persist in seeing intimations of immortality peering through a glass darkly.

February 1, 1965

356

THE WIND RETURNETH

W E live in such times of toil, trouble, and despair as the world has never known—or that anyway is the burden of the lament in the newspapers, magazines, TV documentaries, novels, poetry, sermon, and song. You can scarce escape the refrain.

Wars, riots, and strikes. Revolutions abroad. At home, violence in the streets. A decay of manners and morals. Economic tribulations. Racial hostility. Rebellion and delinquency among the young; a disregard of law among their elders. Disillusionment with the dream of the parliament of man. And so, in fact, it goes *ad infinitum*.

Ah, well; the indictment can hardly be dismissed. Still, it is only the young who can soak themselves in the romantic view of history, although sometimes the middle-aged cling to it, that everything is new, different, and worse than in some halcyon day of yore.

For old men the antidote is memory; if you were born before the turn of the century you may have the queer feeling that you've been here before, although that is perhaps small comfort. For the young, or for those too busy with middle age to have time for memories, the only antidote is a bit of browsing through the history books. Not the solemn history of kings and foreign policy, albeit that too is instructive. It's more curative, and much more delightful, to spend an hour among the volumes of Mark Sullivan's *Our Times,* which were mainly our grandfathers' times, or the *Only Yesterday* of Frederick Lewis Allen, who recounts the days of our youth.

Or lacking these musty volumes you can turn with as much

delight, and equal instruction, to the newest of Doubleday's Main-stream of America series in which Jonathan Daniels brings both research and recollection to *The Time Between the Wars*. It's just plain nostalgic for those lucky enough to have been there, in-structive for those with the misfortune to miss it all.

All that ancient history, that interlude of peace between two global wars. And was it, then, a quiet time with no wars, riots, or strikes? No revolutions abroad, and at home no violence in the streets? A time of settled manners, respect for age and law, of well-ordered morals? A time too free of troubles to give men cause for despair?

Hardly. The time between embraced the Jazz Age, the years of frenzy, the birth of the Red Menace and the Yellow Peril; the crash of an old order, the great depression, the rise of fascism, and the fusing of the scientific explosion soon to ignite the Arma-geddon that was Hiroshima. If you remember the flapper how can you be startled by the mini-skirt? Is it really forty years since that avant-garde magazine, *Civilization*, trumpeted that "the younger generation is in revolt against right-thinkers and forward-lookers . . . It dislikes almost to the point of hatred and certainly to the point of contempt, the type of people who dominate our present civilization, the people who actually 'run things.' . . ."? Is there not something familiar in seeing Greenwich Village described as a "noxious warren where males wore their hair long, females theirs short" and where both sexes were "of doubtful manners and morals"?

Some people may even remember Lewis Mumford—alas, so long ago—lamenting that the bourgeois "lives in an environment which the jerry-builder, the real estate speculator and the in-dustrialist have created." Or Deems Taylor complaining of com-posers who wrote music "that we cannot produce." So many movies have so romanticized the gangster era that it's a shock to be reminded how much violence, lawlessness, and bloodshed filled the streets. And not all the murder was so purposeful; Leopold and Loeb killed retail rather than wholesale, but their slaughter of the innocent was as wanton and paranoiac as yesterday's headline.

As for scandals in Washington, the postwar purveyors of mink coats and food freezers were rather gauche amateurs compared with the masters of another day. Teapot Dome was but the icing on the cake. And how long has it been since we had a President who fathered illegitimate children? So much for the mores. Romanticism has also laid its hand on the great depression. In the little magazines those who were never there have begun to write about it with nostalgia, noting that it was a period of firm national spirit, of reform, of a flowering in literature and the arts.

Lest we forget, it was also a period of misery for millions. If they rallied, it was as people besieged and because they had courage. If there was reform, there was also makeshift and blundering. If there was flowering of literature and the arts, it was because creative people kept their faith in man.

There were, indeed, moments of despair. Robert E. Sherwood, writing in the early thirties, saw ahead only "black doubt, punctured by brief flashes of ominous light . . . Behind, nothing but the ghastly wreckage of burned bridges." But neither he nor the others who gave birth to the flowering were whimperers. If there was a difference, it lies there.

There was excuse for despair elsewhere, too. Today's disappointment with the United Nations was matched by yesterday's with the League of Nations or with the Kellogg Peace Treaty, which, so said the dreamers, banished war forever. Meanwhile, the clouds abroad were even more ominous than those at home. If those were your days you will hardly need reminding that before Pearl Harbor every man could feel the oppressive weight that marked the coming of the storm. If they were not your days, reading about them will give you a glimpse of how quiet, peaceful, staid, and unruffled were the days of your fathers. On the beaches of Iwo Jima those dead are as dead as the dead in a Vietnamese jungle.

The moral, or perhaps reminder is a better word in these times, is inescapable. If ours are the worst of times, so were they all. The question is not whether black doubt lies ahead, but how men at different times meet their different doubts, whether with courage and ironic laughter or with whimpering. The despairing Robert Sherwood would not have understood the whimpering Arthur Miller or Edward Albee.

There is another reminder in such tales retold, at least for those who were there. Men were broken on the wheel of depression; others died in wholesale slaughter; still others merely succumbed to the frenzy and wasted their lives. Yet there are rewards for the survivors; they were exciting times, and we would not have missed them for the world. It will probably be so hereafter. Whatever the outcome of that dirty, messy war in Vietnam the day will come when those who were there, like those at Agincourt, will pity those who were not. And old men someday will sit in nostalgia of these times, frowning at young men trumpeting their revolt and despairing of a world they never made.

When that day comes there need be pity only for those who surrender to self-pity, wailing of such toil, trouble, and despair as the world has never known. From them will come no flowering of the arts, no new dreams; for that matter, no new woes.

But, of course, that is an old man speaking. You have to survive before you can fully savor the storm, or appreciate the exhortation, *Olim haec meminisse juvabit*. In the midst of it you find it hard to believe that someday you may remember even these trials with pleasure. All the same, when you look about at the world around you there's a queer comfort in knowing that time moves around in full circles. The prophet offered not despair but solace when he taught that if the sun goeth down it also ariseth, and that if the wind whirleth continually it also returneth according to its circuits. It's the troubled world that abideth forever.

August 15, 1966

POSTSCRIPT

When this book appeared in 1967, the author faced a dilemma. For he was editor of *The Wall Street Journal,* and his column, "Thinking Things Over," in which the essays in the book had first appeared, was familiar to *Journal* readers. How, therefore, to review his book in the *Journal* without either putting the reviewer on the spot or else resulting in an uncritical eulogy? His solution, which appeared in *The Wall Street Journal* for November 8, 1967, appears below:

THINKING THINGS OVER

By Vermont Royster

Unpaid Advertisement

One of the minor problems that arise now and then around any editorial sanctum is how to handle the reviewing of books written by members of the staff.

Of course they could just be ignored. However, this is hardly calculated to raise staff morale, and besides the readers of the paper might like to know the books exist. Regular reviewers may have conflicts of friendship with a colleague. Calling on outsiders isn't wholly satisfactory either; neither they, the author nor the reader can be quite sure what unconscious compensation can, under the circumstances, affect the praise or blame distributed.

These worrisome little metaphysical problems are compounded when the author happens to be the editor, as with a volume of my own essays just published under the Borzoi imprint of Alfred A. Knopf. The book is appropriately titled *A Pride of Prejudices,* which might unduly influence any hired reviewer conscious that, after all,

361

the editor okays the pay chit and might have some preformed opinions.

That leaves one obvious way to cut the Gordian knot. When the editor reviews his own handiwork you are at least clearly forewarned that the impartial judgments will be from the author's point of view.

One thing that can be said straightaway about *A Pride of Prejudices* is that it is a nice job of book-making. The Lindenmeyer Paper Company of Long Island City, N.Y., has supplied a good stock of comfortable weight that takes the ink well and is easy on the eye. The Book Press Incorporated of Brattleboro, Vt., has done the competent job of composing the type that you would expect from the printers of such outstanding recent works as *The Arrangement, Games People Play* and *Rosemary's Baby*. There is only one typographical error (on page 36) in the book's 361 pages.*

The whole has been put together by Warren Chappell, one of the more imaginative book designers, who also did the dust jacket and binding. For the type-face he picked Times Roman, a design of the late Stanley Morison. The Times here referred to is not the New York one but the London one, which adopted the type in 1932 and still uses it; this just suits the copy, being a nice balance between modernity and old-fashionedness.

For his jacket colors Mr. Chappell chose gold and rust, which I'm told are quite fashionable this season, and has accented them with white and bold black. He also had the wit to see that these vagrant essays needed a unifying motif, so he designed a sort of monogram of the author's initials to set off the chapter headings. Visually, therefore, the book is quite striking.

In short, it is just the sort of book-making that you would expect from the house of Knopf. Mr. Knopf, who despite a penchant for mixing florid neckties with blinding shirts manages to look like a Prussian archduke, is one of the last of the personal publishers with a personal pride in the books that bear his imprint.

Clifton Fadiman once said that Alfred Knopf had first made a profession out of a business and then an art out of a profession. He did this not just by corraling a distinguished list of authors, although his judgment here is sure and among the Knopf family are such as Gide, Camus, Willa Cather, Edmund Wilson, Langston Hughes and Raymond Chandler, to merely sample the names. Nor was his contri-

* – the typographical lapse was quickly corrected in the second printing.

bution merely the care he takes with book-making, although in the 1920s he revolutionized the design and manufacture of books.

What sets Alfred Knopf apart in this day of big corporate publishing is that he brought to the business of book publishing, and still retains, the mental attitude of the artist, a person who is marked first of all by a love of what he is doing and then by a driven desire to put his own mark on what is done.

Ordinarily we think of this attitude as belonging exclusively to the lonely creator. Yet the builder of a cathedral or the director of a symphony must tap the artistry of many others without whom he can accomplish nothing; if he too is an artist he must also satisfy himself that the whole is worthy of its parts.

In a long life Mr. Knopf has had his mediocrities, and perhaps he is not finished with them this morning. But one consequence of his attitude is that for half a century the would-be writers, such as those who waste their hours around the campus bookshop, have dreamed of appearing under the Borzoi colophon. Other publishers might promote them more flamboyantly and garner them more notoriety or more money; they had only to look at his wares on the shelves to know that Knopf would care about what they did and then take care of what they had done.

Rumor has it that Mr. Knopf has mellowed with the years, but that must be a canard. Anyway, there is still a delightful crustiness to his conversation and he can display as many prejudices as the most opinionated of his authors. One that he retains, surely, is the notion that if a book is worth making at all it is worth a pride in the doing.

This much, then, can be said for *A Pride of Prejudices*. It looks good on a coffee table even if you never open it.

If you do open it, you will find inside about what any reader of these columns would expect. That is, some little essays on sundry subjects done in a quaint, meandering style. There are the personality sketches of public persons that are de rigueur for a practicing journalist; the passing thoughts on weighty public questions that an editor must offer to keep his license; the reportage on affairs as distant as Kansas and India by which a reporter tests his craftsmanship.

But there are also, you should be forewarned, essays of no great point or purpose. Nostalgia can be pleasant self-indulgence but others may not be moved by remembrances of yesterday's Depression or of wars past. The borderline between sentiment and sentimentality is very narrow, and therefore easy to step over when recalling a great-grandfather or dreaming over a grandchild.

Finally, one man's prejudice is another man's anathema. Certainly not everyone today will share the belief, expressed therein, that our heritage from the past contains many values worth conserving in the twentieth century. Or amid the troubles of the present find comfort in the reminder that the Dark Ages lasted only five hundred years.

So perhaps the best thing to be said of the book is simply that Alfred Knopf thought it worth publishing.

November 8, 1967